After the Bounty

Related Titles from Potomac Books

The Buccaneer's Realm: Pirate Life on the Spanish Main, 1674–1688
by Benerson Little

A Call to the Sea: Captain Charles Steward of the USS *Constitution*
by Claude Berube and John Rodgaard

Quelch's Gold: Piracy, Greed, and Betrayal in Colonial New England
by Clifford Beal

A Sailor's Account of the Mutiny and Life in the South Seas

James Morrison,
Royal Navy

Edited and Annotated by
Donald A. Maxton

Potomac Books, Inc.
Washington, D.C.

Library of Congress Cataloging-in-Publication Data
Morrison, James, 1763 or 4–1807.
 [Journal of James Morrison]
 After the Bounty : a sailor's account of the mutiny and life in the South Seas / James Morrison ; edited and annotated by Donald A. Maxton. — 1st ed.
   p. cm.
 Includes bibliographical references and index.
 ISBN 978-1-59797-371-7 (hardcover : alk. paper)
 1. Morrison, James, 1763 or 4–1807—Diaries. 2. Bounty Mutiny, 1789. 3. Bounty (Ship) 4. Bligh, William, 1754–1817. 5. Christian, Fletcher, 1764–1793. 6. Oceania—Discovery and exploration. I. Maxton, Donald A., 1951– II. Title.
 DU21.M73 2010
 910.9164'8—dc22

                                              2009039550

Printed in the United States of America on acid-free paper that meets the American National Standards Institute Z39-48 Standard.

Potomac Books, Inc.
22841 Quicksilver Drive
Dulles, Virginia 20166

First Edition

10 9 8 7 6 5 4 3 2 1

In remembrance of James Morrison and Peter Heywood, tenacious survivors of the *Bounty* mutiny, *Pandora* shipwreck, and *Bounty* court-martial.

Contents

Illustrations

Foreword

When I first read James Morrison's journal in Sydney's Mitchell Library, it was as thrilling as any other book of exploration and adventure I had ever read, including the fictional exploits of W. E. Johns's fearless flying-ace Biggles and Enid Blyton's the *Famous Five,* true stories of explorers and shipwrecks, and *The Swiss Family Robinson* and their perilous survival. I would have loved to have been Alexander Selkirk—the real Robinson Crusoe—or his Man Friday. But there was a difference. Morrison's journal was a book about a reality my ancestor Fletcher Christian had seen, smelt, eaten, and lived. It dramatically changed my view of the present as well as of the past. During the 1960s I thought my surfing schoolmates very brave to take up this new craze from the United States. But James Morrison told me, in his own handwriting, that the *Bounty*'s men had seen all this in Tahiti almost two centuries earlier. There have been doubters of the journal's veracity. They demean the work, distrustful that an ordinary seaman could possibly have written such a narrative, or had such a prodigious memory for the minutiae of exotic life. Morrison was neither an ordinary man nor an ordinary seaman. It should be remembered that the *Bounty* was the first naval vessel ever to sail with an all-volunteer crew, which is one reason why others have reckoned the curiosity quotient and intellectual levels aboard were far above the norm. My response to such doubters is to ask them to recall the number of men of apparent simplicity who yet can remember weekly football or baseball scores for decades, further retelling the entire careers of sportsman after sportsman, none of whom they have once met. Morrison lived on Tahiti for almost two years and personally experienced all he recorded.

In bringing Morrison's journal finally into the realms of public access, Donald A. Maxton does many things. He gives twenty-first-century readers direct access to an eighteenth-century adventure that at the time was as uncommon as a man on the moon is today; because the life recorded has disappeared, it is still as startling as when it was written. Equally important, the journal gives back to Tahitians who wish to read about their vanished roots, their complicated—sometimes cruel, always misogynistic—but successful culture, which was totally adapted to their blissful geographical situation. This was not a culture that dissolved itself by inbreeding, self-indulgence, and pointless wars. It was Europeans, first with their firearms and then their arrogant and destructive view of godliness, who destroyed ancient Tahiti and Tahitians. Here is a unique document that reveals the cultural richness lost when the Tahitians' opportunity to adapt to foreign influences in their own way was effectively smothered.

For me it is particularly important that Morrison thus brings vividly to life the Tahitian women with whom Christian sailed away to Pitcairn Island, the silent protagonists in what happened after the mutiny on the *Bounty*. These women were born without rights. They could not eat pork or shark, could be divorced with little or no notice, and were largely forbidden that most potent symbol of womanhood, that of being a mother, with most children conceived on Tahiti being either aborted or killed at birth.

And yet, after untold generations of such treatment, the Tahitian women of Pitcairn created for themselves a new definition, fashioning a socially just type of society seen nowhere else on the globe. Mauatua, Fletcher Christian's partner and my great-great-great-great-grandmother, lived to a great age and in 1838 led the Pitcairn women to become the first in the world to have their right to vote written into law. Born without rights, she died one of the most liberated and powerful women in the world. It is only possible to appreciate the remarkable single-lifetime journey of these women by understanding the culture from which they had escaped. Theirs is the next and the most startling facet of the *Bounty* saga that must be told.

Morrison's journal is a priceless firsthand look into a world that was once real. It is for every adventuring mind the first real opportunity to know what it was like for Fletcher Christian and the men of the *Bounty* to have been on Tahiti in the late 1780s. It is real adventure, experienced by men and women whose direct descendants—I am but one—you can meet today.

There is, of course, the vexing matter of what Morrison says of Bligh. On one hand, he tells how Bligh's officers and men gave him three grateful cheers after he turned the *Bounty* back at Cape Horn to head instead to the Cape of Good Hope. He also recalls the manner in which he insulted his men and emasculated his officers. These comments have often been dismissed. But now that you can read *all* of what Morrison wrote and put his views of Bligh into perspective, you might have to revise your views of his tormented but brilliant nemesis, Fletcher Christian. To dismiss what Morrison says about Bligh is to dismiss his entire journal. I hope the fresh air of universal accessibility to the journal will stop such nonsense for good.

What a truly remarkable, true adventure Donald A. Maxton's book tells. You'll thank him for bringing it to the world as much as I do. And wish you had been there, too.

—Glynn Christian
Author of *Fragile Paradise: The Discovery of Fletcher Christian,* Bounty *Mutineer*

Acknowledgments

Thanks to George Barrowclough, American Museum of Natural History; Karen Barrowclough; Elizabeth Bauman, Naval Institute Press; Paul Brunton, Mitchell Library, State Library of New South Wales; Glynn Christian; Herbert Ford, director, and Patrick Benner, system administrator, Pitcairn Islands Study Center; Kristin Fowler, Boston Public Library; John Hagan; Cheryl Hoskin, Barr Smith Library, University of Adelaide; Herbert Kane; Andrew Lindesay, the Golden Cockerel Press; Alaric Maude; Douglas McCarthy, National Maritime Museum; Lisa Moss; Marie Moss Maxton; Hugh Murphy, *The Mariner's Mirror*; Judith Oringer; Lee Shepard; Sidney Shiff, the Limited Editions Club; and "Midgie," my feline assistant. Special thanks to the Mitchell Library, State Library of New South Wales, for its gracious permission to publish the manuscript *James Morrison: Journal on HMS* Bounty *and at Tahiti, 1787–1792.*

American Museum of Natural History Research Library, New York, New York; Archibald S. Alexander Library, Rutgers University, New Brunswick, New Jersey; Boston Public Library, Boston, Massachusetts; Cambridge University Press; Drew University Library, Madison, New Jersey; Mitchell Library, State Library of New South Wales, Sydney; National Maritime Museum, Greenwich, London; New York Public Library, New York, New York; Pitcairn Islands Study Center, Pacific Union College, Angwin, California; Sterling Memorial Library, Yale University, New Haven, Connecticut; William Andrews Clark Memorial Library, University of California, Los Angeles, California.

Introduction

THE MUTINY ON HMS *BOUNTY*

Many readers of *After the* Bounty*: A Sailor's Account of the Mutiny and Life in the South Seas* will already be acquainted with the infamous rebellion that took place on His Majesty's Ship *Bounty* in 1789. Millions of people have been exposed to this great seafaring saga through the medium of film, typically the 1935 Academy Award winner *Mutiny on the* Bounty, starring Clark Gable and Charles Laughton. Many others have read *The* Bounty *Trilogy*, a popular series of historical novels by Charles Nordhoff and James Norman Hall: *Mutiny on the* Bounty, *Men Against the Sea*, and *Pitcairn's Island*.

These entertaining works have firmly embedded the mutiny and its main protagonists, William Bligh and Fletcher Christian, into our culture. Four additional films and dozens of novels, short stories, poems, and plays have been based on the story of the *Bounty*. Unfortunately, most of these creative portrayals provide an incomplete, inaccurate picture of the events that compose the full tale. For readers unfamiliar with the historical context, a summary of the *Bounty* mutiny and its aftermath follows.

The small Royal Navy vessel HMS *Bounty* (formerly *Bethia*, a merchant ship), under the command of Lt. William Bligh, departed England on December 23, 1787, with a crew of forty-six men. Bligh, an exceptionally skilled navigator who served on Capt. James Cook's last voyage, had Admiralty orders to sail to Otaheite (Tahiti), collect shoots of the breadfruit plant, and transport them to the West Indies, where English planters hoped to cultivate them as a source of inexpensive, nutritious food for their slaves. The mission was set into motion by Sir Joseph Banks, president of the Royal Society, who also suggested that Bligh serve as commander of the ship.

The *Bounty*'s voyage was of little consequence to the Royal Navy, and if it had been successfully completed, this expedition would be a minor footnote in British history, not the most famous of all maritime mutinies.

Although most people think of Bligh as the ruthless, even sadistic commander portrayed on film by Charles Laughton, in reality he was more lenient than many commanders of the period were. He also was a rigid perfectionist, with little patience for others' carelessness or mistakes. Bligh had a quick temper and a penchant for using extremely coarse language, and was prone to humiliating his officers in front of the crew. In his journal, Boatswain's Mate James Morrison recorded a number of events that occurred during the voyage to Tahiti, such as Bligh's alleged theft of the ship's cheese, that led to animosity between captain and crew. Morrison reported several other incidents that Bligh deliberately left out of his own account of the expedition (*A Voyage to the South Sea*, 1792) and even provided a taste of Bligh's harangues at the crew and officers.

The *Bounty* anchored in Tahiti on October 26, 1788, and stayed in this South Seas paradise—with its delectable climate, abundant supply of fresh food, and attractive, compliant women—for almost five months. On April 4, 1789, the ship departed Tahiti with a cargo of young breadfruit plants. The next leg of the *Bounty*'s mission was a passage through the dangerous, poorly charted waters of Endeavour Strait, which runs between the Australian mainland and Prince of Wales Island. On April 28 the ship lay off the coast of Tofua, a volcanic island in the Tonga Group. During the early morning hours, Master's Mate Fletcher Christian led a mutiny against his commander, taking over the ship and forcing Bligh and eighteen of the crew into the *Bounty*'s twenty-three-foot launch.

Bligh's party had little chance of surviving in such a small, overloaded vessel on the open sea, with a pitifully scant supply of food and water. However, Bligh was a superb seaman with seemingly inexhaustible resources of courage and tenacity. His journey of nearly 4,000 miles to the Dutch East Indies is the most celebrated open-boat voyage in maritime history and an astonishing example of endurance under harrowing conditions—one of several events associated with the mutiny that still capture the imagination after more than two hundred years.

When Bligh returned to England, he became a popular hero, celebrated in print and even on the stage. Soon after, the Royal Navy dispatched HMS *Pandora*, commanded by Capt. Edward Edwards, to apprehend the mutineers. Many people are unfamiliar with the *Pandora*'s tragic voyage, which has never been depicted on film. When *Pandora* reached Tahiti on March 23, 1791, Captain Edwards found fourteen members of the *Bounty*'s crew (two of them had died before his arrival) and cruelly confined them on deck in a horrific makeshift jail that the prisoners named "*Pandora*'s Box." Edwards's search for Fletcher Christian's party of mutineers was fruitless, and on August 28, 1791, *Pandora* was shipwrecked on Australia's Great Barrier Reef. Thirty-one of the ship's crew and, thanks to Edwards's callousness, four prisoners perished.

After a grueling voyage to the Dutch East Indies in the ship's small boats, the ten surviving prisoners were returned to England for a court-martial, which took place on board HMS *Duke* in Portsmouth Harbor from September 12 to September 18, 1792. Four crew members, clearly forced by the mutineers to remain on board the *Bounty*—Michael Byrne, Joseph Coleman, Thomas McIntosh, and Charles Norman—were acquitted and released. Morrison, Peter Heywood, William Muspratt, Thomas Burkett, John Millward, and Thomas Ellison were found guilty and sentenced to death. Morrison and Heywood received pardons from King George III, and Muspratt was released on a legal technicality. Burkett, Millward, and Ellison were hung from the yardarms of HMS *Brunswick* on October 29, 1792.

The fate of Christian and his followers remained a mystery until February 6, 1808, when Capt. Mayhew Folger arrived at remote Pitcairn Island in the American sealing vessel *Topaz*. He was greeted by a small group of women and children led by John Adams (alias Alexander Smith), the only surviving mutineer. Captain Folger learned from Adams that the colony's early years were tragically violent, filled with jealousy, alcohol abuse, and murder. However, by the time Folger arrived, Pitcairn Island had evolved into a peaceful, religious community, where descendants of the *Bounty* mutineers live to this day.

JAMES MORRISON'S JOURNAL
Although film and fiction have mostly failed to tell the full true story of the *Bounty*, the *Pandora*, and Pitcairn Island, these works have enticed many viewers and readers to explore the historical background in greater depth. Why the mutiny occurred in the first place is a perennial topic of debate that has been discussed in literally thousands of nonfiction books, articles, and documentaries. Bligh's *A Voyage to the South Sea* is the most widely known firsthand account. This narrative en-compasses the *Bounty*'s voyage to Tahiti, the mutiny itself, and Bligh's perilous open-boat voyage and return to England. Not surprisingly, Bligh tells only his side of the story. He accepts no blame for his crew's rebellion, ignoring information and events that might place him in a negative light. *A Voyage to the South Sea* is rarely out of print, but now an equally important narrative—a journal written in 1792 by the pardoned James Morrison—is readily available.

Morrison was a native of the Isle of Lewis, off the coast of Scotland, and he clearly had sufficient education and experience to rise in the ranks of the Royal Navy. He served on the *Suffolk*, *Termagant*, and *Hind* before joining the *Bounty*. On the *Termagant*, Morrison held the rank of midshipman, a customary stepping-stone for those wishing to rise in the officers' ranks. *Bounty* scholar Sven Wahlroos suggests that Morrison may have agreed to accept the lower ranking of boatswain's mate on the *Bounty* just for a chance to visit Tahiti's fabled shores.

Bligh wrote a description of Morrison's physical appearance after the mutiny: "Boatswain's Mate, 28 years, 5 feet 8 inches high. Sallow complexion. Long black hair. Slender made. Lost the use of the first joint of the forefinger of the right hand. Tattooed with star under his left breast and a garter round his left leg, with the motto *honi soit qui mal y pense*. Has been wounded in one of his arms with a musket ball." (The French phrase—translated as, "Shame on him who evil thinks"—is the Knights of the Garter's motto.)

Morrison's journal is our only firsthand account of the *Bounty*'s adventures after Bligh was set adrift, including Christian's ill-fated attempt to establish a refuge from English law among hostile natives on the island of Tubuai. He tells the full story of this tragic misadventure, including the bloody battles that took place there, and the mutineers' construction of the castle-like Fort George. After Christian failed to colonize Tubuai, the *Bounty* returned to Tahiti. From there, Christian, several of his die-hard followers, and a group of Polynesian men and women sailed away on the *Bounty*, eventually reaching Pitcairn Island.

The rest of the crew remained on Tahiti to await the inevitable arrival of an English ship searching for the missing *Bounty*. Some of these men, including Morrison and Midshipman Peter Heywood, had not played an active role in the mutiny and wanted to return to England to resume their naval careers. The actual mutineers in this group decided that a sensual life on Tahiti was worth the risk of being captured and court-martialed. Morrison provides a detailed account of their eighteen-month sojourn on that island paradise, during which he closely observed virtually every aspect of Tahiti and its way of life and played an active role in tribal politics. Remarkably, he also designed and built the *Resolution*, a thirty-ton schooner that later voyaged into uncharted waters, leaving a fascinating mark on the history of South Seas exploration. The first Europeans to make landfall in the Fiji Islands and establish contact with the natives sailed on the *Resolution*.

Heywood also made the most of his time on Tahiti, learning the language well enough to later compile a Tahitian-English vocabulary.

Morrison records the arrival of *Pandora* and his imprisonment, with the rest of the remaining *Bounty* crew, in *Pandora*'s Box. He narrates Captain Edwards's pursuit of Christian, *Pandora*'s shipwreck, and the survivors' desperate journey to the Dutch East Indies—a little-known adventure that has been eclipsed in fame by Bligh's heroic open-boat voyage. The first part of the journal closes with Morrison's arrival in England. Though he does not provide a personal account of his trial, the court-martial and subsequent events are well documented in a number of other publications.

Throughout the court-martial, Morrison—whose verbal skills evidently matched his writing ability—defended himself with eloquence, winning the respect and admiration of the spectators. A contemporary article from *The Gentleman's Magazine* states, "This ship appears to have abounded with men above the common herd of uninformed illiterates. The boatswain's mate [Morrison] . . . stood his own counsel, questioned all the evidences, and in a manner so arranged and pertinent, that the spectators waited with impatience for his turn to call on them, and listened with attention and delight during the discussion."

Although there was little compelling evidence that Morrison actively participated in the mutiny, the neutral position he took during the affair did not constitute a defense under the Royal Navy's martial law. Heywood's case was similar to Morrison's, and both were condemned. The court, however, petitioned King George III to grant them full, unconditional pardons. Since there was no guarantee that the pardons would actually be issued, both men endured a period of anxious waiting. Heywood, a beloved scion of a prominent family, had powerful parties lobbying on his behalf before, during, and after the court-martial, but Morrison had no such allies. Nevertheless, this ingenious sailor took action that may have influenced the final outcome of his case.

During his imprisonment and trial, Morrison wrote what was essentially a first draft of his journal, entitled *Memorandum and Particulars respecting the Bounty and her Crew*. This forty-two-page document is dated October 10, 1792. In the *Memorandum* and an accompanying letter addressed to Rev. William Howell—a local pastor who attended the prisoners while they were confined on board HMS *Hector*—Morrison made serious accusations about Bligh's honesty and ability as a commander. He also described the inhumane treatment the prisoners suffered under Captain Edwards and implied that his incompetence doomed the *Pandora*: "On the evening of August 29th, the *Pandora* went on a reef, I might say how, but it would be to no purpose."

Accusing Bligh and Edwards of incompetent leadership, possibly illegal behavior, and, in Edwards's case, cruelty and poor seamanship might increase Morrison's chances of receiving the court-recommended pardon—if this information reached the right audience. There is little doubt that Reverend Howell ensured that key people in the Admiralty read the *Memorandum*. The *Bounty* court-martial had attracted a great deal of public attention, and the naval establishment would not want to risk the scandal that might ensue if Morrison's *Memorandum* was widely distributed. There was already a good deal of unrest in the ranks of the Royal Navy that culminated in the Spithead and Nore mutinies of 1797. Morrison and Heywood received their pardons on October 24, 1792, just two weeks after the date of the *Memorandum*.

Following his release, Morrison finished the journal, filling it with vivid observations and descriptions of Tahitian life and culture. The second part, here entitled "An Account of the Island of Tahiti and the Customs of the Islanders," continues to influence anthropological research on Polynesia. If Morrison's journal had been published as planned, Heywood's Tahitian-English vocabulary would have been appended to the volume, making it an even richer work.

Although Heywood's Tahitian-English vocabulary eventually disappeared and Morrison's journal remained unpublished until 1935, the London Missionary Society (LMS) put these documents to use at a much earlier date. The society's first evangelical mission to the South Seas on the *Duff* began on August 10, 1796. The ship was delayed for some time at Portsmouth, which gave Reverend Howell the opportunity to share both manuscripts with LMS director Dr. Thomas Haweis, who eagerly made copies for the missionaries.

In *Peter Heywood's Tahitian vocabulary and the narratives by James Morrison: some notes on their origin and history*, *Bounty* scholar Rolf E. Du Rietz reveals that publication of the journal was suppressed in exchange for Morrison receiving a favorable naval assignment after his pardon. Du Rietz quotes from Samuel Greatheed, an LMS director: "Mr. Howell [Rev. William Howell] had proposed publishing his [Morrison's] papers, but suppressed them on condition that Morrison should be provided for by Government; and he was accordingly appointed to act as a gunner in the navy, the publication being deemed objectionable, as it would have reflected some discredit on Captain Bligh." Nevertheless, a handful of nineteenth-century authors had access to the manuscript and quoted from it when they wrote negatively of Bligh.

Morrison and Heywood soon resumed their careers in the Royal Navy, where they both served with distinction. Morrison saw a considerable amount of action in the Mediterranean and also served for some time as a gunnery instructor. His last position was master gunner on HMS *Blenheim*, under the command of Rear Adm. Thomas Troubridge, one of the navy's most distinguished commanders. In February 1807 the *Blenheim* sank with all hands during a gale off Rodrigues Island in the Indian Ocean.

Heywood became a distinguished hydrographer, rising to the rank of post captain. He retired in 1816 and spent his remaining years in the village of Highgate, London. Before his death on February 10, 1831, Heywood gave his copy of Morrison's journal to Diana Jolliffe (Lady Belcher), his stepdaughter. This precious document remained among the Heywood family papers until 1915, when the Rev. A. G. L'Estrange, a family friend, bequeathed it to the Mitchell Library, State Library of New South Wales, in Sydney, Australia, where it is still preserved.

Morrison's journal was finally published in its entirety by the Golden Cockerel Press (1935), which released it as *The Journal of James Morrison, Boatswain's Mate of the* Bounty, *Describing the Mutiny and Subsequent Misfortunes of the Mutineers, Together with an Account of the Island of Tahiti*, edited by Owen Rutter and illustrated with wood engravings by Robert Gibbings. Most copies of this expensive limited edition (325 copies) are in the hands of book collectors and research libraries.

Since 1935, the complete text of Morrison's journal has appeared in French as *Journal de James Morrison, Second maître à bord du* Bounty (Paris: Société des Océanistes, 1966; Papeete: Société des Etudes Océaniennes, 1966.) The first part of this translation was reprinted in 2002 (Rennes: Editions Ouest-France). A few brief extracts (in English) have appeared in two anthologies: *The Saga of the* Bounty: *Its Strange History as Related by the Participants Themselves* (New York: Putnam, 1935) and *Exploration and Exchange: A South Seas Anthology, 1680–1900* (Chicago: University of Chicago Press, 2001).

After the Bounty: *A Sailor's Account of the Mutiny and Life in the South Seas* is the first complete edition of Morrison's journal to appear in English since 1935. The rarity of the Golden Cockerel Press edition has heretofore limited its audience to scholars with a professional interest in the *Bounty* mutiny, South Seas exploration, or Polynesian culture. This new edition—in which I have made Morrison's eighteenth-century text more reader-friendly by modifying his spelling to make it more consistent with contemporary British usage and by changing his punctuation and grammar to clarify the sense when necessary—puts it within the reach of anyone interested in reading the full story of the *Bounty* and her crew.

Part One

THE MUTINY AND THE SUBSEQUENT MISFORTUNES OF THE MUTINEERS

The Mutiny and the Subsequent
Misfortunes of the Mutineers

A ROUGH START TO A LONG VOYAGE

On the 9th of September 1787, I entered on board His Majesty's Armed Vessel *Bounty*, Lieutenant William Bligh, Commander, then lying at Deptford. On the 18th of October, she dropped down to Long Reach and in a few days after sailed for Spithead, where she anchored on the 4th of November. After several attempts, in one of which the fore-topsail yard was carried away (which was returned at Portsmouth Yard, together with a cable that was rubbed at St. Helens), she sailed on the 23rd of December with a fresh gale easterly, which increased to a heavy gale by the 27th—in which the ship's oars, a spare topsail yard, and topgallant yard were washed from the quarters, one of the eye-bolts being drawn from the side.

She also shipped asea, which broke the boats' chock and tore all the planks from the large cutter's stem and washed some empty casks overboard that were on the deck. Another sea stove in a part of the stem between the deadlights but did very little other damage except breaking an azimuth compass and wetting a few bags of bread in the cabin. The breach in the stem was soon secured, and the ship hove to, as it became dangerous to scud.

January, 1788. When the weather became moderate, we made sail. The carpenters repaired the boat and chock, and the wet bread was got up, dried, and used first. We met with no other accident or anything material till the 5th of January 1788, when we made the island of Tenerife and anchored in the road of St. Croix on the 6th. [The following is written on the flyleaf of the manuscript at this point: "Two Drip stones were purchased here for refining water, and a barrel of Flour and some

Indian corn for the Stock."] Here she completed her water and took on board some wine for the ship's use and several casks for gentlemen in England and the West Indies. Four quarters of miserable beef, a few pumpkins, and a goat and kid (which died soon after) were all the refreshments this island afforded. The beef was for the most part thrown overboard as soon as it was served out by the people, who were not yet sufficiently come to their stomachs to eat what they supposed to be either an ass or mule. Every necessary except wine was here both scarce and dear, nor could the loss of the topsail yard and sweeps be here repaired.

The water being completed and the hold stowed, the boats were got in on the 10th, and on the 11th we weighed anchor and stood to the southwest with a fine breeze and pleasant weather. The ship's company were now put in three watches, and Mr. Fletcher Christian appointed to act as lieutenant by order of Lieutenant Bligh—which order was read to the ship's company. Mr. Bligh then informed them that as the length of the voyage was uncertain till he should get into the South Sea, he was not certain whether he should be able to get round Cape Horn, as the season was so far spent; but at all events, he was determined to try. It became necessary to be careful of the provisions (particularly bread) to make them hold out. For this reason he ordered the allowance of bread to be reduced to two-thirds, but let everything else remain at full. This was cheerfully received, and the beer being gone, grog was served.

The weather still continuing fine a few days after, the cheese was got up to air. On opening the casks two cheeses were missed by Mr. Bligh, who declared that they were stolen. The cooper declared that the cask had been opened before while the ship was in the river by Mr. Samuel's order [marginal note by Morrison: the clerk], and the cheeses sent to Mr. Bligh's house. Mr. Bligh, without making any further enquiry into the matter, ordered the allowance of cheese to be stopped from officers and men till the deficiency should be made good, and told the cooper he would give him a damned good flogging if he said any more about it.

These orders were strictly obeyed by Mr. Samuel, who was both clerk and steward, and on the next banyan day [days on which no meat was served out], butter only was issued. This the seamen refused, alleging that their acceptance of the butter without cheese would be tacitly acknowledging the supposed theft. John Williams declared that he had carried the cheeses to Mr. Bligh's house with a cask of vinegar and some other things that went up in the boat from Long Reach. As they persisted in their denial of the butter, it was kept also for two banyan days and no more notice taken.

As the ship approached the equator the pumpkins began to spoil, and being in general too large for the cabin's use, they were issued to the ship's company in lieu of bread. The people, desiring to know at what rate the exchange was to be, asked Mr. Samuel, who informed them that they were to have one pound of pumpkin in lieu of two pounds of bread. This they refused, and on Mr. Bligh's being informed of it, he came up in a violent passion and called all hands, telling Mr. Samuel to call the first man of every mess and let him see who would dare to refuse it or anything else that he should order to be served, saying, "You damned infernal scoundrels, I'll make you eat grass or anything you can catch before I have done with you."

This speech enforced his orders and everyone took the pumpkin as called, including the officers, who, though it was in their eyes an imposition, said nothing against it. It was plain to be seen that they felt it more severely than the men, who, having yet a good stock of potatoes that they had laid in at Spithead, did not immediately feel the effects of such a reduction of their bread.

As the pumpkin was always served at one pound a man, it was frequently thrown together by the seamen, and the cooks of the different messes drew lots for the whole. The pumpkin was issued every other day till they were all expended. In all probability the grievance would have ended, but private stock began to decrease and the beef and pork to appear very light. Because there had never yet been any weighed when opened, it was supposed that the casks ran short of their weight, for which reason the people applied to the master and begged that he would examine the business and procure them redress.

The master made this known to Mr. Bligh, who ordered all hands aft and informed them that everything relative to the provisions was transacted by his orders—and it was therefore needless to make any complaint, for they would get no redress—as he was the fittest judge of what was right or wrong. He further added that he would flog the first man severely who should dare attempt to make any complaint in the future and dismissed them with severe threats.

The seamen, seeing that no redress could be had before the end of the voyage, determined to bear it with patience and neither murmured nor complained afterwards. However, the officers were not so easily satisfied, and made frequent murmurings among themselves about the smallness of their allowance, and could not reconcile themselves to such unfair proceedings; but they made no complaint, seeing that the men had dropped it, and did not appear either in public or private to take any notice of it. When a cask was broached, they saw with regret all the prime pieces taken out for the cabin table, while they were forced to take their chance in common with the men of what remained—without the satisfaction of knowing whether they had their weight or not, being forced to take it as marked.

This circumstance, while it served to increase their distress and to draw forth heavy curses on the author of it in private, helped to make the men reconciled to their part, seeing that it was not leveled at them alone but that all shared a like fate. Nor were they, as the sea phrase expresses it, able or calculated "to stand the wrangle in the galley" for their peas and oatmeal, which were served in very sparing quantities—so sparing that there never was any of either left for the hogs, which would have starved but for the bread and Indian corn purchased for the poultry.

The usual allowance of peas was seven quarts for the whole complement, which none failed to partake, and of oatmeal nine quarts each banyan day. In the peas was frequently boiled four cakes of portable beef broth and some sauerkraut (salted cabbage). The butter and cheese being expended, oil and sugar were served in lieu, in the proportion of half a gill of oil and one ounce of sugar per man each banyan day.

We caught very few fish while standing across the trades. Near the line [equator] we had heavy rain and filled several casks of water both for ourselves and our stock and crossed the line with the usual ceremony.

March, 1788. We met with no accident or occurrence worth mentioning after leaving Tenerife except speaking the British *Queen of London.* She was bound for the Cape of Good Hope on the whale fishery. On board this ship we sent letters for England, supposing she would in all probability be the last one we should see on this side of Cape Horn. We saw several ships on the coast of Patagonia but spoke none of them. We carried a fair wind and fair weather (except at intervals) with us till we made Tierra del Fuego, which happened on the 23rd of March. The weather being fine we were all in high spirits and hoped soon to get round the Cape, but a few days convinced us that Commodore Anson had not said worse of this place than it deserved. [Commodore George Anson, who circumnavigated the globe in the early 1740s, rounded Cape Horn in very stormy weather.]

March 23rd. One of the sheep dying this morning, Lieutenant Bligh ordered it to be issued in lieu of the day's allowance of pork and peas, declaring that it would make a delicious meal and that it weighed upwards of fifty pounds. It was divided and most of it thrown overboard. Some dried shark supplied its place for a Sunday's dinner, for it was no more than skin and bone.

THE *BOUNTY* BATTLES CAPE HORN

The day continued fine, and we stood along the land crossing the Strait of La Maire; but fair weather in this clime is always a forerunner of foul, and this we found by experience as soon as we were clear of Staten Land. But before it set in, we got the topgallant masts down and made everything ready for it. The appearance of the country is rugged and barren, and the snow on the hills gives it a very inhospitable look at a distance. What it may be on a nearer view I do not pretend to say.

We saw here vast quantities of seals, penguins, shags and other seafowl, and white and black albatrosses, some of which we caught that made an excellent meal. Some of them measured upwards of eight feet from tip to tip of their wings; the black ones we called padries but never caught any of them. We tried for fish but without success.

The weather becoming very sharp as we stood to the southward, the people requested that their rum might be served without water. This was readily agreed to as the water was saved by it, and the allowance of water was now reduced to three pints per day. In such weather as we had this was more than sufficient, having no method of using it otherwise than as drink. This indulgence was not lost on the seamen, whose spirits seemed to have an additional flow from it. They thought nothing of hardship, and notwithstanding fatigue and increasing bad weather, they carried on their duty with alacrity and cheerfulness, anticipating the pleasure and profit they hoped to reap by the success of the voyage.

Wheat and barley were now boiled every morning for breakfast in lieu of the burgoo, but of this the quantity was so small that it was no uncommon thing for four men in a mess to draw lots for the breakfast and to divide their bread by the well-known method of "Who shall have this"; nor were the officers a hair behind the men at it. The quantity of wheat boiled was one gallon for forty-six men, of which they all partook, and of barley two pounds for the like number. The division of this scanty allowance caused frequent quarrels in the galley, and in the present bad weather was often attended with bad consequences. In one of these disputes the cook, Thomas Hall, got two of his ribs broken, and at another time Churchill got his hand scalded. It became at last necessary to have the master's mate of the watch superintend the division of the wheat.

The weather continued to grow worse every day. Hail, rain, sleet, and snow, or rather large flakes of half-formed ice, alternately followed each other in heavy squalls. This often reduced us under bare poles and battened hatches, as the sea made fair breaches over us, running in a manner unknown in northern climes— frequently obscuring the sun when 20° above the horizon, tossing the ship so violently that the people could not stand on the deck without the assistance of a rope or something to hold.

At several times with this violent motion and sudden jerking, Mr. Huggan, the surgeon, was flung down the after ladder into the cockpit and dislocated his shoulder. And a few days after, Richard Skinner met with the same fate in the same place. Peter Linkletter got a hurt in his back by being thrown down in the fore-cockpit, of which he always complained afterwards. Yet, notwithstanding the severity and inclemency of the season and the continued gales and repeated squalls, which seemed to break with redoubled violence and threaten us every moment with destruction, such was the alacrity and carefulness of officers and men that we never lost a spar or a yard of canvas—though frequently we were forced to take the sails in after loosing them before the tacks could be hauled on board or the sheets aft.

Sweet wort was now made from malt, and a pint a man served hot every day, which was very acceptable and nourishing in our present situation; but the intense cold, and being continually wet, the hard duty and continual fatigue that the rigorous season required, and the uncomfortable situation of the men between decks—which were always filled with smoke while the hatches were fast—soon began to lay hold of their constitutions, and several fell sick. The straining of the ship, though perfectly sound, kept the hammocks always wet, which made them very uncomfortable not only for the sick but for the well. As the people began to fall sick, the duty became heavier for those who were well but was still carried on with alacrity and spirit. The behaviour of the seamen in this trying situation was such as merited the entire approbation of the officers and Mr. Bligh's thanks in a public speech.

After a fatiguing, ineffectual trial, it was found that the passage round Cape Horn was not practicable at this season of the year, though we had reached the 62nd degree of south latitude and 79th of west longitude; yet we found that we had lost ground, and though the ship was an excellent sea boat, it was as much as she could do to live in this tremendous sea, where the elements seem to wage continual war. What a deep-waisted ship must suffer in this climate can be only guessed at by those who have not experienced it, but a good account may be seen in Anson's *Voyage*.

April, 1788. On the 18th of April Mr. Bligh ordered all hands aft and, after giving them his thanks for their unremitted attention to their duty, informed them of his intention to bear away for the Cape of Good Hope, as it appeared to him an impossibility to get round Cape Horn. This was received with universal joy and returned according to custom with three cheers. The ship was instantly put before the wind, and the reefed foresail and close reefed main topsail set—which with the mainsail and mizzen staysail were the chief sails that had been in use for some time—but they were seldom in use all at the same time.

A hog was now killed and served out in lieu of the day's allowance that, though scarce anything but skin and bone, was greedily devoured, everyone by this time being fairly come to their appetites. In the evening the wind veered to the northward, which induced Lieutenant Bligh to heave to and try again, though we had run nearly 120 miles to the eastward. But these flattering appearances soon vanished and are always forerunners of something worse, for it shifted again to the west and blew with redoubled fury.

We again bore away on the 22nd, seeing our hopes in vain while we continued in this inhospitable climate. The thermometer was seldom at the freezing point, but we always thought it much colder than the thermometer seemed to indicate, which might be partly owing to the continual sleet overhead and the ship being drenched alternately with seas—so that no man could keep dry for one minute after he came on deck.

After we bore away, we got the hatches opened, which we could not very often do before, being forced to keep them almost constantly battened down. We also got the stoves to work airing and drying the ship between decks, and the sick recovered fast, as we got into a more temperate climate. We met with nothing during this passage worth mentioning, nor could we find the Isles of Tristan da Cunha according to their situation on the chart, though we hove to and lay by part of a night for that purpose. This perhaps is owing to their [position on the chart] not being well laid down.

THE CAPE OF GOOD HOPE

May, 1788. We made the Cape on the 23rd of May and anchored in False Bay on the 25th. Here we found several Dutch and French ships, and soon after arrived and watered here. The Honourable East India Company's ship *Dublin* also sailed and left us here.

June, 1788. Fresh provisions were now procured, with soft bread and wine for present use. The peas, oatmeal, oil, and sugar were stopped, except oatmeal for Mondays, which by general consent was kept for thickening the broth. We also hauled the seine with various success and caught several fine fish with hook and line, called here Romans and Hottentots, and a few seals on a rocky island in the middle of the bay called by us Seal Island—where those animals resort in great numbers and lay basking themselves like swine in the sun.

On this island we found part of a boat that had been dashed to pieces and several bundles of sealskins, which were for the most part rotten. As the island is an entire rock, it affords shelter for no animals but the seals and seafowl, with which it abounds. On firing a musket they rise up in vast flocks, making a great noise and, in a manner, forming a cloud over the whole island, which is not more than half a mile in circumference. The birds are gannets, shags, boobies, gulls, Cape Hens, petrels of sorts, and penguins. We found here a large bird of the size of a goose of a grey colour that seemed to us unable to fly, several of which we knocked down. From their darting immediately at the eyes of those who came in their reach, we called them eye-peckers. They were fully as heavy as a goose, but their flesh rank and coarse, and were indifferent food.

On enquiry concerning the boat, we found that this place used to supply the settlement with oil, but that the boat had been lost in a gale of wind and her crew of seven hands drowned; the Dutchmen had never been so curious as to enquire how. The landing being very bad, it is possible she might have been dashed in pieces in attempting to land, as part of her was there in our time. As we saw no bones we supposed the men never reached the shore. The governor has never sent a boat there since; this island lays about three leagues east of Symons Bay.

While we remained here the ship was refitted, the rigging overhauled, and the sails repaired. The armourer set to work to make new hinges for the weatherboards that had been washed away. The carpenter and his mates, with two Dutch caulkers, caulked the sides and repaired the weatherboards. The hold was unstowed to get the iron stocked anchor up, the sheet put down in lieu, the water filled, and several longboat loads of stones got in for ballast. The bread was sifted and an additional nine hundred pounds got in for sea store, and three barrels of brandy and two of arrack with some flour and raisins. The powder was taken on shore and aired, to which also was added two barrels of fine Dutch powder from the fort. Hay and barley were procured for the stock of sheep, goats, and poultry.

July, 1788. Everything being complete by the 1st of July, we sailed, having on board five live sheep for the ship's company's use and some pigeons. We stood to the eastward with a fine breeze; as we edged to the southward, the wind increased to a fresh gale and continued with little alteration. We passed close by the island of St. Paul but saw no place where a landing might be made with safety. The island is high and barren, affording but a very few trees and shrubs; but as this was the dead of winter, it may have a better appearance in summer. We saw no appearance of water on any part, and a heavy gale coming on prevented our further examination. We arrived at Adventure Bay in New Holland without any material accident on the 2nd or 3rd of September, where we wooded and watered, and sailed about the middle of the same month for Tahiti. This is a large, spacious bay with good anchoring in any depth from twenty to five fathoms and a white sandy bottom; any number of ships might ride here in safety.

EXPLORING ADVENTURE BAY

The country is mountainous and clothed with wood from the beach to the tops of the mountains. The trees are of several kinds and run to a prodigious size; we measured one that had fallen, by being burnt at the root by the natives, that was twenty-seven yards to the first branch and nine in circumference.

The surf on the beach makes the labour of wooding and watering very severe in the winter season, and the water, though plentiful, is neither good nor convenient. The soil near the beach is sandy but on the hills is a strong, red loam, and in clear places affords excellent grass that we cut and dried for the sheep and goats. On the east part of the bay were planted some vines, pear trees, and bananas that we brought from Tenerife and the Cape with several kinds of seeds, marking the adjacent trees with the ship's and commanders' names and the date of the year. We saw no quadruped but a dead opossum, but there were various kinds of birds, among which were black swans, ducks, hawks, parakeets, sea pyes, and several others that we could not name, with numbers of gannets and other seafowl.

We hauled the seine but had no success, catching very few fish. We saw several of the natives' huts, which consist of nothing more in structure than several pieces of bark set up against a tree, and round them several marks of fire and a number of crab, mussel, and other shells. A few days before we sailed, some of the natives came down on the rocks on the west part of the bay, where Mr. Bligh, accompanied by Mr. Nelson, went in the cutter to see them and made them several presents—of which they seemed to take very little notice.

As they approached the boat the women stayed at some distance, and the men, in number ten, threw away their short sticks and came close down on the rocks. Their colour was nearly black, but they appeared to be smutted in several parts with charcoal. Their heads were all closely shorn, so that we could not tell whether they were woolly or not, but thought that the short remains looked more like wool than hair. Their countenances were by no means agreeable, and their teeth black and uneven; they were quite naked and appeared harmless, miserable creatures.

Among them was one very much deformed, which Mr. Nelson declared to be the same he had seen here on a former voyage.

Though they did not appear in the least curious to examine anything given them, they talked a good deal, which none of us understood, and would frequently jump up and shout, seemingly pleased when the boat rose higher than common on the surf and again when she fell. As we did not land, it was not possible to see into their method of living, but from the number of shells at different places, we supposed that shellfish was their chief food. We saw no canoes among them, though they appeared by their lights in the night to be numerous. We therefore supposed that they depend on what the sea throws up and, on the whole, appear the most miserable creatures on the face of the earth.

TEMPERS FLARE

While we were here, the carpenters sawed some plank while the wooding and watering was going on. Bread was served at full allowance and water gruel boiled for breakfast, but as soon as we put to sea we returned to the former allowance. Here also were sown seeds of eternal discord between Lieutenant Bligh and his officers. He confined the carpenter and found fault with the inattention of the rest to their duty, which produced continual disputes, everyone endeavouring to thwart the others in their duty. This made the men exert themselves to divert the storm from falling on them by a strict attention to their duty, and in this they found their account and rejoiced, in private, at their good success.

Soon after we sailed, we discovered a group of small islands to the eastward of New Zealand, which we called the *Bounty*'s Isles. James Valentine was let blood, and his arm festered and turned to a mortification, of which he died. Several of the seamen, particularly the oldest, began to complain of pains in their limbs, and some symptoms of the scurvy began to make their appearance. Weakness and debility began to be observed throughout the ship's company, for which essence of malt was given; to those who appeared worse, with portable soup and rice from the surgeon's chest; the salt provisions were also stopped and flour given in lieu.

October, 1788. During this passage, Mr. Bligh and his messmates, the master and surgeon, fell out and separated, each taking his part of the stock and retiring to live in their own cabins. Afterwards they had several disputes and seldom spoke but on duty, and even then with much apparent reserve. Previous to making Tahiti, a dispute happened between Mr. Bligh and the master relative to signing some books that the master had refused to sign for reasons best known to him. All hands were called aft and the Articles of War read, and some part of the printed instructions, after which the books and papers were produced with a pen and ink. Mr. Bligh said, "Now sir, sign those books." The master took the pen and said, "I sign in obedience to your orders, but this may be cancelled hereafter." The books being signed, the people were dismissed to return to their duty.

TAHITI LANDFALL

On the 24th of October we made the island of Myetea (or Osnaburgh Island) and stood close in with it. Several of the natives came down on the rocks on the north part and waved large pieces of white cloth, but none attempted to come off. In the afternoon we bore away for Tahiti, which we made between five and six in the NW. At eight we hove to, and at four in the morning of the 25th, made sail and anchored at ten in Port Royal (or Matavai Bay).

We were presently surrounded by the natives in their canoes, who brought off hogs, breadfruit, and coconuts in abundance, and a trade for nails, hatchets, etc., soon commenced. The sick were urged to drink plentifully of the coconuts, and this contributed so much to their recovery that in a few days there was no appearance of sickness or disorder in the ship. The plentiful provisions with which the natives supplied us soon renewed their strength.

Immediately on anchoring, an order signed by Mr. Bligh was stuck up on the mizzenmast, prohibiting the purchase of curiosities or anything except provisions. There were few or no instances of the order being disobeyed, as no curiosity struck the seamen so forcibly as a roasted pig and some breadfruit—and these came in abundance, because every species of ship's provision except grog was stopped.

November, 1788. As soon as the ship was moored, a tent was pitched on Point Venus, and Mr. Nelson and his assistant went on shore to collect plants. The gunner also went to the tent to trade for hogs for the ship's use—it being found more convenient than trading alongside the ship, as the canoes came so thick as to put a stop to all work. Mr. Fletcher Christian, Mr. Heywood, Mr. Peckover, the gunner, and four men were also sent on shore as a guard in case the natives should behave amiss.

A shed was built for the reception of the plants and the pots carried on shore as Mr. Nelson filled them. Meantime, the carpenter and his mates fitted the cabin for their reception. Some hands were employed cutting wood and filling water for present use. The forge was set up, and the armourer set to work to make trade. All the salt in the ship was soon expended in curing pork for sea store, and everything seemed to go on in a prosperous manner.

While the salting time lasted, provisions were in great plenty, as each man was allowed two pounds of the bones and such parts as were not fit for salting per day—which, with what they could get by purchase themselves, was always sufficient to enable them to live well.

December, 1788. On the 11th of December Mr. Thomas Huggan departed this life, and the next day his remains were interred on Point Venus and a board fixed to a tree near his grave with an inscription on it to his memory. The sailmaker got the sails on shore to repair.

The market for hogs beginning now to slacken, Mr. Bligh seized on all that came to the ship, big and small, dead or alive, taking them as his property and serving them as the ship's allowance at one pound per man per day. He also seized on those belonging to the master and killed them for the ship's use, though he had more than forty different sizes on board of his own. There was then plenty to be purchased, nor was the price much risen from the first. When the master spoke to Mr. Bligh, telling him the hogs were his property, Mr. Bligh told him that "everything was his as soon as it was on board, and that he would take nine tenths of any man's property, and let him see who dared say anything to the contrary." Those of the seamen were seized without ceremony, and it became a favour for a man to get a pound extra of his own hog.

The natives, as well as the people, observing that the hogs were seized as soon as they came on board and not knowing that they would be seized from them, became very shy of bringing a hog in sight of Lieutenant Bligh either on board or on shore. They watched all opportunities when he was on shore to bring provisions to their friends. Mr. Bligh observed this and saw that his diligence was likely to be evaded, and he ordered a book to be kept in the binnacle, wherein the mate of the watch was to insert the number of hogs or pigs, with the weight of each, that came into the ship. To remedy this the natives took another method, which was cutting the pigs up, wrapping them in leaves, and covering the meat with breadfruit in the baskets, and sometimes with peeled coconuts. By this means, as the bread was never seized, they were a match for all his industry, and he never suspected their artifice. By this means, provisions were still plentiful.

On the 20th we had heavy rains and a strong gale of wind from the NW, which brought with it a heavy sea from that quarter, breaking so violently on the Dolphin Bank that the surge ran fairly over the ship. The carpenter, who was the evening before confined to his cabin, was now released to secure the hatches. Several things were washed overboard, and had not the cables been very good, the ship would have gone on shore.

Map of Tahiti, 1767–78

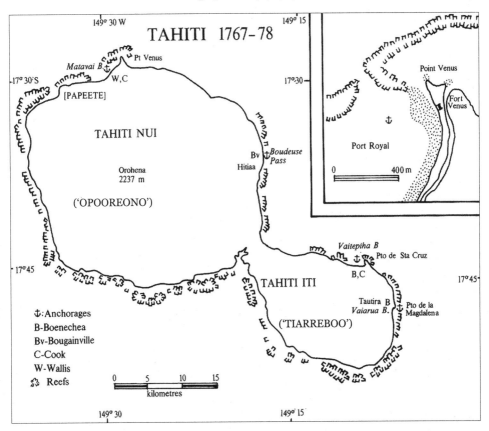

"Tahiti 1767–78," a map from O. H. K. Spate's *Paradise Found and Lost,* marks the points where the first explorers of Tahiti anchored, as well as the many reefs surrounding the island. The *Bounty* and the *Pandora* both anchored near Point Venus in Port Royal, Matavai Bay, enlarged in the upper right-hand corner of the map.

The next day the gale abated, but the surf ran very high on the shore so as to prevent landing either in canoes or boats. However, several of the natives found a way through it; they brought bunches of coconuts with them that were so full that one of us could barely haul it up the side, though they had swam off with them through a tremendous surf. As the weather moderated the canoes came off, and of them we learned the situation of the party on shore, who had been in danger of being washed away by the overflowing of the river. We observed them opening a sluice in the bank that soon assumed the appearance of a large river.

As soon as a boat could land, the sails were got off and bent, the plants got on board, and the ship unmoored. The master was sent to examine Oparre Harbour, as Matavai Bay was judged unsafe to remain in any longer. He returned with a favourable account of the place, and on the morning of the 25th, the tent was struck and sent down in the launch. At ten the ship weighed anchor and followed, but standing in she ran on a coral rock that had escaped the master's sight. The sea breeze gave us some trouble before we got her off, which however we did before night. We moored with one bower and the kedge until morning, when we moored with both bowers. We got the plants on shore, and a house was provided by Otoo, or Matte (the chief mentioned by Captain Cook), in lieu of a tent for the shore party, and a place fenced in for the plants.

Having got the ship in order, we kept our Christmas on the 28th. Each man had a double allowance of grog, which was stopped from those who had not crossed the equator before this voyage. On the 1st of January 1789 this was repeated, after which the grog was reduced to half the allowance. As we had plenty of coconut milk the grog was not missed, and the natives took care to keep us well supplied with it—notwithstanding the frequent seizures made by Mr. Bligh, who drank nothing else in his grog.

A LONG, EVENTFUL STAY ON THE ISLANDS

January, 1789. It would be difficult to account for every transaction that happened while we lay at this island, and I shall only make a few remarks—

On our first arrival, the ship was visited by numbers of the inhabitants of all descriptions. There were several chiefs who brought large presents and were presented in their turn by Mr. Bligh, who found some of his old acquaintances, as did Mr. Nelson and Coleman, who had been here before. Every officer and man in the ship were provided with new friends, though none understood the language. Yet, we found it very easy to converse by signs, at which these people are adept.

Some of the women who came on board became very intelligible in a short time and soon brought their former husbands into a method of discourse by which everything was transacted. Through them we found that the stock left by Captain Cook was for the most part destroyed, there being but one sheep in the island that was killed by dogs soon after our arrival. I observed that this sheep, contrary to those in most warm climates, had not lost its wool. The only horned cattle on the island were an old bull and a young cow (the rest being destroyed and carried away by the Morea people soon after Captain Cook had left the island). These were kept at a distance of twenty-five or thirty miles from each other. Mr. Bligh purchased them, and they were brought to Matavai and put under Poeno's care—Poeno was chief of Matavai, and he had the charge of Captain Cook's picture, which he brought on board to get repaired. It remained in the ship till she sailed. [This portrait had been painted by John Webber during Captain Cook's last voyage and had been presented to the chief of Matavai. The natives held the picture in great veneration, and it became the custom for the commanders of visiting ships to record on the back of it the date of their arrival and departure.]

We also learnt through them that O'Mai was dead, though we could not learn by what means he died. [In 1773 Captain Furneaux, of the *Adventure*, the consort to Captain Cook's *Resolution,* had taken O'Mai with him to England, where he had received much attention. He returned with Captain Cook in 1777.] It was thought that he had been killed for the sake of his property, but we were better informed afterwards, as shall be shown in its proper place.

Otoo, the chief whom we supposed to be king, and Eddea, his queen, often slept on board the ship. They frequently entertained Mr. Bligh and the officers on shore with heivas (or dances, plays, etc.,) and such diversions as they thought most pleasing, and from which he generally returned with presents of cloth, etc. They also informed us that the name of Otoo, or Too, was now transferred to the son (of the man whom we knew by that name), who was now earee rahi, or king, and that the name of the father was now Matte and that he was only regent during his son's minority.

Our imperfect knowledge of the language prevented us from enquiring into these mysterious customs; however, we learned that as soon as a child is born, the honours and titles of the father immediately become his or hers, and the father becomes guardian to his child and honours it as his superior. The present Too, king of Tahiti, is a boy of nine or ten years old, but for reasons to be explained hereafter, he never came on board, although Mr. Bligh went once to see him on shore. He frequently paddled round the ship in his canoe and received homage from all who saw the canoe. He was generally carried on the shoulders of a man who sat on the bow of the canoe, it being the custom of this country to prefer the bow to the stern.

When any strange visitors came, they were entertained by Mr. Bligh, who gratified their curiosity by firing a gun, at which they appeared much amazed. They always stopped their ears and fell down as soon as they saw the flash, and a pistol was to all appearance as much dreaded as a four-pounder. Mr. Bligh took the opportunity at such times to show them the effects of round and grape shot, which to them appeared wonderful. They always exclaimed in amazement when they saw the shot fall, scarcely giving credit to what they saw.

While we lay in Matavai Bay, the nun buoy was cut from the best bower anchor, the cutter's rudder stolen, several hooks and thimbles cut from the rigging, and several other things missed; Mr. Bligh applied to Otoo, or Matte, to have them returned. Some of them were brought back, but the buoy and rudder were destroyed, and only some pieces of the wood brought. As these things were readily found, it was thought that the chiefs were accessories to the thefts. The numbers that frequented the ship and tent rendered it impossible to observe all their actions. As the thefts were not very considerable, and large allowances were being made by Mr. Bligh in favour of the natives, the best method to prevent thieving was by keeping things as much out of their way as possible—by fixing wooden buoys and placing all the loose ironwork into the storerooms until wanted—few accidents of this kind happened afterwards.

While we lay at Oparre we cut wood for sea store, filled our water, and over-hauled the blocks, sails, and rigging. Here, the ship began to swarm with cock-roaches. Every method was tried to get rid of them but to no purpose. After repeated washing and carrying every chest and box on shore, where the clothes, etc., were cleared of them, they appeared as plentiful as ever in two or three days. The cables appeared alive with them, and they seemed to increase instead of diminish, though great quantities were destroyed every day. Hot water was now applied twice a week, and the cables and every part of the ship from stem to stern washed with it, but to no purpose. They flew to the hold rigging and mastheads and returned as before. Our attention was now drawn to the sail room and storerooms, where the hot water had found its way but had done no other damage than wetting everything in them. The hot water was now disused, and the sails, canvas lines, etc., were got on shore, washed with salt water, dried, and made up while the carpenters caulked over the store and sail rooms.

DESERTION AND PUNISHMENT

On the 24th of January at four in the morning, the small cutter was missed. Lieutenant Bligh was acquainted with it, and the hands being called, it was found that Charles Churchill, John Millward, and William Muspratt were missing. As Mr. Hayward, a midshipman, had been asleep on his watch, and a small bag with trade being found on deck, it was readily supposed that they had taken the boat—especially as it was known that Millward was sentry from twelve till two.

On examination, it was found that from the cutter's arms chest they had eight stand of arms complete and eight cartouch boxes of ammunition. The large cutter was hoisted out, the master sent in her to Matavai in quest of the boat, and Mr. Hayward ordered to be placed in irons. The master returned about eight o'clock, having met the cutter with five natives who were coming to the ship. They informed us that the three men before named had brought her to Matavai and left her, took the arms chest on board a canoe, and sailed for Tetooroa—a number of small islands enclosed by a reef, eight leagues north of Point Venus.

On examining Churchill's chest, a paper was found containing his own name and that of three of the party on shore, which Churchill had written. Lieutenant Bligh went on shore to the house and informed Mr. Christian of the business, calling the men and challenging them with being in league with Churchill and intending to desert. They persisted in their innocence and denied it so firmly that he was inclined from circumstances to believe them and said no more to them about it.

He then went in quest of Matte, who was by this time informed by his men of the affair and was coming to the tent. As soon as Mr. Bligh saw him, he told him the affair and asked him to have the men brought back, which he promised to do. Several canoes under the command of Moana, an old chief, and Areepaeea (chief of Oparre, Matte's brother) were dispatched after them, with instructions on how to proceed to take them by stratagem.

Three weeks elapsed before any account was heard of them. On the 15th of February, Hetee-hetee [This man had spent seven months with Captain Cook on board the *Resolution* in 1773–74, visiting the Friendly Islands, New Zealand, Easter Island, and the Marquesas.] (the same mentioned by Captain Cook), came on board and informed Mr. Bligh that they were landed at the upper part of Tettahah, about six miles to the westward, on which Mr. Bligh manned the launch and went after them. On coming to the place, he learned from them that they had been overset within the reef, had lost a musket, and were nearly drowned. The night being very bad, he did not return to the ship until next morning, when they were put in irons. After a month's confinement, they were punished, Churchill with two dozen [lashes] and the others four dozen each. They were returned to duty, and Mr. Hayward, after receiving a severe rebuke for his neglect of duty, was also set at liberty and returned to his duty.

February, 1789. A little time after, the small bower cable was observed to be cut through two strands at the water's edge. As the cable hung slack under the bottom, it was not observed until a squall from the westward brought it to bear ahead. We hove it in and spliced it before the wind became sufficiently strong to part it.

This gave rise to many opinions and strict enquiry was made, but no person on board could give any account of it. It was the private opinion of the men, as well as officers, that no native had been so bold as to attempt it; some supposed they had, thinking to be well paid for their trouble in diving after the buoy, which was sunk, as they had been paid for their assistance in clearing the cable off the rocks when the ship got on shore coming in. They were expert at this and had passed a lead line round a buoy rope before in seventeen fathoms, the buoy having sunk. However, although they are not very guilty of keeping secrets, this remained a profound one and was not found out while the ship remained here.

While we were watering, the casks were all got on shore, and the cooper set to work to put them in order at the tent. After a dark, rainy night, a puncheon was missing, together with some of the gunners' bedding, and an azimuth compass broken (which was kept at the tent for the purpose of surveying), and part of it carried away. Mr. Bligh had made a strict survey of the harbour and Matavai Bay, and as soon as Mr. Bligh heard of this, he went on shore and rebuked the officers at the tent for neglecting their duty. The officers alleged that the night was so dark and the rain fell so fast that they could not see or hear each other, and that the thief had taken a full cask, though the empty ones stood close by. He then went in a passion to Matte and insisted on having the thief delivered up.

In a short time, the thief and cask were both brought to the tent, and Matte told Mr. Bligh to shoot him, which he said would make the others afraid to steal. As soon as he was delivered up, he was tied and brought on board, where he was punished with a hundred lashes and put in irons. Mr. Bligh intended to keep him prisoner until the ship sailed, but he found means to get out and make his escape without being perceived by anyone but the gentry. They heard him plunge overboard but never saw any more of him, the darkness of the night favouring his escape. We heard no more of him. It seems he had observed the yeoman putting the marlin spikes in by the foremast, near which he lay in the galley; with one of them he twisted the lock to pieces without being heard and, going up the forescuttle, jumped overboard.

FAREWELL TO PARADISE

Towards the latter end of March, we put the rigging in order and bent the sails. Mr. Nelson, having collected upwards of a thousand fine breadfruit plants, with many others of value, we got ready for sea, getting them on board by the 1st of April. The natives, to show the last token of their friendship, loaded us with presents, and the ship became lumbered with hogs, coconuts, and green plantains for sea store. The plantains were all taken aft, and such hogs as Mr. Bligh thought fit to keep were penned up in the waist. The rest were either killed or returned, as the owners thought fit.

Every cask being filled and a good store of firewood on board, on the 4th we placed buoys in the channel. The morning being calm, we weighed anchor and towed out; a breeze sprang up and we hove to, to stow the boats and anchors, but on fishing the best bower, the stock, being much worm-eaten, broke and fell overboard. Captain Cook's picture was now sent on shore by Poeno, with the *Bounty*'s name and the intent of her voyage put on the back.

April, 1789. We were followed out by a number of our friends. Matte and Eddea, with several others, remained on board the ship until three in the afternoon, when the small cutter was sent to put them on shore. Their parting with the lieutenant and officers was truly a tender scene. The rest being gone in their canoes, Mr. Bligh gave Matte a musket, two pistols, some powder, and ball flints, etc., and a chest to keep his trade and ammunition in. The chest also was filled with the presents Mr. Bligh had made him. The carpenter also gave him an American musket. He seemed highly pleased but was quite at a loss how to express himself on the occasion. When they landed, they loaded the boat with coconuts and returned; the coconuts were hoisted in.

As the labour of the day had been very great, a double allowance of grog was given to all hands. Everything being secured at five in the evening, we bore away and made sail to the WNW, passing Morea or Eymayo in the night. Everybody seemed in high spirits and began already to talk of home, affixing the length of the passage and counting up their wages. One would readily have imagined that we had just left Jamaica instead of Tahiti, so far onward did their flattering fancies waft them.

At ten a.m. we made Hooaheine. The hands were mustered, and as usual most of their grog was stopped for not being clean. At noon we hove to off Farree Harbour to enquire about O'Mai but could get no other information other than that he was dead for some time. The natives brought off a few yams and a hog or two, which

Map of the Bounty at Tubuai

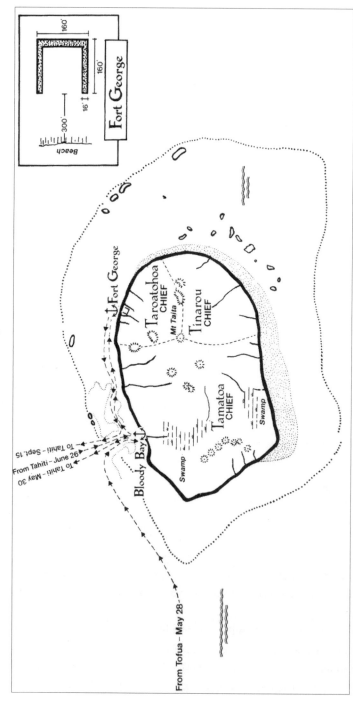

A map of Tubuai charts the *Bounty*'s visits during Fletcher Christian's failed attempt to colonize the island and shows the location of Bloody Bay, as well as Fort George, which was constructed by the mutineers. The diagram of Fort George is based on a drawing by Glynn Christian. Reprinted with permission of Cambridge University Press.

were purchased for Mr. Bligh. In the evening we made sail, leaving Ryeatea on the starboard hand standing to the SW until midnight—when we altered our course to the westward, having passed the islands of Ryeatea and Tahaa, etc., and now took a farewell of the Society Isles.

Plantains were now served in lieu of bread at six per man per day, with one pound of fresh pork. When they were expended, the yams and taro were issued at one pound per day until we arrived at Annamooka.

On Sunday the 12th we exercised backing and filling, making and shortening sail, etc. The wind, coming to the westward and blowing hard, gave us an opportunity to exert our abilities in earnest. On the 13th we discovered an island that we sailed nearly all the way around; it appeared to be surrounded by a reef, inside of which was deep water and five or six small keys.

Three of the natives came off in a canoe on the 15th, the weather being now calm and fine. They seemed much surprised at everything they saw. As soon as they came on board they fell down and kissed Mr. Bligh's feet, giving him the pearl shells that they wore on their breasts, suspended by collars of braided hair. In return he gave them each a knife and some beads, of which they seemed very fond though they knew not the use. He also gave them a young boar and sow, as we found they had no such animals.

Their language seemed to differ from that of the Society Isles, though they knew the breadfruit plants by the same name. They were loath to leave the ship and one of them would have stayed while the others went on shore for some coconuts, but it growing late, we could not stay. They called the island Wytootache, and when they left us they seemed reluctant, still looking at the ship as they paddled away. The canoe differed from those of the Society Isles, being alike at each end but indifferently built.

In the evening a whirlwind passed us between seven and eight o'clock that almost hove the ship about, after which a breeze sprang up. We made sail and on the 16th passed Savage Island at ten at night.

On the 19th we made the islands of Caow and Toofoa, two of the Friendly Isles, but calms and currents prevented us from reaching Annamooka till the 23rd. This is a low island, one of the eastern range of the Friendly Isles (of which there are many). It lies about sixteen or seventeen leagues to the ESE of Tofua, which is a high lump with a large volcano on the top. Caow is a high peak like a sugar loaf and may be seen ten or twenty leagues off in clear weather. These two are not more than three leagues distant from each other. On the 24th a party was sent to wood and water.

Annamooka, or Rotterdam, was first discovered by Tasman, the Dutch navigator, who reduced the natives to good behaviour. Their present behaviour seems to be such as the dread of firearms produces, for they were very rude and attempted to take the casks from the waterers and the axes from the wooding party. If a musket was pointed at any of them, it produced no other effect than a return of the compliment, by poising their club or spear with a menacing look.

TENSIONS RISE

As it was Lieutenant Bligh's orders that no person should affront them on any occasion, they were emboldened by meeting no return to their insolence. They became so troublesome that Mr. Christian, who had the command of the watering party, found it difficult to carry on his duty. Of this he informed Lieutenant Bligh, who damned him for a cowardly rascal, asking him if he was afraid of a set of naked savages while he had arms—to which Mr. Christian answered, "The arms are no use while your orders prevent them from being used."

On the morning of the 25th Mr. Fryer was armed and sent with the cutter to attend the launch. He had not long been at a grapnel before the natives found means of unbending it from the rope by stirring up the mud, thickening the water, and then diving down as they flocked about the boat. One man was ordered to hold the rope in his hand, but they carried it clear off before the boat drove or the man in the bow perceived the rope slack. Mr. Fryer applied to the chiefs to have it returned, but to no purpose, being obliged at present to put up with the loss. When the boats returned, he informed Lieutenant Bligh of what happened—that he applied to some of the chiefs who were then on board, but to no purpose, although they made fair promises.

During our stay here the natives flocked to the ship in great numbers to traffic for hogs, fowl, yams, coconuts, etc., all of which they seemed to know the value of. They would not part with a single plantain without something in return. Several chiefs and principal men were constantly on board, and frequently not less than a hundred canoes of different sizes were about the ship.

NATIVE CULTURE AND CUSTOMS

Their canoes will carry from two to forty men; they have both double and single canoes equipped for sailing, with well-made rope and large sails, which they work in different methods. Some are hoisted up by halyards, and in others the yard is fixed to swivel about on the masthead, having the weather yardarm confined by a strong tack of five- or six-inch rope.

The rope is made of coconut husk plaited into sinnet and then neatly laid and well twisted in three strands. The sails are of a triangular form, with a yard and boom—they are made of matting, doubled and quilted. Some of those booms were longer and bigger than our main yard. Those that hoist and lower their sail work to windward in the same manner as the flying proa of the Ladrones, with both ends alike; but the others are different and always sail one end first. They are neatly built and well finished and sail at an amazing rate in smooth water—but in a rough sea they can never answer.

Their fishhooks are made of pearl, bone, and tortoiseshell, of which they have plenty. Their weapons are clubs about three feet long, of hardwood neatly carved and inlaid with bone and pearl; long spears with barbs of three inches, fixed at equal distances for three feet in length; bows of about six or seven feet long of a very elastic wood; arrows pointed with the stings of the sting ray; and slings made of the husk of the coconut.

Their clothing is in both sexes alike and is mostly one piece of cloth or matting tied round the waist and descending below the knees. The matting is chiefly worn at sea or in wet weather and is of several sorts, neatly made. Their cloth is made of the bark of the cloth tree. They have a method of glazing it to make it keep out wet, and stain it with brown and black, which gives it a very handsome appearance.

Both sexes dress their hair with lime or burnt shells, which though originally black, soon turns to red, purple, and white. Though the countenances of the men are open, yet they have something in it that gives an unfavourable impression to strangers; perhaps this might have been heightened in our eyes by their actions, which did not correspond with their name.

We saw here several well-made earthen vessels and many curious pieces of workmanship and ingenuity. Their canoes appear to be the best made and the neatest work of any we had seen. Though not so large as some, they are well calculated for their seas, which are mostly smooth, owing to the number of islands with reefs round their eastern side and the shallow water about them.

Both men and women run of the common size; they are of a copper colour and are well made. The women are handsome and know how to set a price on their favours. The men are tattooed from the knee to the waist, which somewhat resembles a pair of breeches; the women are not tattooed, but have on their shoulders several circles, indented with burning hot bamboos of different sizes. Many of both sexes lack a part, if not the whole, of their little fingers, which we understood were cut off as a tribute to the memory of their deceased friends.

Having filled all the water and got on board some wood and large quantities of yams, coconuts, plantains, etc., on the 26th we hoisted in the boats. Having but a light air, we got all ready for weighing anchor. The three chiefs who were on board had promised that the grapnel should be restored if Mr. Bligh would wait till the canoe returned—which they said was gone to another island after it. Two hours' liberty was given to the people to expend their trade. As this was likely to be the last island where iron currency was the most valuable, everyone got rid of their trade as fast as they could. They purchased mats, spears, and many curiosities, and a quantity of yams for private store, with coconuts, etc., and everything the natives had or would dispose of. With yams and clubs in all quarters, the ship was so lumbered that there was scarcely room to stir in any part.

About noon we weighed anchor and stowed the anchor. The fore-topsail being loose, we stood to the westward with a light air. The ship's company was armed and drawn up, and the chiefs made prisoners. The canoes were ordered to cast off and keep astern. At this, the chiefs seemed much displeased. They were ordered down to the mess room, where Mr. Bligh followed them and set them to peel coconuts for his dinner. He then came up and dismissed all the men but two who were under arms, but not until he had passed the compliment on officers and men, to tell them that they were a parcel of lubberly rascals and that he would be one of five who would, with good sticks, disarm all of them. He aimed a pistol at William McCoy and threatened to shoot him for not paying attention.

About four in the afternoon we hove to, the canoes being all gone but one double one, on board of which were some women who wept bitterly and cut their faces and shoulders in a terrible manner—as did the oldest of the chiefs, who struck himself several violent blows on the face and cut himself on the cheek bones with his fists. Mr. Bligh now ordered the canoe alongside, seeing no appearance of the grapnel, and dismissed them with presents. The youngest would have stripped and left his mat on board if he had been permitted, but the others seemed as if they only smothered their resentment. Seeing that they could not revenge the insult, however, they went away and stood in for the island. It was the opinion of most on board that if a weak-manned ship came their way, they would remember this day's transaction and make them suffer for it.

The produce of these islands is much the same in every respect as the Society Isles, but they take much pain to cultivate the earth here. The yams here are the largest in the world and equally as good as those of the East or West Indies, but they are indifferently watered—the only water at Annamooka being a stagnant pool that, in a very dry season, may entirely dry up. This is not much felt by the natives, who use very little water in dressing their food; the coconuts supply them with drink in the driest season.

Their animals are the same as those of the Society Isles, but their hogs are in general small; the reefs abound with a variety of fine fish. The coconuts here are very large, but the shells are of a coarse, open grain. Some of them will hold five pints, and the natives use them to carry water in their canoes.

Our stay here being short, it was not possible to examine the manners and customs of these people, but as Captain Cook has been very minute in his description of them, I must refer the reader to his voyage and return to a more interesting part of the business. When the chiefs were gone we made sail, but the wind being light and frequently flattening to a calm, we made very little way during the night. As we neared Tofua, we observed vast columns of smoke and flame issuing from the volcano, which appeared to be a very large one.

THE BREAKING POINT

The weather continuing the same all day, we altered our position very little, being within seven or eight leagues of the island all the day, with no appearance of a breeze. On the afternoon of the 27th, Mr. Bligh came up and was taking a turn about the quarterdeck when he missed some of the coconuts that were piled up between the guns. He said that they were stolen and could not have disappeared without the knowledge of the officers, who were all called. They declared that they had not seen a man touch them, to which Mr. Bligh replied, "Then you must have taken them yourselves," and ordered Mr. Elphinstone to go and fetch every coconut in the ship aft.

He then questioned every officer in turn concerning the number they had bought, and coming to Mr. Christian, asked him. Mr. Christian answered, "I do not know sir, but I hope you don't think me so mean as to be guilty of stealing yours." Mr. Bligh replied, "Yes, you damned hound, I do—You must have stolen them from me or you could give a better account of them—God damn you, you scoundrels, you are all thieves alike, and combine with the men to rob me—I suppose you'll steal my yams next, but I'll sweat you for it, you rascals, I'll make half of you jump overboard before you get through Endeavour Strait." He then called Mr. Samuel and said, "Stop these villains' grog, and give them but half a pound of yams tomorrow, and if they steal then, I'll reduce them to a quarter." The coconuts were carried aft, and he went below.

The officers then got together and were heard to murmur much at such treatment, and it was discussed among the men that the yams would be next seized, as

Lieutenant Bligh knew that they had purchased large quantities of them, and set about secreting as many as they could.

MUTINY BREAKS OUT

The night being calm, we made no way, and in the morning of the 28th, the boat-swain came to my hammock and waked me, telling me to my great surprise that the ship was taken by Mr. Christian. I hurried on deck and found it true—seeing Mr. Bligh in his nightshirt with his hands tied behind him and Mr. Christian standing by him with a drawn bayonet in his hand and his eyes flaming with revenge. Several of the men were under arms, and the small cutter hoisted out, and the large one getting ready. I applied to the boatswain to know how I should proceed, but he was as much at a loss as I and in a confused manner told me to lend a hand in clearing the boat and getting her out, which I did. When she was out, the small one was got in.

Mr. Christian called to Mr. Hayward and Mr. Hallet to get into the boat and ordered Churchill to see the master and clerk into her. Lieutenant Bligh then began to reason, but Mr. Christian replied, "Mamu, sir, not a word, or death's your portion." Mr. Hayward and Mr. Hallet begged, with tears in their eyes, to be suffered to remain in the ship, but Mr. Christian ordered them to be silent.

The boatswain and carpenter came aft (the master and gunner being confined below) and begged for the launch, which with much hesitation was granted, and she was ordered out. While I was clearing her, the master came up and spoke to Mr. Bligh and afterwards came to me, asking me if I had any hand in the mutiny. I told him I had not, and he then asked me to try what I could do to raise a party and rescue the ship, which I promised to do—in consequence of which, John Millward, who was by me at the time, swore he would stand by me and went to Muspratt, Burkett, and the boatswain on that score. But Churchill, seeing the master speaking to me (though he was instantly hurried away by Quintal, ordering him down to his cabin), came and demanded what he had said. I told him that he was asking about the launch, but Alexander Smith, who stood on the other side of the boat, told Churchill to look sharp after me, saying, "Tis a damned lie, Charles, for I saw him and Millward shake hands when the master spoke to them, and called to the others to stand to their arms, which put them on their guard."

As I saw none near me that seemed inclined to make a push, and the officers busy getting the boat in order, I was fain to do so too and the boat was got out. Everyone ran to get what they could into her and get in themselves as fast as possible. The officers were hurried in, and when Mr. Bligh found that he must go, he begged Mr. Christian to desist, saying, "I'll pawn my honour, I'll give my bond, Mr. Christian, never to think of this if you'll desist," and mentioned his wife and family, to which Mr. Christian replied, "No, Captain Bligh, if you had any honour, things would not have come to this; and if you had any regard for your wife and family, you should have thought on them before, and not behaved so much like a villain." Lieutenant Bligh attempted again to speak, but was ordered to be silent. The boatswain also tried to pacify Christian, to which he replied, "Tis too late, I have been in hell for this fortnight past and am determined to bear it no longer. And you know, Mr. Cole, that I have been used like a dog all the voyage."

The master begged to be permitted to stay, but was ordered into the boat. Mr. Christian gave Churchill orders to see that no arms went in the boat. In getting the things into the boat, a dispute happened between Churchill and the carpenter about the latter's tool chest, which Churchill wanted to keep in the ship. By Mr. Christian's orders, it was allowed to go in the boat, but he told Churchill to keep the carpenter's mates and the armourer on board. The boat's masts and sails were got in and all the new, light canvas with nails, saws (hand, whip, and cross-cut), trade, and the lieutenants' and master's clothes, two gang casks of water, four empty breeves, three bags of bread with Mr. Bligh's case, some bottles of wine, and several other things, insomuch that she almost sunk alongside.

Lieutenant Bligh then begged that some of the people would stay and asked Mr. Christian to let the master stay with them, but he answered, "The men may stay but the master must go with you." Mr. Bligh then said, "Never fear, my lads; you can't all go with me, my lads; I'll do you justice if ever I reach England." He was then brought to the gangway and cast off his hands, and he went into the boat. While the boatswain was getting his things into the boat, I told him my intention was to stay and take my chance in the ship, telling him of the captain's promise, and as he saw the situation of the boat, which was scarcely seven inches free, I had no occasion to point out the danger to him. He repeated Lieutenant Bligh's promise, saying, "God bless you, my boy; were it not for my wife and family, I would stay myself."

After Mr. Bligh was in the boat, he begged for his commission and sextant; the commission was instantly given him, with his pocket book and private journal, by Mr. Christian's order. Christian took his own sextant, which commonly stood on the dripstone case, and handed it into the boat with a *Daily Assistant*, saying, "There, Captain Bligh, this is sufficient for every purpose, and you know the sextant to be a good one." [Thomas Haselden's *Seaman's Daily Assistant, Being a Short,*

Easy, and Plain Method of Keeping a Journal at Sea, first published in London, 1757, and later in Philadelphia, was a practical guide for sailors. Haselden was a teacher of mathematics in the Royal Navy.]

The boat was now veered astern and several things thrown overboard to make room, having on board nineteen hands. When the boat was put to rights, Mr. Bligh begged for a musket. This was refused, but Mr. Christian ordered four cutlasses to be handed in, and I handed in twenty-five or twenty-six four-pound pieces of pork and two gourds of water. Several other things were handed in over the stern, and as the ship made little way, they got ready for rowing and were cast off, when they stood in for the land about eight or nine leagues distant.

It was now about eight o'clock in the morning. The large cutter was hoisted in and stowed, and the arms collected and put into the chest, when the whole that appeared were ten muskets, two pistols, and two cutlasses. The pistols had been taken from the master's cabin and were loaded with powder for the purpose of firing the guns.

The behaviour of the officers on this occasion was dastardly beyond description. None of them ever made the least attempt to rescue the ship, which would have been effected had any attempt been made by one of them, as some of those who were under arms did not know what they were about. Robert Lamb, who I found gentry at the fore-hatchway when I first came on deck, went away in the boat. Isaac Martin had laid his arms down and gone into the boat, but had been ordered out again.

Their passive obedience to Mr. Christian's orders even surprised himself, and he said immediately after the boat was gone that something more than fear had possessed them to suffer themselves to be sent away in such a manner, without offering to make resistance. When the boat put off, Mr. Stewart and Mr. Heywood, who had been confined in their berth, came up. Mr. Christian related the cause of this sad affair to the following effect: Finding himself much hurt by the treatment he had received from Mr. Bligh, he had determined to quit the ship the preceding evening and informed the boatswain, carpenter, Mr. Stewart, and Mr. Heywood of his resolution, who supplied him with some nails, beads, and part of a roasted pig, with some other articles he put into a bag that he got from Mr. Hayward (the bag was produced and I knew it to be the same that I had made for Mr. Hayward some time before).

The bag was put into the clew of Robert Tinkler's hammock, where he found it at night, but the matter was then smothered and passed off. He also had made fast some staves to a stout plank that lay on the larboard gangway, with which he intended to make his escape; but finding he could not effect it in the first and middle watches, as the people were all stirring, he went to sleep about half past three in the morning.

When Mr. Stewart called him to relieve the watch, he had not slept long and was much out of order. Stewart begged him not to attempt swimming away, saying, "The people are ripe for anything." This made a forcible impression on his mind, and finding that Mr. Hayward, the mate of his watch (with whom he refused to discourse), soon went to sleep on the arms chest that stood between the guns and Mr. Hallet not making his appearance, he at once resolved to seize the ship. Disclosing his intention to Quintal and Martin, they called up Churchill and Thompson, who put the business in practice. With Smith, Williams, and McCoy, he went to Coleman and demanded the keys of the arms chest (which Coleman, the armourer, always kept), saying he wanted a musket to shoot a shark that happened to come alongside.

Finding Mr. Hallet asleep on the arms chest, he roused him and sent him on deck. The keys were instantly procured and his party armed, as were all the rest who stood in his way, without their knowing for what purpose. In the meantime, Norman had waked Mr. Hayward to look after the shark, at which he was busy when Mr. Christian came up the fore-hatchway with his party. He left Thompson to take care of the arms chest, arming Burkett and Lamb at the hatchway, and commanding Mr. Hayward and Mr. Hallet to be silent. He proceeded to secure Lieutenant Bligh, whom he brought on deck, placing two sentries at the master's cabin door to keep him in, and to keep the gunner and Mr. Nelson in the cockpit— and proceeded as before described.

About nine o'clock, a breeze sprang up and sails were trimmed. When asking the opinion of his party, it was agreed to steer for Tahiti and stood to the southwest. When Mr. Christian had related his plan to leave the ship, I then recollected seeing him make the staves fast to the plank the night before and hearing the boatswain say to the carpenter, "It won't do tonight." Afterwards I saw Mr. Stewart and Mr. Christian several times up and down the fore-cockpit, where the boatswain's and carpenter's cabins were, and where Mr. Christian seldom or ever went.

At noon, Tofua bore NE ten leagues, the boat out of sight under the land.

Mr. Christian, having as, before said, determined on his route, hauled to the southward in order to proceed to Tahiti, touching at Tubuai on the way. [Tubuai, one of the Austral group, lies about three hundred miles south of Tahiti. No Europeans had landed on it, but Captain Cook had sailed past it on his third voyage and had put it on the charts.] He divided the men that remained on board into two watches, appointing George Stewart to the charge of one and kept the other himself. He ordered me to take charge of the stores and act as boatswain, Thomas McIntosh as carpenter, and John Mills as gunner. However, this is not to be considered as a point of authority. It was for no other purpose than taking care of the stores and that he might have some person to call on in these departments, everyone doing their duty alike and obeying his orders. Here it may not be improper to explain the affair more clearly by giving a list of those who went in the boat as well as who remained. Those who went in the boat were:

William Bligh, Lieutenant and Commander
John Fryer, Master
William Elphinstone, Master's Mate
William Cole, Boatswain
William Purcell, Carpenter
William Peckover, Gunner
Thomas Hayward, Midshipman
John Hallet, Midshipman
John Samuel, Clerk
Thomas Ledward, Surgeon's Mate
Robert Tinkler, Midshipman
John Norton, Quartermaster
Peter Linkletter, Quartermaster
George Simpson, Quartermaster's Mate
Lawrence Labogue, Sailmaker
John Smith, Captain's Cook
Thomas Hall, Ship's Cook
Robert Lamb, Butcher
David Nelson, Botanist
In all 19

Those who remained in the ship were:

Fletcher Christian, Acting Lieutenant
George Stewart, Midshipman
Edward Young, Midshipman
Peter Heywood, Midshipman
James Morrison, Boatswain's Mate
Thomas McIntosh, Carpenter's Crew

John Mills, Gunner's Mate

Charles Norman, Carpenter's Mate

Isaac Martin, Able Seaman

Charles Churchill, Master at Arms

Joseph Coleman, Armourer

William Muspratt, Captain's Steward

John Sumner, Able Seaman

John Williams, Able Seaman

John Millward, Able Seaman

William McCoy, Able Seaman

Matthew Thompson, Able Seaman

Matthew Quintal, Able Seaman

Alexander Smith, Able Seaman

Thomas Burkett, Qr. Gunner

Henry Hillbrant, Cooper

Michael Byrne (blind), Able Seaman

Richard Skinner, Master's Servant

Thomas Ellison (a boy), Able Seaman

William Brown, Botanist's Assistant

In all 25

By these lists it would appear that Mr. Christian had the strongest party. However, this was not the case. Lieutenant Bligh himself did, and he has already acknowledged it [in *Narrative of the Mutiny*, 1790]. The fact was that none seemed inclined to dispute the superiority, and Mr. Christian, at the head of eight or nine men, was permitted to proceed as before described. Even after the boat was gone, some of them hardly knew what part they had acted in the business.

CHRISTIAN ASSUMES COMMAND

Mr. Christian, now finding himself master of the ship, ordered the plants to be thrown overboard to clear the cabin, which was finished by the 1st or 2nd of May. The effects of the officers were collected into it with the Tahiti and Friendly Isles cloth and curiosities, and Christian took possession of Mr. Bligh's cabin.

May, 1789. As I had reason to believe from the countenance of affairs that the ship might yet be recovered if a party could be formed, and as I knew that several on board were not at all pleased with their situation, I fixed on a plan for that purpose.

I soon gained several to back my opinion. We proposed to take the opportunity of the night when the ship anchored at Tahiti, when we could easily get rid of those we did not like by putting them on shore. In all probability, our design might be favoured by an extra allowance of grog.

These matters being settled, I had no doubt that everyone would stand to the test; and to prevent the others from knowing our design, affected a shyness towards each other. But I soon found to my unspeakable surprise that Mr. Christian was acquainted with our intentions, some of his party overhearing some part of the business. But as he was not positive how many were concerned, he took no further notice than threatening Coleman that he should be left on shore at Tubuai until the ship returned from Tahiti.

He got the arms chest into the cabin, taking the keys from Coleman, who had always kept them. They were now given to Churchill, who made his bed on the chest. Each of Mr. Christian's party was armed with a brace of pistols. Mr. Christian himself never went without a pistol in his pocket, the same one that Lieutenant Bligh formerly used. A sharp lookout was kept by his party, one of which took care to make a third when they saw any two in conversation.

On the 9th, being in the latitude of 30° south, the wind shifted to the westward in a heavy squall that split the fore-topsail. This was the first accident of the kind we experienced during the voyage and was chiefly owing to the sails being much worn. However, it was soon replaced, and the wind continued fair till we made Tubuai, which happened on May 28th.

During this passage, Mr. Christian cut up the old studding sails to make uniforms for all hands, taking his own for edging, observing that nothing had more effect on the mind of the Indians as a uniformity of dress—which, by the by, has its effect among Europeans, as it always betokens discipline, especially on board British Men-of-War.

When we got in with the island, the small cutter was sent with George Stewart to examine the reef and find the opening described by Captain Cook. While he was on this duty, he was attacked by a number of the natives in a canoe, who boarded him and carried off a jacket and some other things. He had no arms but a brace of pistols, one of which misfired, and they were not certain that the other did execution. The natives were armed with long spears that became useless at close quarters, by which means the boat's crew escaped being hurt. The natives, being frightened by the report of the pistol, made off.

The cutter came to a grapnel to mark the passage for the ship, which got in and anchored in the afternoon of the 29th, and next morning weighed anchor and warped in to a sandy bay, mooring with one bower and the kedge in three and one-half fathoms, two cable lengths from the shore.

BATTLE AT "BLOODY BAY"

The natives now began to assemble on the beach, and numbers flocked round the ship in their canoes. At first they were very shy, paddling round and blowing their conch shells, of which they had one or two in every canoe. After viewing the ship they paddled on shore to those on the beach, who appeared armed with clubs and spears of a shining black wood, with a number of conchs blowing. Their dress, being red and white, gave them a formidable appearance.

They kept off all day, and all we could say to persuade them to come on board (though they seemed to speak the Tahitian language) was of no use. Next morning we observed their numbers to be much increased, both in men and canoes, which had arrived in the night. At last an old man, whom we supposed was a chief, came on board. He appeared to view everything he saw with astonishment and appeared frightened at the hogs, goats, dog, etc., starting back when any of them turned towards him. Mr. Christian gave him several presents, and he went on shore seemingly satisfied, promising to return again. We supposed that his visit was not for the purpose of friendship, as he had been particular in counting our number. The arms were therefore got to hand that we might be in readiness to receive the promised visit. Their ferocious aspects gave us plainly to understand in what manner we might expect it.

About noon we observed them making a stir upon the beach and launching their canoes, which were filled with men, and soon moved towards the ship. Among them was a double canoe, full of neatly dressed women, their heads and necks decorated with flowers and pearl shells. As they approached the ship they stood up and beat time to a song given by one of them, who appeared to be a person of some consequence.

Afterwards, we found out that she was the daughter of a chief. They were all young and handsome, having fine long hair that reached their waists in waving ringlets. They came on board without ceremony, being in number eighteen. Six men paddled the canoe, followed by five others. In the meantime, about fifty canoes manned with fifteen or twenty men each paddled round on the other side, closing in and blowing their conchs. On seeing this we supposed that the women had been sent as a snare to catch us, as they came so readily on board. Being on our guard, which they observed, and having changed our dress, they were disappointed and made no attempt.

The women were treated with civility and presents made to each, but the men who followed them began to steal everything they could lay hands on. One of them took the card off the compass, the glass being broke. [A compass card is a card labeling the 360° of the circle and the named directions such as north, south, east, and west. Part of a compass, the circular card is graduated in degrees. It is attached to the compass needles and conforms to the magnet meridian-referenced direction system inscribed with direction. The vessel turns, not the card.] Mr. Christian observed him secreting it and took it from him, but not before it was torn. As he refused to part with it, and being a stout fellow, a scuffle ensued; however, he was worsted. Mr. Christian gave him two or three smart stripes with a rope's end and sent him into the canoe. The others, who had not been idle, followed him, as did the women, whom we did not think prudent to detain.

When they were put off in the canoes they began to show their weapons, which till now they had kept concealed, brandishing them with many threatening gestures. One of them got hold of the buoy and cut it away. He was paddling off with it when he was observed by Mr. Christian, who fired a musket at him; a four-pounder was fired with grape and they all paddled to the shore. The boats were now manned to follow them, but on coming to the beach, the landing was vigourously disputed by them, plying the boats smartly with stones. They did not seem to pay any attention to the muskets till they saw some of their party fall, when they took to the wood. In a few moments, all were out of sight.

As they had left several canoes on the beach, Mr. Christian ordered them to be towed off and made fast astern of the ship, thinking to make them instrumental in making peace; but the wind coming to the NW and the canoes filling with water, they broke adrift in the night and drove on shore. As the natives made no further appearance, they were suffered to remain there. We found a number of cords in the canoes, which we supposed were intended for binding us had they succeeded in their plan. Afterwards, we found this to be their purpose.

This bay lies on the NW part of the island, abreast of the opening (the only one in the reef) described by Captain Cook. From this time we called it Bloody Bay.

On the morning of the 30th, the natives not appearing, the boats were manned and armed and went round to the east end of the island, carrying a white flag in the bow of one and a Union Jack in the other. Mr. Christian landed in several places, leaving presents of hatchets, etc., in their houses, but saw none of the natives. Although he made a diligent search, he was forced to return without seeing one.

Next morning, the 31st, some of them came down and hauled the canoes up, at which they were not disturbed; they retired before the boat could reach the shore. A boat was sent to land a young goat and two pigs that were sickly and returned without seeing any of the natives. The anchors being weighed, we put to sea, steering to the NNE for Tahiti.

ATTEMPTS TO COLONIZE TUBUAI

Mr. Christian, having formed a resolution of settling on this island, was determined to return as soon as he could procure sufficient stock of hogs, goats, and poultry, of which we saw none on the island—although breadfruit, coconuts, and plantains appeared to be plentiful. The island was scarcely eighteen miles in circumference, he supposed the inhabitants to be but few, and he had hopes of bringing them into friendship, either by persuasion or force. As the anchorage for ships was not enticing, he judged that none would make choice of this island when they could reach Tahiti and that he would be permitted to live here in peace. This was all he now desired, knowing that he had taken such steps as had forever debarred him from returning to England or any civilized place, and dreamt of nothing but settling at Tubuai.

However, I cannot say that ever I agreed with Mr. Christian with respect to the plan he had formed. Nor did I ever form a favourable idea of the natives of Tubuai, whose savage aspect and behaviour could not gain favour in the eyes of any man in his senses, but were fully capable of creating distaste in anyone.

June, 1789. On the passage to Tahiti, Mr. Christian gave orders that no man should tell the name of the island or mention it to the natives. If any person was found to mention the real name, he would punish him severely, and declared that if any man deserted, he would shoot him as soon as he was brought back. Everyone knew he had the power to perform this, and having appointed his own party to keep constant guard, he distributed the trade among all hands, desiring them to make the best market they could, as it was to be the last they would ever have the opportunity of making.

He also made several distributions of the clothes, etc., that had been left by the officers and men who went in the boat. These were made out in lots by Churchill and were drawn for by tickets, but it always happened that Mr. Christian's party was always better served than those who were thought to be disaffected. However, as they had different views, no notice was taken of it at present.

On the 6th of June we anchored in Matavai Bay, where the natives flocked on board in great numbers. They were glad to see us and enquired where the rest were, what had brought us back so soon, and where we had left the plants—as they knew our stay had been too short to have reached home from the account we had formerly given them of the distance. To all these questions, Mr. Christian answered that we had met Captain Cook, who had taken Mr. Bligh and the others, with the plants and the longboat, and had sent us for hogs, goats, etc., for a new settlement that the king had sent him to make, which he described to be on New Holland.

This being made known to the people, none dared to contradict what he said, knowing if they said anything contrary, it would soon reach his ears, as the Tahitians are not remarkable for keeping secrets. But if this had not been the case, there were few who could explain the matter properly, as they were not so well versed in the language.

While we lay here, the armourer was set to work to make trade, and Churchill and myself were sent on shore to purchase hogs, goats, etc. Meanwhile, Mr. Christian entertained the chiefs on board, plying them with wine and arrack, of which they became very fond. Everyone on board was busy purchasing stock and provisions for themselves, and although the general opinion when we sailed before was that we had impoverished the island, we were now convinced that they had not missed what we got, as we now found the country full of hogs that they had kept out of sight. They appeared now better able to supply a fleet than they seemed before to supply our single ship.

The demand for ironwork increased so fast that the armourer could not supply them, though he was constantly employed. There also was a tolerably good, ready-made stock found in the ship that had not been expended during our former stay. On the 10th, William McCoy, being sentinel, fired upon a number of the natives who thronged the gangway and did not get as fast out of his way as he thought proper. But, as no damage was done, no notice was taken of it. On the night of the 14th, Churchill observed a canoe ahead of the ship and hailed her, but getting no answer, he fired at them and they paddled off.

It may here be observed that Mr. Christian's account of himself passed very well with the natives, who had not yet been informed of Captain Cook's death. Mr. Bligh had given orders that no person should mention his death, but tell the natives that he was yet alive in England and that he would probably come again to Tahiti. Mr. Christian informed them that he would come to Tahiti as soon as he had settled the country, which he called Wytootache. They were perfectly satisfied, and as they were more intent on trading than anything else, they made but few enquiries and thought little about it.

We remained here till the 16th, during which time we were plentifully supplied with every necessary by the natives, our old friends. Nor do I think they would have thought any worse of us had they known the truth of the story or been any way shy of supplying us, as Mr. Christian was beloved by the whole of them. On the contrary, none liked Mr. Bligh, though they flattered him for his riches, which is the case among polished nations, those in power being always courted.

The grand object of these people is iron, and like us with gold, it matters not by what means they get it or where it comes from, if they can only get it.

By the 16th we had mustered about 460 hogs (mostly breeders), 50 goats, a quantity of fowl, and a few dogs and cats. For a few red feathers, we got the bull and cow, on which they set little store. With these and a quantity of provisions for present use, we prepared for sea, having on board 9 men, 8 boys, 10 women, and a female child, some of which hid themselves below till we were at sea. When we shortened in the cable, the ship drove, and dropping near the Dolphin Bank, we were forced to cut away the anchor and make sail.

When we were out, a number made their appearance, among which was Hetee-hetee and several of our old friends. Mr. Christian found it too late to put them on shore. At the request of some of his party he consented to proceed to sea with them, but told them they would never see Tahiti again—at which they seemed perfectly easy and satisfied, never betraying the least sign of sorrow for leaving their friends—nor did I observe that they ever repined afterwards.

The weather proving rough during the passage, the bull that could not keep his feet and would not lie down received several falls, which killed him. Having no method of slinging him and his weight being more than he could support, we were forced to heave him overboard. Although the hogs and goats were trampling over each other for want of room, we lost but four hogs and one goat during the passage and arrived with the rest in good order, anchoring in Bloody Bay on the 23rd. The pigeons were now let loose, and a pair of them went on shore, but never returned.

We now found the natives quite friendly, and they appeared a different people, coming on board in a peaceable manner without weapons or conch shells or the least appearance of hostility. This induced Mr. Christian to land the cow and two hundred hogs on the island, at the sight of which the natives were more terrified than they had been before at the firearms. The remainder of the stock was landed on the keys, where we could more conveniently visit them, but those landed on the island were suffered to take their chances.

Landing the stock took up several days, and in the meantime, our Tahitians, come fast into the Tubuai tongue, served us as interpreters. They soon made

Reconstructed Track of the Bounty

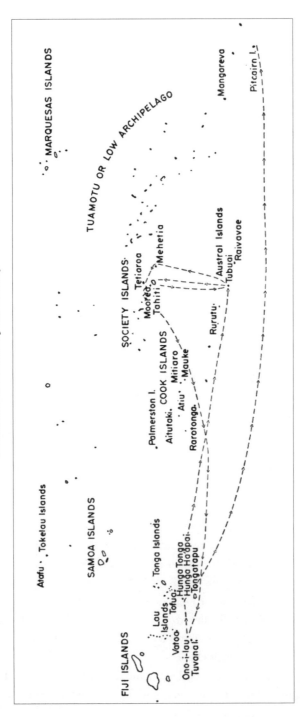

This map traces the route of the *Bounty* from the day of the mutiny to Pitcairn Island. It illustrates a famous article by H. E. Maude titled "In Search of a Home: From the Mutiny to Pitcairn Island [1789–1790]." Courtesy of Alaric Maude.

friends with the natives, who informed us that eleven men and a woman had been killed in the affair at Bloody Bay—who they said belonged to a chief on the east part of the island, called Tinnarow. As we had only seen two of them fall, we were forced to take their word. They also showed us some of the musket balls, which had struck the toa trees and fell down. They wore these round their necks in a string.

July, 1789. The chief of this part of the island, called Tummotoa, made Mr. Christian his friend after the manner of the island. Mr. Christian was going on shore to his house when he was taken to the morai and seated on a large parcel of cloth placed there for the purpose, and surrounded by all the chief's relations and the heads of families subject to him or belonging to his district. The chief first made a long speech, presenting him with a young plantain tree (which here is the emblem of peace) and a root of yava, saluting him by the name of Tummotoa, it being the custom to exchange names on making friends.

His relations came next in rotation, each performing the same ceremony, but with this difference: Each of them presented him with a piece of cloth besides the plantain and yava. After them came the landed men, each attended by a man (to the number of fifty), loaded with two baskets of provisions and a piece of cloth. The provisions consisted of raw and dressed fish, breadfruit, taro, plantains, coconuts, etc.—all which were placed before him.

The women of the chief's family came next and followed in the same manner. When all was finished the men took the cloth, provisions, and yava, and carried them to the boats. The chief came on board with Mr. Christian, where he remained all night, the most of which he spent in prayer at Mr. Christian's bedside. In the morning Mr. Christian gave him several presents, consisting of hatchets, red feathers, Tahitian cloth, and matting, with which he seemed highly pleased; but he seemed to value the red feathers more than all the rest.

Mr. Christian now went on shore with him in order to pitch upon a place to fix his residence. When he found none to please him in Tummotoa's district, he went to the next district to the eastward, which belonged to a chief called Taroatchoa— who was not in alliance with Tummotoa. He received Mr. Christian in a friendly manner and invited him to come to his land when he knew his intention, wanting him to bring the ship up and choose any part of his district. Mr. Christian accepted this offer, as he had observed a spot that he thought would answer his purpose, and exchanged names accordingly.

This made Tummotoa jealous, and he did all he could to persuade Mr. Christian not to go. Finding he could not, he grew angry. Mr. Christian promised him that he would still be his friend, which however did not satisfy him. He and Tinnarow combined together against the new alliance, prohibiting their subjects from coming to the ship or having any intercourse with Mr. Christian, who endeavoured to win them with presents, but without any effect. As he was bent on pursuing his own plan, Mr. Christian took no notice of their proceedings at present, though by their prohibiting their people from coming to the ship, the supplies of provisions were much reduced. Taroatchoa's district, being small, could not supply us with as much as we wanted.

Mr. Christian went several times to Tinnarow's, but could never obtain an interview, as both he and his dependents always fled on his approach. He now determined to fix himself on shore before attempting anything further. He gave the necessary orders respecting the frugal expense of sea provisions and the care of the stock. Mr. Christian now thought of nothing but getting on shore to live, and having fixed on a place about four miles to the eastward of the opening, prepared to warp the ship up to it as fast as possible. This proved a laborious task, the water being shallow, and the passage so beset by patches of coral rock that it was impossible to proceed in a direct line. The sea breeze, which sets in about ten or eleven in the forenoon and blows till near four in the afternoon, frequently stopped us. Our boats were not by any means calculated to carry long warps and anchors, the largest being only a light cutter of twenty feet.

After we had got about halfway, it became necessary to lighten the ship by starting the water; but that not being sufficient, the booms and spars were got out and moored at a grapnel. It started to blow fresh and they went adrift, and we saw them no more. However, Mr. Christian thought it no great loss, as he never intended to go to sea anymore.

On the 8th of July we reached the place appointed and moored the ship with both bowers (head and stem) in three fathoms, at the easternmost point of the island, in sight bearing ESE and the westernmost key N by E. We were offshore half a cable's length, and we unbent the sails and struck the topgallant yards and masts.

BUILDING "FORT GEORGE"

On the 10th Mr. Christian went on shore to make choice of his ground to build a fort on. He pitched on a spot abreast of the ship and received permission from the chief Taroatchoa (who met him there) to make what use of it he thought proper.

On his return on board, he found that John Sumner and Matthew Quintal were gone on shore without leave and did not return till next morning. He called them aft and enquired how they came to go on shore without his leave, and they answered, "The ship is moored, and we are now our own masters," upon which he clapped a pistol (which he always kept in his pocket) to one of their heads and said, "I'll let you know who is master," and ordered them both put in irons. This resolute behaviour convinced them that he was not to be played with, and when they were brought up the next day, they begged pardon and promised to behave better in the future, on which they were released.

However, to prevent the like happening again, he gave liberty for two hands to sleep on shore each night, and as many as pleased to go on shore every Sunday. He also made a distribution of red feathers to all hands, but some of them were missed out of his cabin. Thomas Ellison, who waited on him and was frequently there, was charged with having taken them, on which he was brought to the gangway, stripped and tied up; but as he persisted in his innocence, and no person having seen him with any, he was cast off.

Mr. Christian ordered that one boat crew should go every Sunday to the keys to see the stock. Things were settled for the present, and the forge got up. The armourer was set to work to make iron rammers for the muskets, the wooden ones being mostly broken. When these were completed, he set to work to alter the junk axes and make them fit for cutting wood and felling trees.

As soon as the axes were ready, the following work regulations were made:

William Brown and one Tahitian to clear a piece of ground and plant yams; Joseph Coleman and William McCoy to work at the forge, making spades, hoes, and mattocks; Henry Hillbrant to cook the provisions; Michael Byrne and Thomas Ellison, with some of the Tahitian boys, to take care of the boats; and the rest to go on shore, armed, to work. The arms were to be left under the care of a sentinel in a convenient place while the others cleared the ground; and one boat to return to the ship and the other to be kept at a grapnel near the beach.

On the 18th we went on shore, where we were met by the chief and some of the friends, who presented Mr. Christian with two young plantain trees and two roots of yava, by way of a peace offering. The ground was measured out for the fort and possession of the land taken by turning the turf and hoisting the Union Jack on a staff. On this occasion an extra allowance of grog was drunk and the place named Fort George. Finding the place overrun with rats, several cats were brought on shore and let loose among them.

While we were employed in this business, we were alarmed by a great noise of hideous shrieks and yells, which we supposed at first to be a war cry. We took to our arms, sending some of the Tahitians to enquire what it was, who soon returned and informed us that it proceeded from a funeral ceremony. It was the custom in this island that when a man of any rank dies, all his friends and relations, and all who wish him well, attend his funeral. When the body is put into the grave, a priest makes a long prayer and the bystanders rend the air with horrid cries, cutting their heads and breasts with shells and smearing their body with blood; after which the grave is filled up and they depart, leaving the near relations of the deceased to enjoy their mourning in private. Having had this information, we returned to our work.

The ground being cleared, the fort was laid out in a quadrangular form, measuring one hundred yards on each square outside of the ditch. The width of the ditch was eighteen feet, depth twenty feet from the top of the works, thickness of the wall at the base eighteen feet, on the top twelve feet, with a drawbridge on the north side fronting the beach; on this, the ship's ordnance was to be mounted in the following manner: one four-pounder on each corner and on each face two swivels, with two for reserve to be shifted as occasion might require. By this means two four-pounders and four swivels could be brought to bear in any direction, and in some directions, three four-pounders and six swivels.

Everything being settled, we proceeded to work, though not a man knew anything of fortification. Some cut stakes, others made battens, some cut sods and brought them to hand, some built, and others wrought in the ditch. The carpenters made barrows and cut timber for the gates and drawbridge. The work began to rise apace. Nor was Mr. Christian an idle spectator, for he always took part in the most laborious part of the work. An extra half a pint of porter was served twice a day.

August, 1789. We continued at work without any interruption from the natives, who visited us in numbers every day, bringing provisions. Nor did they now seem so much inclined to thieving as at first; the only things they fancied were red feathers, and the cocks with red hackles became a valuable article, being esteemed far superior to the black or grey ones. The natives seemed to view them with particular attention, but ironwork or our cloth they held in no esteem. Although they saw us using our axes and other iron tools, they set no value on them and never seemed inclined to have them in their possession, for which we were no way sorry. As their cloth is glazed so as to turn rain, they preferred it to ours and would sooner have a piece of fine Tahitian cloth than the best article of clothing we had. However, our Tahitians were not so ignorant, for they knew which was best; and though these people preferred their stone adzes to our axes, the Tahitians never attempted to alter their opinion.

On the 20th of August Mr. Christian and some others sailed round the island in the large cutter. He landed on the south side, was well received by a chief called Heetererre, and was invited on shore at several places; but the foulness of the shore prevented him from accepting. When they got off the east end, Tinnarow sent a man off with a peace offering of a young plantain tree and a root of yava and an invitation to land. He received the offering, but the shore being rocky, he could not come within three-quarters of a mile of the beach with the boat, and was forced to decline the invitation and return to the ship.

On the 25th the Tahitian men and boys were sent in quest of some coconuts, but were set upon by some of the natives, who drove them off and nearly killed one of the men with a stone. This news being brought to the fort by the boys, Mr. Christian ordered the party to arms and marched to the place where a number of the natives were in arms. Two muskets were fired among them and they fled; we returned to the fort. Next day, we learned that one man was killed; as they had carried him off, we saw nothing of him.

After this we remained quiet some days. But as the people were fond of sleeping on shore, some of them were decoyed by the women into Tinnarow's district, where they were stripped; Alexander Smith was kept prisoner at Tinnarow's house. As soon as Mr. Christian was informed of it, he resolved to punish the offenders, and marched the party into Tinnarow's district, but Tinnarow fled at his approach. When he arrived at Tinnarow's house, the woman with whom Smith had been conducted him to the place without any clothes but his shirt, the rest being taken away by Tinnarow's men.

Mr. Christian then sent several messengers to Tinnarow, asking him to return the things and make friends, both of which he refused. After waiting some hours and sending repeated messengers, who all returned with the same answer, he resolved to burn the house, which was done accordingly. Before it was set on fire, we took out some clubs and spears, and two curious carved images of their household gods, which were decorated with pearl shells, human hair, teeth, and nails, cut in a very curious manner. Round them was placed a kind of grove of red feathers from the tail of the tropic birds.

As Mr. Christian supposed these images to be of value to the owner, he ordered them to be secured, hoping that the return of them might help to make the peace. The house being now in flames, he returned to the ship. The young woman who had been Smith's companion came with him on board of her own accord, saying that her countrymen would use her ill for her friendship towards him, if she stayed on shore among them. When she found some companions on board, she was perfectly satisfied and pleased.

September, 1789. We returned to work again, and though it did not seem to go on as well as at first, it still continued to get forward. By the 1st of September, the gateposts were fixed and three-quarters of the walls completed. On the 2nd, Tinnarow came with a great number of attendants, loaded with baskets of provisions, which he presented to Mr. Christian with a peace offering. At the same time, he begged that his household gods might be restored. Mr. Christian promised to do that on condition that he restored the things his men had taken away and that he would promise not to use any of his men ill when they came into his district.

Tinnarow readily agreed and ordered some yava to be prepared, of which he wanted Mr. Christian to partake. Christian refused, upon which Tinnarow got up in a passion and departed abruptly, followed by his attendants. He found Mr. Christian aware of his treachery, his party having come armed within a small distance of the works, where they hid their spears. One of the Tahitian boys, having seen them, informed Mr. Christian, who ordered the party to arms. Tinnarow thought it fit to depart without taking his leave, as he saw that Mr. Christian had ordered his men on the top of the works where they were in good order to receive him.

The boy was sent privately off to the ship with orders to Coleman; as soon as he saw them appear on the beach armed, he fired a four-pound shot among them, at which they fled. The shot did no other damage than passing through a house, where it cut away a rafter to which a man was hanging a gourd of water. He was so terrified that he left the house, as did all who saw it, being alike surprised. The shot being lost, and the house not in sight of the ship, they could hardly be persuaded that it came from her, but readily believed it to be something supernatural and could not be persuaded to return to the house to live, judging it unsafe.

On the 3rd came old Tahoohooatumma with his son Taroatchoa, Mr. Christian's friend, and daughters. One of them was the young woman who had come on board at our first anchoring. She was called Wyakka. He brought a number of attendants loaded with provisions, which were presented to Mr. Christian. At the request of the old man, the young women performed a dance, beating time and singing. They went through the performance with much regularity, after which the Tahitian women entertained them with a dance in turn; when they took their leave, Mr. Christian invited them to see a heiva next day, which they readily accepted.

Before they arrived in the morning, two of the women were neatly dressed, and two men dressed in parais, the mourning dress of Tahiti. When the company arrived they were entertained with a heiva after the manner of the Society Isles, at which they seemed highly pleased; they were quite taken with the dress of the women and appeared astonished at the parais. This was conducted by the Tahitians, during which time the party was under arms.

Mr. Christian now began to talk of taking the masts out and dismantling the ship when he intended to erect houses and live on shore. As I had some hope that I could reach Tahiti in the large cutter, I spoke to George Stewart about the affair, who told me that he and Peter Heywood had formed the same plan. I knew that after the masts were taken out, I could put it out of Mr. Christian's power to get them in again by destroying the purchase blocks and fall; then we could reach Tahiti with no danger of being pursued.

I then advised him to get the cutter repaired, but he said Mr. Christian would not have the boats repaired till he was on shore; to prevent any suspicion, he said we had better say nothing about our plan, and he was determined to take the cutter as she was. As we had some reason to suppose that others were of the same way of thinking as us, we resolved to take the first opportunity and provided accordingly. But Providence ordered things better, and we had no need to make this rash attempt. Though the passage was short, and it might perhaps be made with safety in five or six days, yet if we met with bad weather, our crazy boat would certainly have made us a coffin.

Mr. Christian's party, finding that the natives still kept their women from living among us—though they had no objection to their sleeping with them at their own houses—began to murmur, and insisted that Mr. Christian would heed them and bring the women in to live with them by force. They refused to do any more work until every man had a wife, and as Mr. Christian's desire was to persuade rather than force them, he positively refused to have anything to do with such an absurd command. Three days were spent in debate, and having nothing to employ themselves in, they demanded more grog. This he also refused, and they broke the lock of the spirit room and took it by force.

Mr. Christian, to keep them in temper, ordered a double allowance to be served every day, but all to no purpose; and finding all his endeavours to be in vain, on the 10th he called all hands aft to ask their opinion of what was the best plan to proceed on. It was soon moved that we should go to Tahiti, where they might get women without force and there separate. This proposal was at first overruled, but was carried the next day: On a call for a show of hands, sixteen appeared for Tahiti. It was agreed that those who went on shore should have arms, ammunition, and part of everything on the ship. The ship would be left in charge of Mr. Christian, in a proper condition to go to sea, with her sails, tackle, and furniture. Everything being settled, we began to get ready for sea, filling the water and bending the sails, etc.

A party was now sent to get sufficient stock and search for the cow, which we had not seen since she was landed; but they were set upon by the natives, who beat and plundered them, and sent them to tell Mr. Christian that they would serve him the same way. This happened on the 12th, when we found that the Tubuaiian woman had returned to her friends without giving any previous notice.

WAR ERUPTS ON THE ISLAND

As the party returned without finishing their errand, Mr. Christian ordered twenty men to be armed on the 13th to go in quest of stock and to chastise the offenders. They took the nine Tahitian men and four boys, one of whom always carried the Union Jack. The party had not proceeded more than a mile from the landing before they were surrounded by about seven hundred of the natives. They had formed an ambush, into which we got before we perceived them. They were all armed with clubs, spears, and stones, and fought with more fury than judgement; otherwise, the whole party would have fallen into their hands. However, the case was otherwise, and after many obstinate and furious efforts, they gave ground and retired with great loss. The stock was collected without further trouble.

As we had some reason to think that they would be troublesome, each man was provided accordingly with twenty-four rounds of ammunition, six of which contained one musket and two pistol balls. Hetee-hetee, being an excellent shot, was armed with a musket; the rest of the Tahitians were unarmed. When we landed at the fort, we were met by Tahoohooatumma, Taroatchoa, and Taroamiva, his younger brother, and several of their friends, who informed Mr. Christian that Tinnarow had armed a number of men and was determined to dispute his right to the stock. Mr. Christian then wanted his friends to remain at the fort, lest any of them should suffer by mistake. He drew up the party, placing one Tahitian (who now armed themselves with clubs from our friends) between two of us.

Having given the necessary precautions to all, they marched in silence and good order through the wood to Tinnarow's district. We had scarcely got a mile from the fort when we got into a hollow path, beset with thick bushes on each side. Orders were given to keep a good lookout. Burkett, thinking that he heard something stir in the bush, stepped to look and received a wound in the left side with a spear. The Tahitian who was next to Burkett instantly leveled the man and seized his spear. Before Burkett could either speak or fire his piece, they started up in a swarm all round us, rushing on us with great fury and horrid yells, on which we instantly halted.

Facing different ways, we gave a smart fire, which we repeated several times with good effect. Notwithstanding, they kept pouring in from all quarters, seeming not to regard death or danger. We now found it necessary to retreat to a rising ground, at a small distance in our rear. By this time, the Tahitians were all armed with the enemies' long spears and behaved manfully. When we gained the rising ground, they followed up with redoubled fury, mocking us (as we were only a handful compared to them), even though many fell by our constant fire as they approached. However, the bush being thick above us, they plied us smartly from there.

Several of the Tahitians being wounded, and Mr. Christian having in his hurry hurt his hand on his own bayonet, we thought it prudent to retreat to a taro ground at the distance of about two hundred yards. We effected this in good order, keeping up a constant fire to cover our retreat, retreating and firing alternately till we gained the clear ground. Having posted ourselves on the banks that intersected the taro ground at right angles, we halted to receive them.

They followed close till we were out of the thicket, plying us with volleys of stones, but did not like to quit the bush. However, some of the most daring attempted to rally their men and lead them on to renew the attack. One in particular (appearing to be a chief) came out, inviting his men to follow and making many menacing gestures. He was singled out and shot, though at a good distance, as were several others who attempted to follow him. This proved a check on the others, who observed that all who came in sight were either killed or wounded. They gave ground and retreated to some distance.

In the meantime, Burkett growing faint and Skinner, having disabled his musket by putting the cartridge in whole, was ordered to take Burkett and convoy him to the boat. We stayed some time on the ground, but finding that they were not inclined to try us again, we gave them three cheers, on which they fled and left us masters of the field, leaving their dead at our disposal. Our Tahitians loaded themselves with such spoils as they thought proper, chiefly their clubs and spears, of which they were very fond.

And here it may not be improper to observe that before we quitted the field, one of the Tahitian boys desired leave to cut out the jawbones of the killed, to hang round the quarters of the ship as trophies, which he said would strike others with terror. He was much displeased when his request was denied. It was only the fear of being put to death that prevented him from setting about it, begging at least that he might be suffered to take one for himself. None of the others seemed inclined that way, as they were perhaps better pleased with the plunder, and saw that it was contrary to our inclination.

When we returned to the fort we were met by the old chief and his friends, who expressed much joy at our success. Here also Skinner joined us, having sent Burkett on board. A party was now sent to gather in what stock we wanted, and the cow was brought to the fort without opposition.

When we came on board, we found that Burkett had got his wound dressed, which was in a fair way of doing well, the spear having struck against one of his ribs. The spear thrust did not break it, and in a short time it got healed. However, this affair gave us a very poor opinion of our bayonets, though several natives had fallen by them. This always broke the neck of the bayonet and left us the socket on our musket, while the blade remained in their bodies. Our ammunition were all we had to depend on, without which they would have been an overmatch for us man for man—their spears being so long that our bayonets could be of little or no use. We observed that though their onset was furious and without order, yet every party of eighteen or twenty men had a leading man who appeared to have some authority and to whose orders they paid some regard.

On the 14th we killed the cow, which proved excellent meat. This evening the young Chief Taroamiva and two of his friends came on board. He informed us that sixty men had been killed, along with six women who were supplying them with spears and stones. A great number of wounded were among the killed, including several of note and Tinnarow's brother, who had been killed by Mr. Christian himself. Taroamiva said he had been so much Mr. Christian's friend that if he stayed on shore, he should be killed. Mr. Christian told him that he was going to Tahiti, at which he seemed rejoiced and asked if he would let him and his two friends go with him, to which Mr. Christian agreed.

They expressed much satisfaction, and having filled sufficient fresh water, we weighed our anchors on the 17th and dropped down to the opening without much trouble, the ship being much lighter than before. Having got clear of the reef, we lay by and filled with salt water to keep the ship on her legs.

At noon we made sail, leaving Tubuai well stocked with hogs, goats, fowl, dogs, and cats, the former of which were increased to four times the number we landed. But before I take my leave of the island, it may be proper to give some account of it and its inhabitants.

TUBUAI AND ITS PEOPLE, COMPARED WITH TAHITI
Tubuai lies between 22° and 23° south and about 209° east longitude, is about six miles in length from east to west, and about twenty-two miles in circumference. It is surrounded by a reef a full mile from the shore and on the east part near three miles, having but one break or entrance on the NW part, where the passage is indifferent; in some places there is four or five fathoms. Within the reef are six small keys covered with wood, chiefly the toa, a hardwood of which the natives make their clubs and spears. Four of these islands or keys are on the NE part and the others on the SE.

The island is mountainous, with a border of flatland running almost a mile or a mile and a half wide, a great part of which is covered with trees and underbrush—which makes it difficult to pass by any other road than the beach. To the eastward the land is fertile, and the low land broader than on either side, but the west end is rocky and barren. Off this part, the water is, in general, very shallow, and the reef nearest the shore. The lowland is, in general, coral sand or rock covered with a fine black mould, which in many places is not more than a foot thick, though in some places it runs to a good depth.

Near the foot of the hills are numbers of large, flat stones, and the earth is of a reddish colour, covered with fern, reeds, and bamboo. On the top of the ridges are naked rocks of hard, brown stone, though the water is shallow in some parts. In others, there was no bottom, with forty fathom of line.

It produces breadfruit, coconuts, yams, taro, plantains, and almost everything common to the Society Isles. The reef affords plenty of fish and large turtle. The cloth tree here grows to a larger size than in the Society Isles, though they do not cultivate it. Most of the trees are in common with the other islands, and they have also a species of the primrose.

The island is watered with innumerable rivulets from the hills, which being banked up for the cultivation of taro, affords shelter to the wild ducks, which are here in plenty. It also affords plenty of fine eels, shrimp, prawns, and a fish like the miller's-thumb. The island is full of inhabitants for its size, and may contain 3,000 souls. Their colour is nearly the same as that of the Society Islanders, but they are more robust and have a more savage appearance. This is heightened by the turmeric and the oil that they use to colour their cloth, which gives them a yellow, disagreeable look.

The men wear their hair and beards in different forms as they please. The young women wear their hair long, flowing in ringlets to their waist, dressing it with the white leaves of the fwharra, or palm-like ribbands and odoriferous flowers. They also make necklaces of the seeds of the ripe palm apple and flowers elegantly disposed—which not only sets their persons off to advantage, but also affords a continual nosegay to themselves and all who sit near them. They are in general handsomer women than any we saw in those seas—nor do they make use of the lewd motions or gestures in their dances so much in use in the Society Isles— though they are equally good at that diversion, and move with a becoming grace. Their dances seem more like those of the Friendly than the Society Isles.

Children of both sexes go naked till they are five or six years old. The boys have their heads mostly shorn, but the girls' hair is suffered to grow long, which—as it is not of a strong, wiry nature, but flows in ringlets—when they arrive at fourteen or fifteen sets them off to much advantage. The old women cut off their hair when they mourn the loss of their relations, but we observed no marks of this kind on any that appeared capable of child bearing. They never kill their children here as at the Society Isles; they are careful of them and use them very tenderly. They have no marriage ceremony, but join and live as man and wife while they agree, nor is virtue deemed of any consequence among them. While they agree they live on the estate of either, and if they part after having children, the man takes the boys and the woman the girls, and each retire to their own estate. The children are no obstacle, being no hindrance to their getting other partners.

They have no tattooing, nor do they cut the foreskin, but keep away all superfluous hairs from the body. As they seldom bathe in the sea, they are but indifferent swimmers or divers, the rivers being too shallow for that exercise, and few or none of the women know how to swim at all.

Their dress is similar to that of the Society Isles, and both sexes wear pearl shells in form of a gorget, with collars of hair neatly plaited. These shells are common, but as we saw no pearls, it is possible—as they always find them on the reef, frequently dry—that the oysters may lose their pearls while they lay open and half-dead with the heat of the sun, after the surf has thrown them up.

Their temper appears in many respects similar to the Indians of North America than any of their neighbours. They seem rather serious than lively and appear to be always ruminating on some important business.

When they go abroad, they have each a large piece of glazed cloth of a purple colour that they carry folded up, except when it happens to rain they wear it like a cloak. If the rain continues, they strip and tie a girdle of grass and leaves about their middle, if they have no matting on. They wrap their clothes up in their cloak and proceed home, or to the next house, when they have dry clothes to put on.

Their cloth and matting are made from the same materials and after the same manner, but are much coarser. But they have a method of dying and glazing it so as to make it turn the rain, and scenting it with sweet flowers and perfumes. They prefer the cloth plant or Chinese paper mulberry to any other. Though they have several other trees and shrubs fit for that purpose, this is the most durable. They do not bleach it so well as the Society Islanders, and their principal colours are purple, red, and yellow. The latter they extract from the turmeric, which grows in abundance here, but we could not learn how they prepared the others.

Their houses are built of an oval form and at a distance resemble a long haystack. They are from forty to eighty feet long and from fifteen to thirty broad and about as much in height. The ridge is a strong beam supported by two or more pillars, chiefly toa. The sides and top are framed of strong timbers, squared to five or six inches and firmly lashed together. The thatch is neatly and well made of fwharra or palm leaves, which will last several years. The thatch reaches the ground on the back and ends, and on the front within about six feet.

The front is closed with timber, neatly carved and painted with a reddish colour, and has several openings about four feet high and two and a half wide. They have shutters, answering the double purpose of doors and windows. These shutters are also carved with rude figures of men and women. The inside is neatly lined with reeds, about four or five feet up. The floor is covered with grass, to a good thickness, and a division in the middle with a tier of stones to part the men and women.

At the end, belonging to the men, is a place separated from the rest for the purpose of burying the males of the family. This place is fenced by a tier of flat stones, set up on end four or five feet high, and here the women must not come. In this place they keep the images of their forefathers or titular deities, as they believe that their souls are fond of seeing respect paid to their remains and that they always hover about the place of these representatives. They are curiously carved and decorated with human hair, the teeth, and nails of their departed friends; red feathers; and pearl shells neatly disposed.

The chief of their furniture is mats for sleeping on, baskets of several sorts, neat platters of different sizes for holding their provisions, stools for beating pudding on, and a stone or pestle for that purpose. The stools and platters are made of the tummannoo, or calophyllum mophylum, with the nut of which they scent their cloth. When they go to sleep, they beat the mosquitoes out and make a fire at each door to keep them out. These are very troublesome, and together with fleas and lice keep them employed till sleep gets the better of them. The rats run

over them all night in droves, but as we left several cats, it is possible that in time
they may reduce their numbers. They have no snakes or anything more venomous
then a centipede or scorpion, and their birds and insects are common to all the
Society Isles.

Their food is chiefly breadfruit (which they preserve as the Society Islanders
do, making it into a sour paste called mahee), yams, taro, plantains, coconuts,
wild roots, and fish, which they bake in the same manner as at the Society Isles.
They always cook out of doors, and the women and their servants are under the
same restrictions. Nor can a woman touch what her child has touched while the
child remains sacred. [Morrison discusses the Tahitian concept of children being
"sacred," which he says was a custom "from time immemorial," in part II, pages
176–78.] The women are prohibited from eating the turtle, cavally, dolphin, and
albacore, but may eat all the rest. They have abundance of the white salmon and
plenty of delicious rockfish, with shellfish of several kinds, among which are a sort
of cockle that is excellent when stewed. The turtle is also sacred to the men and are
only used as sacrifices or eaten by the chiefs and priests.

Their canoes are differently built from any of the other islands' that we have
seen and are from thirty to forty feet long and carry from twelve to twenty-four
men. They are narrow at the bottom, spreading out to sixteen or eighteen inches at
the gunnel, and carry their bearings to the top. They are about two feet deep and
sharp towards the head and stern, the head resembling the head of some animal
with a large mouth. The stern rises into a scroll, neatly finished and carved.

The canoes are built of several pieces, well trimmed and joined together by
seizings of coconut fibers, and the whole painted with a reddish paint. The sides
are stuck with breadfruit, pitch, the scales of the parrot fish, and small shells in
a number of arches, which have a handsome appearance. They are built of tummannoo and breadfruit, and are well finished, considering their tools, which are
no other than a stone or shell adze, bones, and shark teeth with coral and sand to
rub them smooth—after which the skin of the stingray, nourse, and shark serve to
polish the work. These were all the tools we saw them use.

Their paddles are from three to four feet long and the blade is circular, having
a ridge on one side like our oars, but the other is hollowed out instead of being flat.
Their fishing gear is hooks and lines, large seines, and spears of different kinds
pointed with toa that every fisherman makes for himself. Their hooks are of pearl
shell, which they grind into form with a stone and sand; they drill a hole with
a piece of a shell or a shark's tooth fixed in a long stick that they work between

their hands, after the manner of a chocolate mill—after which different sizes of the branchy coral serve for files to cut the hollow of the hooks to their fancy. They have no beards to their hooks, but turn them with the bow, more rounding and the point close to the back. They are of different forms as the fisherman fancies. Their lines and nets are made from the bark of the roaa and are well twisted in three strands.

They have no sailing vessels and never leave the land unless they are blown off, as all the islands of which they have any account are at too great a distance for them to hold any intercourse. When they fish within the reef, they seldom use their paddles, but get along with long poles, or staves, to prevent frightening the fish they may be chasing. The white salmon and the turtle they catch with their nets, some of which are very large, and they have several fine white beaches to haul their seines on.

They have an abundance of the yava, or intoxicating pepper, which grows without cultivation, and they use it in the same manner as the Society Islanders, preferring the method of chewing it to any other. They cultivate nothing but the taro, a root of the nature of a yam that grows in watery ground, the tops of which make excellent greens. In the cultivation of this root, both men and women labour, taking great pains to level the ground and bank it up, so that the water may cover the whole of it. Their only method of digging is with a pointed stick and hauling the brush up by the roots. When they find it necessary to level a piece of ground, they carry the earth about in baskets, saving the stones for embankments, and find whether it is properly leveled by turning a stream of water into it.

As some of them are always employed weeding or planting, they always carry with them a long staffer wand, with which they knock down the ducks that come within reach; at this they are expert and frequently come on them unperceived, the leaves of the taro keeping them from the sight of the ducks till they are within reach.

Their war weapons are made of toa. They include spears or lances, eighteen or twenty feet long, regularly tapered from within about twelve or fourteen inches of the heel to the point; clubs that answer the double purpose of club and spear, from nine to twelve feet long, two-thirds of which is a round staff about the size of the common sponge staves—the remaining part is a flat blade about four inches wide in the middle and tapering from the middle, each way. The point is sharp enough to pierce a man's body. On the head of the staff, where the blade commences, is wrought a double diamond, the whole polished and finished in a style that some good artists would be surprised at.

The old men have walking staves and handles of fly flaps, made of the same wood and highly finished. On the top of their staves, they generally carve a double figure of a man, representing a figure with one body and two heads, and sometimes of two standing back to back. Their fly flaps are made of coconut fibers, twisted and plaited very curiously.

When they are accoutered for war, they bind a piece of red cloth or matting, or both, round their waist with a sash made of coconut fibers plaited into sennet; at each end hangs a tassel of the same. Round their waist, they fill all the folds with a number of flinty stones. The shoulder is mostly bare and on their breast a pearl shell hangs in a collar of braided hair. Their head is defended by a cap made of coconut fibers wrought after the manner and something in the form of a beehive; they are covered with white cloth, and on the top is a bunch of black feathers from the man-o'-war bird. With a spear or club, they are completely equipped. Some of these caps have a pearl shell on the front with a semicircle of feathers from the wild duck's wings round it, but these are more for show than use. The others will resist a severe blow, and a cutlass will make no impression on them.

They use neither slings nor bows in war, and though their weapons bespeak them to be warriors, yet it does not appear that they destroy each other's habitations, as they do in other islands; many houses appear to have stood several years. But they perhaps satiate themselves with blood, for they appear to fight furiously.

Their musical instruments are drums about twelve inches in diameter and four feet long, hollowed out after the Tahitian manner and covered with sharkskin— others are about eighteen or twenty inches high and ten in diameter; conch shells with long tubes; flutes of a larger size than those of Tahiti, but used in the same manner. The sound of the whole of them is more harsh and disagreeable than those of the Society Isles, though the workmanship is superior.

Their morais, or places of worship, differ from those of the Society Isles, being all flat pavements and having a number of large flagstones placed on end, in tiers or rows in the center. They are planted with the tee, or sweet root, having a long stalk about six feet long and as thick as a man's finger. These places each have a little house on one side and bear some resemblance of a burying ground. Here they offer sacrifices of men and turtle.

When a sacrifice is to be made, all the males in the district assemble at the morai, and the old men and the priests (who are numerous) always bring their walking staves in one hand and a young plantain tree in the other. These are thrown in a heap with long prayers when (if the sacrifice is to be a human one) the victim is pointed out and knocked down. They soon dispatch him with their staves, which are sharpened at the point for the purpose. The body is instantly dissected with bamboo knives. Each takes a part, which he wraps in the leaves of the tee and carries to his own morai, where it is again offered with a plantain tree. The head, bones, and bowels are interred in the morai and a stone put up, not to perpetuate the memory of the man, but as a mark for the number that have been offered there. Some of these morais have numbers of these marks.

A feast is then made and eaten in the morai by the priests, of fish, bread, taro, etc., part of which is also offered with long prayers. The friends of the victim, if he happened to have any, put up with it quietly for fear that they should follow him on the next occasion. We knew of no more than two being offered during our stay, both of whom were young men.

Besides the general morai, each father of a family has one where it makes frequent, though not regular, prayers and offerings. If they are taken sick, they believe it to proceed from the anger of the Eakooa (or Deity) or from some of their relations. Should they go to war in a wrong cause, they think that any sickness that befalls them at the time is sent as a punishment for their fault.

On our first anchoring in Bloody Bay, most of the inhabitants of the island flocked to that place, the land surrounding it an uncultivated swamp. In the course of the few days that they remained there for want of their usual bedding, they caught colds, agues, sore eyes, running at the nose, etc. All these they said fell on them through our means, and because of this we found such an alteration in their behaviour when we anchored the second time.

The priests, who seemed to have all the authority and be nearly on a footing with the chiefs—seeing that we were no more than common men, liable to accident like themselves—could not bear to see such superiority as the Europeans, in general, usurp over those who differ from themselves. They became jealous of us with respect to their religious authority, seeing that we not only refused to take notice of their authority but even ridiculed it. For this reason, they used all the means in their power to keep the chiefs from making friends, thinking perhaps that if we stayed on the island, their consequence would be lessened, which in all probability would have been the case.

The island is governed by three chiefs, Tinnarow, Tahoohooatumma, and Heetererre before named, each of whom is absolute in his own district. Two of these are related by marriage, Tinnarow having the sister of Tahoohooatumma to wife. Even so, they do not agree; and although their territories are small, they are continually at war.

There are other chiefs, who reside as private gentlemen; Tummatoatobe was one who, on our first coming, acted for Heetererre, and Taroatchoa acted for his father. One of these is always in commission and the other on half pay. If one is removed by war, death, or otherwise, the other always supplies his place, receiving his honours; nor does the deposed chief suffer no more than the loss of command. He is always treated with respect, but no man can ever arrive at that dignity unless his father was a chief. Their classes are the same as at the Society Isles, but the priests seem to have more influence and appear to be next to the chiefs in point of authority.

Their language is a dialect between the Society and Friendly Isles, but not so much different from either as to prevent its being understood by both. It is more than probable that they are all descended originally from the same stock, though so much different in their manners, customs, and appearance.

In other countries, it is observed that the inhabitants of the northern and southern climes are more robust in general than those within the tropics. It also is to be observed in those seas, in islands at an inconsiderable distance from each other in a north and south direction. Perhaps this may be occasioned by the different degrees of fertility of the islands, which are generally more fertile near the line [equator] than at a distance from it. The inhabitants of those isles where every necessary is supplied by nature have no occasion to cultivate the earth and are less robust and vigourous than those who must exercise and labour to procure their food.

The inhabitants of those islands drive about in their canoes to an amazing distance, and I am, therefore, led to think that the whole of the islands in these seas might have been peopled from South America, notwithstanding the difference of their language, manners, and customs—all which are liable to change in length of time. Yet, the present language of all the islands in these seas differ no more than English in different counties. On one of their morais, we found part of a canoe that we knew to belong, by its form, to some of the Society Isles. On making enquiry, one of our Tahitians (named Toobyroo, Coleman's friend) declared that she was the same that had been driven off from Tahiti with six or eight more, of which he related the following story:

Some years before our arrival at Tahiti, the districts of Heedeea, Matavai, Fwhapyeano, Yunnowheaa Teearey, and Oparre (commonly called Tepirreonoo or Teeahhoroa) were at war with Attahooroo, sometimes called the Orapaa. Each district furnished its proportion of men and canoes, to one of which, he (Toobyroo) belonged, being then resident in Fwhapyeano. The canoes were assembled at

Oparre, and they proceeded to a place in Attahooroo called Terooaboo, where they landed and attacked the Orapaa. They were repulsed and forced to retire to their canoes, but they brought off several of the enemy's dead, one of which was put into Toobyroo's canoe. In the meantime, the Orapaa fleet came up and closed with them so vigorously that they were forced to fly, and at last to jump overboard and take to the shore at Taboona (another part of Attahooroo). They left their canoes to the enemy, who followed them on shore without seizing their canoes, and were forced to fly to Oparre. The wind being offshore, some of the canoes were driven on the reef and dashed to pieces. Eight or nine drove to sea, among which Toobyroo's was one, and these they saw no more of.

This story agreed exactly with the account of the natives of Tubuai, and we had no doubt of the part of the canoe found here being the same that Toobyroo described, as the time of her coming on shore agreed. Part of a man was found in her with the flesh decayed and eaten off the bones by the birds. She must have been some days in drifting here, as the distance is nearly six degrees of latitude, but nearly on the same meridian of longitude.

This circumstance led us into further enquiry to know if any such thing had happened before. We found that the present Tummotoa was great-great-grandson to a chief of the island of Ryeatea (an island 120 miles NW of Tahiti) who had been driven off in a fishing canoe. After being driven about for some time he landed on this island, which was then but thinly inhabited by some people. They had been driven to it in the same manner from an island that they called Paroodtoo, which they described to be at a great distance to the westward, and some others from an island that they called O'Gweeva, to the eastward. On his arrival, he settled himself not knowing his way home and was acknowledged as a chief by these people. He also gave names to three districts from the three islands of Ryeatea, Tahaa, and Hooaheine, which they still retain.

This was further confirmed on our return to Tahiti, where we learnt from Obirreroa, the present Queen Dowager and mother of Otoo (or Matte), who informed us that her great-great-grandfather, named Tummatoa, a chief of Ryeatea, was lost or blown away in a fishing canoe and had never been heard of since. The young Tubuai chief was immediately acknowledged as her relation and adopted the friend of Matte, who wished to make a voyage to Tubuai to claim his kindred with Tummatoa. The time of these circumstances agreed so well with both of their accounts that we remained in no doubt of their being facts.

These, with an account of several islands that they described in different directions, were the principal information we were able to collect from these people. Though from their savage appearance we at first supposed them cannibals, yet we found that though they had no animal for food, they detested the idea of eating human flesh.

RETURN TO TAHITI—THE CREW DIVIDES
And now to return to the ship—we stood to the NNE with a fine breeze and fair weather, and during the passage Coleman was employed in making trade. On the 20th we made the island of Myetoo, or Myetea, under which we hove to and divided the trade, ammunition, arms, wine, slops, etc., in lots that were put into the cabin for safety till the ship should come to anchor. On the 21st we bore away and anchored on the 22nd in Matavai Bay, where everything being settled, the following men went on shore:

Charles Churchill, Master at Arms
George Stewart, Midshipman
Peter Heywood, Midshipman
James Morrison, Boatswain's Mate
John Millward, Able Seaman
Charles Norman, Carpenter's Mate
Thomas McIntosh, Crew
William Muspratt, Able Seaman
Matthew Thompson, Able Seaman
Richard Skinner, Able Seaman
Thomas Ellison, Able Seaman
Thomas Burkett, Able Seaman
John Sumner, Able Seaman
Michael Byrne, Able Seaman
Joseph Coleman, Armourer
Henry Hillbrant, Cooper

Those who remained in the ship were:

Fletcher Christian, Acting Lieutenant
John Mills, Gunner's Mate
Isaac Martin, Able Seaman
William Brown, Gardener
Edward Young, Midshipman

William McCoy, Able Seaman
John Williams, Able Seaman
Matthew Quintal, Able Seaman
Alexander Smith, Able Seaman

And with them the two friends of the young Tubuaiian chief, who were now very fond of Mr. Christian and would not leave him, and the young Tubuaiian chief. They were also instantly joined by a number of fresh Tahitians, both men and women, which increased their number to thirty-five.

As soon as the ship was at anchor, those who intended for the shore began to land their chests, hammocks, etc. Having only one boat that would swim and a tolerably high surf going, it was night before we got all on shore, being afraid to venture much in the canoes of the natives at one time, though they made a much better hand of landing them in the surf than we could have done with the boat. As we were fearful of the canoes, we were forced to wait for the boat to carry the ammunition, which was not landed until everything else was on shore, and then not more than two men together.

Having landed our baggage, we found the Tahitians ready to receive us with every mark of friendship and hospitality. Among us we found the whole of them striving to outdo each other in civility towards us, and we found our old friends ready to receive us with open arms. All were glad when we informed them that we intended to stay with them.

Among the things that we carried on shore were the carpenter's mates' and part of the armourer's tools: a pig of iron for an anvil, a grindstone, some bar iron; a suit of colours; some iron pots and a copper kettle; about three gallons of wine per man; and for each man (except Byrne) a musket, pistol, cutlass, bayonet, cartridge box, seventeen pounds of powder, a quantity of lead to make ball, and some spare belts. Having a musketoon and two spare muskets, the former was left in my care, and the muskets fell by lot to Charles Norman and Thomas Burkett. Because Byrne was blind and of a very troublesome disposition, we thought that arms put into his hands would only help him to do some mischief, and he was therefore kept without them.

We wanted the saws, of which there were a whip and cross-cut in the ship, but Mr. Christian told us he wanted them himself and gave us some trade in lieu. He also gave us two spyglasses and an old azimuth compass, for which I provided cards and glasses privately. He also told us to take the swivels on shore, but they were no use to us. The sails and canvas that he thought he would not want were also divided among us. The Tubuaiian images were put into my hands as a present for the Young King.

It being late before everything was landed, Mr. Christian told us that he intended to stay a day or two. He hoped that we would assist him to fill some water, as he intended to cruise for some uninhabited island where he would land his stock (of which the ship was full, together with plants of all the kinds that are common in these islands) and set fire to the ship. He hoped to live the remainder of his days without seeing the face of a European other than those who were already with him.

Having formerly made Poeno (chief of Matavai) my friend, and Millward having made friends with Poeno's wife, we were now invited to live with them, which we accepted. We were treated like the rest of the family, but with more attention and respect. The others also went to the houses of their former friends, where they were treated in like manner.

FAREWELL TO THE *BOUNTY*

In the night we saw the *Bounty* under way, standing out of the bay, but it proving calm in the morning she was not out of sight till noon, during which time she stood to the northward on a wind. We were all much surprised to find the ship gone, as Mr. Christian had proposed staying a day or two to give us time to get on shore the things we might want or had forgotten to take. This gave us reason to suppose that he either was afraid of a surprise or had done it to prevent his companions from changing their minds.

On the 23rd Muspratt, McIntosh, Norman, Hillbrant, and Byrne went to live in Oparre with Areepaeea (uncle to the Young King), chief of that district. The others remained in Matavai, Mr. Heywood and Mr. Stewart living together on the land of Stewart's wife, whose father was also Mr. Heywood's friend; Coleman and Thompson at Coleman's friends'; Churchill by himself at his friend's; Skinner by himself at his wife's fathers'; and Sumner, Burkett, and Ellison at Sumner's friends'.

Immediately on landing they informed us that a vessel (*Mercury*, commanded by Captain Cox) had been there lately, and had left a man who they called Brown, who was then at Tyarrabboo with Matte, settling some business with Vay-heeadooa, chief of that peninsula. As we heard they told strange stories of him, we wished to know what had been the true cause of his stay, and therefore appointed Churchill and Millward to go to Tyarrabboo and take presents to Matte—and at the same time see who this man was.

On hearing our story now in the proper manner, Wyetooa (Matte's brother), who had been Mr. Hayward's friend, told us that it was by his order that the cable was cut at Oparre, he being angry with Lieutenant Bligh for putting Mr. Hayward in irons. He said if Mr. Hayward had been punished with Churchill, Muspratt, and Millward, he would have killed Lieutenant Bligh, having taken his station behind him, armed with a club for that purpose. On his describing the circumstances, we recollected seeing him on board and close by Lieutenant Bligh on that day.

They also informed us that Captain Cox had told Matte of Captain Cook's death and had left them the picture of it. On that score they were angry that we had not told them before, and accused Mr. Bligh of imposing on them by saying that he was alive in England and that he was Captain Cook's son. They were informed to the contrary by Captain Cox, who told them that Captain Cook's son was then in England.

[Wyetooa] said that as soon as he had seen Mr. Hayward receive the first blow, he intended to level Lieutenant Bligh and escape by jumping overboard, and diving till he reached the shore, which he said he could reach in one dive—and be out of sight before anyone could know who it was that had done it.

He said his reason for cutting the cable was to let the ship come on shore, where he hoped that she would bilge, or at least receive so much damage as to prevent her going to sea. By that means he hoped to get his friend out of Mr. Bligh's power, as he supposed all hands would be forced to live on shore if the ship received much damage. He cursed Mr. Christian for not killing Lieutenant Bligh, which he said he would do himself if ever he came again to Tahiti.

A SECOND STAY ON TAHITI

On the 27th, having appointed that we should meet at Oparre and make our presents to the Young King, we marched in a body under arms, taking with us the Tubuaiian images and several other presents of red feathers, Friendly Island and Tubuai cloth, matting, war weapons, ironwork, etc. We were joined by those who were at Oparre and were welcomed to the district by the priest, who made a long oration and presented each of us with a young plantain tree, with a suckling pig or a fowl.

Having made known our business to Areepaeea, he told us that we must not approach the Young King, as he was yet sacred, unless we stripped the clothing off from our head and shoulders. This we refused, telling him that it was not customary to remove any part of our dress except our hats; and if we were under arms, it was not our country's manner to remove our hat, even to the king. However, that we might not seem to be deficient in point of good manners, each of us was provided with a piece of Tahitian cloth to put over our shoulders and take off in the Young King's presence.

We marched to his house in procession, each attended by a friend to remove the Tahitian cloth that we had on. All the Tahitians stripped as they entered the sacred ground, the men to the waist and the women uncovering their shoulders, and tucking their clothes up under their arms. Our Tahitian clothes were removed, and we were followed by a multitude of both sexes, all of who observed the same rules in their homage.

Having got to the opposite bank of the river, facing the farre raa, or sacred house, the Young King appeared, sitting on the shoulders of a man. He had a large piece of white cloth round his shoulders, his head almost hid with a garland of black and red feathers. As he approached the bank he saluted us with the word "manoa" (welcome), which he repeated to each, calling us by the name of our Tahitian friends. Having placed himself over against us, Hetee-hetee stripped himself naked to carry the presents, and the party drew up on the bank for that purpose.

The Tubuaiian images were first sent in the name of the whole, with which Hetee-hetee told a long story, and which from the number of red feathers were thought a valuable present. They produced a general exclamation of wonder when they were held up to public view on the opposite bank of the river. After these were delivered, everyone sent his present separately, which consisted of red feathers, cloth, etc. The whole being finished, the party formed three divisions and discharged their arms, at which the young chief was so much pleased that he told us to follow our own country's fashion in everything and take no heed of their ceremonies.

We retired and were now conducted to Areepaeea's house, where a feast was provided for us of a baked hog, fish, bread, taro, coconuts, plantains, etc.—after which a proportion of land was pointed out for the use of the whole when in this district. In the evening we returned to Matavai.

On next day, the 28th, a messenger arrived from Matte with a hog and a piece of cloth for each of us and pointed out two pieces of land for the use of the whole; the one (Point Venus) for coconuts, and the other well-stocked with breadfruit trees near the spot where Poeno's house stood. These were ordered for our present use, though we stood in no need of his care, having an abundance of everything supplied by our friends.

However, as Millward and Churchill set out this day for Tyarrabboo, they were loaded with presents for Matte, that we might not appear to be behind hand.

Among the presents were several large roots of Tubuaiian yava and a bottle of wine. The yava was a grand present, and the wine he gave to a sick man, as he had been informed by someone that it was good for sick people.

October, 1789. They were well received by all the chiefs at whose houses they stopped on their way, but particularly by Matte and Vay-heeadooa, who loaded them with presents. Matte desired that we should make his land our own, and Vay-heeadooa gave strong invitations to come and see Tyarrabboo. Tommaree, chief of Papaara, also used them extremely civilly, asking them to send some of the others round, that he might form an acquaintance among them. They missed Attahooroo, having but an unfavourable account of it, although Tetowha, the chief, sent to invite them while they went past in a canoe.

AN UNWELCOME GUEST

They returned to Matavai on the 10th of October, bringing with them the Englishman who called himself Brown, alias Bound, who said he had been left on shore from the brig *Mercury*, T. H. Cox Esqr., Commander, of London. He said he had stayed at his own request, having had a dispute with some of his shipmates. He had cut one of them across the face with a knife. This and some other things that he related of himself was sufficient to give us a very good idea of his character and to put us on our guard against one who appeared to be a dangerous kind of man. However, we each gave him some addition to his stock of clothes, and he soon mustered as good a stock as any of us had. What he brought on shore was either very slender or soon expended. He had got from Captain Cox an augur, some gimbals, and a plane, which were the whole of his tools. As he had no work to do, these were more than he had any occasion for.

He also informed us that Captain Cox had given Matte a musket and some pistols with flints and ammunition, but had left none with him, nor had he an axe or saw, though Captain Cox had left numbers of each on the island. He set out on the 18th in company with Burkett, who went to Tyarrabboo to see Matte.

When he was gone, Poeno produced a letter signed T. H. Cox, wherein the vessel is called His Swedish Majesty's Armed Brig *Gustavus IIIrd*, and wherein he calls Brown, "an ingenious handy man when sober but when drunk a dangerous fellow." This letter was put on shore at Tetooroa and brought to Poeno, and this agrees with Brown's account, as he said she was bound to the Sandwich Isles and from thence to China. As Brown found this letter in Poeno's possession, afterwards he secured it himself to prevent it from being of any further use in pointing out his character, which according to his own account was black enough.

He had, according to his story, been a sergeant in the Portsmouth Division of Marines, but being broke, had gone to India in the frigate *Euryidice*. There, he left her and stayed in the country and was cook to Colonel Bailly, when he was taken by *Hyder Ally*, into whose service he entered. Turning musselman, he was made an officer; this service he soon left and coming down to Fort St. George, soon found an opportunity in company with some others to seize on a small vessel loaded with company goods, which they carried off. He was afterwards taken and tried, but for want of evidence against him he escaped punishment, but was sent to England. He soon found the country too hot for him, and having made a cruise in HMS *Pomona*, he left her and got on board the brig *Mercury*, from which he was put on shore in this island.

November, 1789. Finding ourselves settled, I began to think it would be possible to build a small vessel in hope of reaching Batavia, and from thence to England. I communicated this to McIntosh and Millward, and the matter was agreed on; but we resolved to keep the real motive a secret and to say that she was only for the purpose of pleasuring about the island.

Having observed that Matthew Thompson had a quadrant (formerly Mr. Hallet's) and some of Mr. Hayward's books, though he could neither read nor write, I was determined, if possible, to get possession of them. With a little persuasion, I got the quadrant for six small trade adzes and a gallon of wine, but when I wanted the books he began to have some suspicion and was sorry that he had let me have the quadrant, which I told him was only for amusement. He said he had no cartridge paper, and the books would answer that purpose. I told him that I would give him paper in lieu, which would answer that purpose better, but this only served to confirm his opinion; however, as I had a *Seaman's Daily Assistant*, I took no further notice and affected to be easy about them, though I was sorry that I could not get them.

MORRISON BUILDS A SHIP

Norman and Hillbrant having agreed to be of our party, they and McIntosh moved to Matavai on the 1st of November, bringing their effects with them. We prepared houses on a square piece of ground raised above the level, where we fixed a flagstaff to hoist the colours on Sundays. We were also joined here by Burkett (who returned on the 2nd and brought Brown with him), Sumner, Ellison, Churchill, and Byrne. Having appointed Divine Service to be read on Sundays, everything at present seemed right. I now made a public proposal to build a small vessel to cruise about the island, which was agreed to. McIntosh said it was possible to put one together and he had no objection, Norman and the cooper being the workmen, while the rest of us could chop off the rough parts, ready for their use.

Having agreed on this, I informed Poeno that we intended to build a little ship, as we did not understand the method of handling canoes. I told him that we could carry him and Matte with some of our friends to the neighbouring islands. He was well pleased and told us to cut down what timber we pleased, as there was plenty in Matavai.

On the 6th, Brown and Ellison set out for Tyarrabboo and returned on the 11th. Brown, having taken Ellison's cutlass, had been playing some tricks with it at Attahooroo. He had it taken from him by the natives, one of whom had cut him across the hand with a piece of bamboo. In the scuffle he had lost his cloth, which had been part of the tick of a bed that he wore in the country style.

On their return, Brown applied to us to recover the things, but on enquiry we found that he had been the aggressor, and as we did not think the natives to blame, we told him that he must endeavour to live peaceably and not bring himself into trouble; otherwise, he must stand to the consequence, and as he found that we would not support him, he contented himself for the present. Poeno had given him a house and a piece of ground, and he remained quiet in Matavai for some time. The natives never troubled him, as they supposed he was under our protection, though they knew he was a stranger to us. He often used them very ill, which on our account they took no notice of, and they always allowed for his not understanding their language or customs.

On the 11th we began to cut down trees for our intended vessel, and having cleared a place near the square under the shade of some trees, we laid the blocks. On the 12th, we laid the keel, which was thirty feet. We drew the plan to the following dimensions:

Length of the keel: 30 feet
Length on deck: 35 feet
Length of the sternpost: 6 feet, 6 inches
Stem: 7 feet, 2 inches
Breadth: 9 feet, 6 inches on the midship frame
Depth of the hold: 5 feet
Breadth of the floors and timbers: 4 inches to 3½, thickness 3¼ to 2½
Keel, stem, and sternpost: 8 inches by 4

Saturday, 14th. Employed trimming stuff for molds and cutting trees down for planks.

16th. Having got some molds made, I took part of them and got some of the natives to assist me when I procured three or four floors and some timbers. Churchill also took some and went to Oparre and Tettahah on the same errand. He returned on the 20th with some pieces of poorow, but only one answered to the present molds. In the meantime, McIntosh superintended the cutting down of trees and splitting them for plank. I had collected several more pieces of poorow, which was the best to answer the purpose of timbering, and the breadfruit for plank.

20th. Having collected several more floors, we set about trimming them for use. I assisted by doing part of the rough work while McIntosh and Norman fitted them. In the meantime, the rest were busy cutting down trees and splitting them for plank, which were laid up to season—but at this the progress was but slow, it being as much as we could do to trim one plank of thirty feet long in two days—and what work we had now cut out lasted us all the week.

Monday, 30th. This day we erected a shed to work under, to keep off the heat of the sun, which we found very intense, and to prevent us from being interrupted by the rain—which we now began to expect from the appearance of the weather.

December 1st. This day we received a present of hogs and provisions from Poeno, by order of Matte. And according to our expectation the rain began and lasted with some few intermissions for near three weeks, during which time no work was done outside the shed. In the meantime, we fitted what floors and timbers we had trimmed, the stem and sternpost, and plank of two and a half inches for the stern.

21st. The weather being fair, we set to search for more timbers and set up the stem and sternposts. It must here be observed, that as we had but few molds, we were under the necessity of altering them to every frame; the timbers being scarce in the lowlands, we were only able to procure one and some knees, nor was this the only difficulty that we laboured under. We found that several of those, which were already trimmed and fitted, had started and became straight, so as to alter their form some inches. The remedy that answered our purpose best was only to side them for the present and let them dry before we took them in hand to finish them, or put them in their places. The removing of those timbers that had started and siding the others kept McIntosh and myself employed till Christmas, while Norman and the rest were making plank.

We kept the holidays in the best manner that we could, killing a hog for Christmas dinner and reading prayers, which we never omitted on Sundays. Having wet weather, we were not able to do anything out of doors for the remainder of the year.

We informed the natives of the reason of our observing these holidays, and especially Christmas Day; all of which they seemed to regard with attention, and readily believed all that we could inform them of, never doubting that the Son of God was born of a woman. They always behaved with much decency when present at our worship. Though they could not understand one word, several desired to have it explained to them. Some of them wished to learn our prayers, which they all allowed to be better than their own.

Those who were constantly about us knew when our Sunday came and were always prepared accordingly. Seeing that we rested on that day, they did so likewise and never made any diversions on it. One of them was always ready to hoist the ensign on Sunday morning, and if a stranger happened to pass and enquire about the meaning, they were told that it was Mahana'Atooa (God's Day). Although intent on their journey, they would stop to see our manner of keeping it and would proceed the next day, well pleased with their information.

January, 1790. On the 4th, the weather being fair, I set out to the hills accompanied by some of Poeno's men and one who lived with myself constantly, in quest of timbers. We returned with several, the poorow being plentiful in the mountains, but mostly at a good distance, as the natives always take the first at hand for their own use. These we sided as usual and laid them to dry. The natives frequently assembled about us to see our work and seemed much surprised at our method of building. They always assisted willingly to haul the trees to hand and hew off the rough. They are very dexterous at splitting, but as they have no idea of working by rule, they could be of no use in trimming the plank.

Among our visitors came a blind man, who they led to the place. He examined the work by feeling every part and asking the use and intention. He seemed amazed at the construction of the vessel, of which he seemed to have a good idea, saying to his countrymen, "Our canoes are foolish things compared to this one." He asked us many questions and received answers, with which he went away well satisfied.

7th. This day we got more timbers and trimmed them as before, Norman and the others still making plank. As we wanted iron nails, the cooper (Hillbrant) was set to work to cut amai for that purpose, this being the best wood that we could find for that use.

11th. Went in search of more timbers and had tolerable success. The business of searching for timber always took up a whole day, having several miles to go before any could be found to answer our purpose. When we found them, we frequently had the misfortune to break them by tumbling them down the precipices, which we could not avoid, it being impossible to carry them along the steep cliffs. What we cut in one day would keep McIntosh and myself employed for three or four, having as before observed the molds to alter for each frame.

Nor was the making of plank less troublesome. Having no saws (except hand-saws), the largest tree would afford no more than two thicknesses of plank. Some of the trees cut for that purpose measured six feet round, which took a deal of labour to reduce into plank of inch and a quarter with axes and adzes. As we had but two adzes, we were forced to make the small trade hatchets (such as are sold in London) answer that purpose. We lashed them to handles after the manner of the natives, which answered our purpose very well.

And here I may also observe that a deal of labour might have been saved by workmen who understood their business, by trimming the timber in the mountains, which would have made a considerable difference in the weight; but of this I was not a sufficient judge. I was therefore obliged to bring it home in the rough and trim it afterwards. However, this appeared but trifling in point of difficulty and was not sufficient to make us abandon our project.

18th. Brought home some more timber, and having got several dry enough to work, we cut up a plank for ribbands and set up several frames to guide us in our work. As we had little ironwork, we made shift with iron nails, putting a spike in every other floor and iron nails in the rest. This kept McIntosh and myself employed till the 30th, as Norman could not be spared from making plank—it being necessary to keep one workman in each branch of the business.

February, 1790. On the 1st of February our attention was drawn from our work by a heiva, which, according to custom, was performed in our neighbourhood before the chief of the district. All the inhabitants of the district were assembled to see it.

Everything being ready, Captain Cook's picture was brought (by an old man who has the charge of it) and placed in front. The cloth with which it was covered being removed, every person present paid the homage of stripping off their upper garments, the men baring their bodies to the waist—Poeno not excepted—and the women uncovering their shoulders.

The master of the ceremonies then made the oodoo (or usual offering), making a long speech to the picture, acknowledging Captain Cook to be chief of Matavai and placing a young plantain tree with a suckling pig tied to it before the picture. The speech ran to this purpose—"Hail, all hail Cook, Chief of Air Earth and Water, we acknowledge you Chief from the Beach to the Mountains, over Men, Trees, and Cattle over the Birds of the Air and Fishes of the Sea, etc., etc."—after which they proceeded to perform their dance, which was done by two young women neatly and elegantly dressed in fine cloth and two men. The whole was conducted with much regularity and exactness, beating drums and playing flutes, to which they kept true time for nearly four hours.

On a signal being given, the women slipped off their dresses and retired. The whole of the cloth and matting, which had been spread to perform on, was rolled up to the picture, and the old man took possession of it for the use of Captain Cook.

Several baskets of provisions, consisting of fish, plantains, breadfruit, taro, and coconuts were brought and presented to us. At Poeno's request, we fired the musketoon, which we charged with slugs. Firing into a large apple tree, we brought down several of the fruit, at which they expressed much wonder and departed well pleased.

On the 2nd came another heiva, which Poeno brought to the square. This was conducted in the same manner and attended by the inhabitants as before, but Captain Cook's picture was not present. Poeno received the cloth and matting, which he divided among us, the whole amounting to nearly one hundred fathoms. After the people departed we missed the flag halyards, a pair of trousers, and three pigs from the sty. On enquiry, we found that the thief was in Oparre, where we followed and apprehended him, finding the halyards in his possession; but the trousers and pigs were gone.

We brought him to Matavai, where we gave him one hundred stripes. Brown, having lost a hog, cut off his ears, though he could not be sure that he had stolen it. Poeno advised us to shoot him, saying he will now go and steal from everybody without fear. However, we thought he had been punished sufficiently and let him go. He quitted the district amidst the shouts and jeers of his countrymen. Another, having stolen a knife some days before, was also brought to the tree and received a smart flogging.

We soon found that this method of proceeding had the desired effect, and few instances of the kind happened after. Though they had many opportunities to steal our tools, they never meddled with any of them. They knew that we would find them out, as they cannot keep anything to themselves. We began to get hold of their language so fast that we could understand everything they said and make a good shift to discourse with them.

On the 3rd we returned to work as before, collecting more timbers and making plank.

On the 6th we received a visit from Eddea, who had come down to visit her son, the Young King, at Oparre. She brought presents of cloth for each, as did her sister Teano (wife to Vay-heeadooa, chief of Tyarrabboo) who accompanied her. She stayed at the square some days, and the vacant space near the square was made use of for dancing, wrestling, and throwing the javelin. The young men and women frequented this place for their amusement when the weather permitted, so that we were entertained with a dance almost every evening while we remained here, without going from home to see it.

When she saw the vessel, which now began to show in frame, she told me that she had got a handsaw from Captain Cox that she would give me. A man was sent away to Tyarrabboo to bring it. He returned within a few days, and it proved to be a very good one. We supposed that it cost at least five shillings in London; it was quite new and had not been used. We stood in great need of it, as our own tools were much the worse for wear.

As the frame of the vessel began to assume some form, we had frequent visitors who all wanted to examine every part, curious to know how every part was secured. Most of them were doubtful whether she would ever be finished, saying the job was too long and wondering how we could keep at it without being tired.

Before Eddea took her leave, she gave orders that we should be well supplied with provisions of hogs, fish, etc., but this was needless, as everyone who came to visit us brought something with them. We never wanted for anything.

8th. We had hitherto gone on with our work without anything to obstruct us except rainy weather, but now an accident happened that put a stop to it for some time. The affair was this: Thompson, who resided with Coleman at Point Venus, had ill-used a young girl, for which her brother, in revenge, knocked him down and fled. Coleman was at this time just recovering from a fit of sickness, when Thompson came home vowing revenge on the first person who offended him.

VIOLENCE ERUPTS

A number of strangers had arrived at the Point (where they generally stop on their passage round the island, to take the opportunity of getting to windward in the morning before the sea breeze sets in) and had flocked round the house as usual to see the Englishmen. Thompson ordered them away, but as he spoke English they did not understand him and paid no regard to the order. Thompson took his musket and firing among them, killed a man and a child that he held in his arms. The shot passed through a woman's lower jaw, breaking both the bones, and grazed another man on the back, at which they all fled.

The man was one of Vyeooreedee, who was going around the island on a party of pleasure with his family, of which the child was one. We expected that this would be revenged, but no notice was taken of it. Mr. Heywood gave the man's wife a white shirt, and Churchill (who had always been aspiring at command) thought this a good time to offer himself as head of the party, in case an attack should be made upon us by the natives. But as we all looked upon the affair as murder, we declined either making him our chief or taking any part in the business. He then sent Brown to Tyarrabboo, to Vay-heeadooa for canoes to carry him to Tyarrabboo, where he intended to stay. The canoes came, and on the 20th he set out, accompanied by Brown and Thompson.

22nd. Finding that the natives made no stir and blamed none but Thompson for the murder, we set to work again and collected more timbers and trimmed them as before, making plank.

Ellison's pistol was stolen this day out of the house.

March, 1790. Peter Heywood had set out on a visit with his friend, and we were this day informed that he was killed at Vyeooreedee; but he returned to Matavai on the 6th of March, bringing with him part of the barrel of Ellison's pistol, which he had found at Heedeea. The thief had escaped. He informed us that he had stopped one night in Attahooroo, where he was well received by Tetowha the chief, but heard some of the people propose to plunder him, on which he made the chief a present of his hat and a knife, which were all the English things he had about him. He was suffered to pass unmolested. He next went to Papaara, where he was well received. Staying one night with Tommaree, he set out for Vyeooreedee for the purpose of seeing Obirreroa.

When he arrived in Vyeooreedee, Mr. Heywood was seized by the hair by one of the natives, who held a stone in one hand with which he was about to knock out his brains, but was prevented by another, who seized his arm. The man, who was brother to the man that Thompson killed, had mistaken Mr. Heywood for Thompson. The other who prevented him was brother to his wife. He remembered Mr. Heywood at Matavai, when he came to see the man and his child and had made the wife some presents when she was weeping over her husband and child. As soon as the man found his mistake he was very sorry and begged that Mr. Heywood would not be angry, inviting him to his house. He refused and proceeded to Obirreroa's.

Mr. Heywood stopped there all night and proceeded to Tyarrabboo, calling at Moenannoo's as he passed through Vyeerre, where he was well received. When he arrived at Tyarrabboo he was kindly received and loaded with presents by Vay-heeadooa, who pressed him to come and live with him. He then proceeded to Matte's, who treated him in the same manner, but begged that he would not quit Matavai, as he understood that Churchill, Thompson, and Brown had come to live there. Mr. Heywood promised him that he would not quit Matavai and pursued his journey homewards by the north side of the island, being well received by every person where he stopped in his way.

8th. This day I went in quest of more timber with tolerable success. A messenger came from Vay-heeadooa with presents and an invitation for Millward and myself to come to Tyarrabboo, making us large offers. A letter from Churchill contained the same invitation, seconding Vay-heeadooa's request and promising us large possessions in Tyarrabboo. At the same time, the letter told us that Thompson's arms had been stolen by the natives, which was bad encouragement for strangers to go there—but as we were glad to be rid of them, we declined the kind invitation of Vay-heeadooa and sent him presents in return.

9th. This morning a messenger came from Oparre to request our attendance there, as Mottooarro was expected there from Morea with a fleet. Having on board a large quantity of hogs and cloth for the Young King, the Attahooroo men had threatened to plunder it. We repaired to Oparre under arms, and a feast was made ready for us. The fleet arrived without being molested and we returned to Matavai. On our way we were accosted by the Young King, who, to thank us for our attention to him, desired us to take fish out of his canoes whenever they came to Matavai and to make no ceremony about taking anything that belonged to him. In return, we fired our muskets as a compliment.

12th. In the night between ten and twelve came Thompson, and having made known the loss of his arms, Norman supplied him with his spare one. He set off before day for Tyarrabboo, having told Norman that he had been informed that some of Matte's men had taken his arms, and swore that he would put the man to death as soon as he found him out. He said that his reason for returning so soon was to prevent the news of his being at Matavai from reaching Tyarrabboo before him. The true reason was that he did not wish to be seen by Coleman, who he had robbed while he was sick.

He also said that he and Churchill had quarreled and parted and that they lived separately: he at Towtirra and Churchill at Vyeowtaya, at the distance of eighteen or twenty miles. As his arms had been taken away in the night, he had no suspicion that Churchill had any hand in the theft, though the natives said publicly that he had taken them away. On my asking Poeno about it, he informed me that Vay-heeadooa's man told him that Churchill had them.

On the 14th a messenger from Matte arrived, asking that none of us quit Matavai or Oparre. He also confirmed the account that Churchill had taken Thompson's arms. We were satisfied of the truth of this and promised the messenger that we would not go to Tyarrabboo.

Monday, 15th. The frame being now complete, we began to trim the timbers for planking. Coleman being quite recovered, we proposed that he make the ironwork for the rudder, bowsprit, etc., to which he agreed on condition that a pair of bellows be made and coals procured to get sufficient heat. We immediately fixed on a plan for making the bellows, and Hillbrant was set to work to assist Coleman.

The breadfruit planks made a tolerable set of boards. Canvas supplied the place of leather, and the iron handle of a saucepan made the nozzle. A frame of plank filled with clay was made for the forge, and Coleman cut a hole through a stone to point the nozzle of the bellows through. The pig of ballast made a good anvil, and the carpenter's maul answered the purpose of a sledge. In the meantime, we got charcoal burnt, and the forge was got to work. We found it necessary to keep the canvas constantly wet to make it keep in the wind, which answered the purpose very well. Coleman, having Hillbrant to assist him, soon got some part of the ironwork into form, making eye bolts instead of braces for the rudder, with a bolt to go through the whole.

16th. Sumner set out for Tyarrabboo on a visit to Matte and did not return till the 26th, during which time the work still went on well. By this day we had got to planking and had got four streaks on the larboard side. Sumner brought Churchill with him, who informed us that Thompson's arms were restored. He had brought Norman's musket with Thompson's thanks for lending it. He said that the arms had been taken by some of the natives who were stopped by Vay-heeadooa's men going across the isthmus; this passed very well, as we did not depend on what the natives said.

He also informed us that Vay-heeadooa had died suddenly and that Churchill was put in full possession of the sovereignty of Tyarrabboo by the name of Vay-heeadooa, his friend, who died without issue. He made us all promises of large possessions in Tyarrabboo if we would go and live with him, but all refused, seeing what he aimed at—which was none other than making himself great at our expense. When I told him that I would rather be one of Poeno's friends than chief of Tyarrabboo, he dropped any further persuasions.

During Sumner's absence, he had made friends with Tommaree, chief of Papaara. Being in alliance with Matte, he had no objection to his going to Papaara to live, and he brought canoes from Tommaree for the purpose of carrying him and Burkett there. They were both tired of the work and seemed to think, like the natives, that it would never be finished.

April, 1790. On the *1st*, Burkett, Sumner, and Churchill set out for Papaara, and Byrne and Ellison went to live at Oparre. Our number being reduced, we divided ourselves thus: Norman and Millward to make plank, McIntosh and myself to put them on, and Coleman and Hillbrant to make the ironwork. By Easter Sunday we completed six streaks on the starboard side. Our manner of proceeding was this: After McIntosh had fitted one plank and placed it, he left me to bore it off and prepared another. When it was bored off, he secured it by driving one nail, and one iron nail in each timber, and three nails in each butt.

During the holidays we learned from the natives that Churchill had fired upon some natives at Tettahah for frightening away the ducks at which he was about to fire. One man was wounded in the back and a boy in the heel. The boy's wound mortified, and he died soon after.

12th. Muspratt arrived from Tyarrabboo, on his way to Oparre where he resided still. He informed us that he had set out with Burkett, Sumner, and Churchill. He confirmed the report of the natives and told us that Churchill had his collarbone broken at the same time. He had left them at Papaara on the 4th and proceeded to Tyarrabboo to see Matte, where a dispute had taken place between Brown, who was now with Matte, and one of Muspratt's men; Brown got one of his arms broken. Muspratt set it for him and took his leave. He related the story to this purpose:

On his arrival at Tyarrabboo he was feasted by Matte, according to custom, and had invited Brown to partake. After dinner the provisions were delivered to his people, and some of them being absent, it was taken care of by one of the others, to whom Brown went and demanded some for his dog. The man told him that the dog should be served when the rest of the men came, which much displeased Brown, who attempted to strike the man. He warded off the blow so effectually that Brown's arm broke against his. Brown ran for a pistol to shoot the man, but he escaped before he could find it.

As we were likely to be soon out of plank, it being now a whole week's work to make one of thirty feet, we therefore set about the beams and knees till there should be some more plank ready, having now completed eight streaks on each side. For the knees I was forced to go to the mountains while McIntosh fitted the beams. In the meantime, the Morea people having rebelled against Mottooarro, chief of that island and brother-in-law to Matte, he wanted to know if he should send his arms over to quell them. We agreed, but told him to send his own people to use them. Hetee-hetee, being present, was appointed to the command. The arms being brought to us, we cleaned and put them in order when they set off.

Arriving at Morea soon brought them to subjection, Hetee-hetee having himself killed the inspired priest of the rebels and their chief (the adopted son of the late Maheine). Tayreehamoedooa, forced to fly to Attahooroo, left the island in possession of Mottooarro, whose right it was. He had been kept from it by his Uncle Maheine and his party till the *Bounty* had sailed in April '89, when, having formed a strong party, was called home from Tahiti, where he then resided. Having strengthened his party from Tahiti, Mottooarro was admitted as joint chief with Tayreehamoedooa, who now became jealous of his power and took up arms to drive him out again. But the firearms gave Mottooarro such strength that Tayreehamoedooa was forced to relinquish all claim and fly to Tahiti for refuge. From Attahooroo he went to Papaara, where Tommaree gave him land and where he now resides privately with his mother and aunt (Wa Vaheine), who was the wife of Maheine, deceased.

15th. Employed fitting the clamps and getting the beams ready, making plank, etc. This day we received a letter from Burkett informing us of the death of Churchill and Thompson, and a letter from Brown to the same purpose. Next morning, the 16th, came Brown himself, having been sent by Matte to inform us by word of mouth, as he thought that he could not explain it by letter. He now gave us the following particulars:

Soon after their arrival at Tyarrabboo, they had a quarrel (which we were sensible Brown had fomented) and parted. Thompson made friends with Teetorea, the chief of Towtirra and uncle to Vay-heeadooa, and Churchill went to Vyeowtea to a house prepared for him. Brown went to live with Matte, who was then at Towtirra. Thompson, growing jealous of Churchill, threatened to shoot him if any difference or distinction was made between them. This coming to Churchill's ears, he got a canoe and came down in the night when Thompson was asleep. His men soon found Thompson's arms and brought them out to him, but being sent in for the powder, Thompson waked.

But the night favoured their escape and they returned to Churchill's house. Thompson, missing his arms, soon got a light and went to his friend, who lay in a house close by, asking him to man a canoe and telling him what had happened. The canoe was got ready and he reached Vyeowtea by sunrise. Churchill, being informed of his approach, was up, and desired him to keep off. Thompson replied, "You have nothing to fear, for I have no arms, and I am only come to tell you that I lost them last night and desire your assistance to recover them." On Churchill's appearing, convinced that he had no evil intent and showing his bayonet as the only arms he had, he was permitted to come in. Their former animosity being dropped, they began to reason with each other and found that Brown had been active in promoting their quarrel.

They now agreed to live together, and Thompson set out for Matavai to borrow Norman's musket while Churchill promised to use his endeavours to recover the arms. Thompson returned and they soon came to an understanding when the arms were recovered, as if by Churchill's interposition. Thompson, being told that they had been taken from some of the natives crossing the isthmus, was perfectly satisfied and made no further enquiry about the business. Soon after, Churchill, being bound on a visit round the island, left Thompson to take care of the house. Churchill also sent Norman's musket, with thanks for his civility in lending it. In the meantime, one of the natives, a man who had been at Lima (called Mydiddy) and who had been beaten by Churchill, came to Thompson and told him everything relating to the taking away of his arms—Mydiddy being one of the principal hands concerned. This exasperated Thompson and he resolved to shoot Churchill, which he put into execution immediately on his return, for which the natives put him to death.

Burkett wrote thus: "Churchill having broke his collarbone shooting at some ducks, I persuaded him to stay with us till he should get well. But he refused, and desired me to accompany him home on the 10th, which I did and we went together to Vyeowtea, where Thompson received us in a friendly manner. We supped together, after which Thompson dropped a hint that he had found out the thief, but said no more."

REVENGE

"Next morning I went to the beach to put my canoe in order, as I intended to return home after breakfast. While I was getting the canoe ready, I heard the report of a musket and ran up to the house. But I was stopped by Thompson, who stood in the door loading his musket. He asked me if I was angry. As I had no arms, I saw it was in vain to say yes and therefore said no, and said, 'I hope you don't mean to take the advantage of me.' He told me, 'No—since you are not angry,' and then said, 'I have done him.'

"Upon my nearer approach I saw that Churchill was dead, the ball having passed below the shoulder through his body, entering at his back. I now thought it high time to be off, and interred the body as fast as I could. Thompson seized on his effects. I asked him for some of his books, but he refused, and I left him and returned home. I intended to have asked your opinion about the affair, but have since heard that Thompson has been killed by the natives in revenge for his having killed their chief, and his body carried to the morai."

We knew not what to think of this business, as we were inclined to think that Thompson's death was more on account of his having the property of both than for killing Churchill; but the natives insisted that it was for killing him who they acknowledged to be a chief, in consequence of his friendship with the late Vay-heeadooa, whose name he also bore.

As I wished to be particularly informed of the manner of their deaths and to see Matte about getting some rope and mats for sails, I set out for Tyarrabboo on the 17th in company with Brown. We arrived at Towtirra, where I was well received by Matte, who begged that I would not think of coming to live in Tyarrabboo—which he said would prevent the people from submitting to his son. I promised him that I would not quit my friend Poeno, and told him I had only come now to see him and hear how Churchill and Thompson were killed.

I told him also that I wanted some rope and mats for the vessel, which I described to him. He promised they should be made. On my enquiry into the manner of Churchill and Thompson's death, a man was called whom I knew to be one of Churchill's favourites. He related everything in the same manner that Burkett had done, as he had been with Churchill and steered his canoe in his journey round the island. I then asked him how Thompson was killed and by whom, at which he seemed rather doubtful. He said to me, "Don't be angry, it was I that killed him, seeing that he had killed my chief and my friend."

The manner was this: Patirre (for such was the man's name), being sorry for his friend's death, was determined to be revenged on Thompson. Having got five or six more men (who, when they knew the cause, were equally enraged), they went to Thompson's house and saluted him by the name of Vay-heeadooa, told him that he was now chief, and such like flattering stories till Patirre got between him and his arms. Being a stout man, he knocked him down. The others whipped a short plank (which happened to be at hand) across his breast, and placed one on each end while Patirre ran for a large stone, with which he dashed his skull to pieces. They then cut off his head and buried the body.

In the meantime, Mydiddy secured their arms and the house was plundered. Patirre brought the head to the morai at Towtirra, where he left it. He said if I had a mind to see it, he would show it to me. I accordingly went to the morai with him, when he produced part of the skull, which I recognized by a scar on the forehead. I asked him why they had not brought him to us at Matavai, and he replied, "The distance is too great, and our anger would be gone before we could get there; and we should have let him escape when we were cooled and our anger gone, so that he would not have been punished at all, and the blood of the chief would have been on our heads." I promised the man that he should not be hurt by me for what he had done, as I looked on him as an instrument in the Hand of Providence to punish such crimes.

I stayed here three days, during which time I was feasted every day by Matte, who also informed me that the nephew of Vay-heeadooa (a boy of about four years old) was appointed to his name and honours, and his father Tyepo as regent. The people of Tyarrabboo refused to acknowledge Young Too, who they said was a bastard and not the son of Matte. However, as he had some possessions, he was resolved to keep footing in Tyarrabboo and had hopes of gaining a party in his son's favour. When I took my leave, he presented me with a large hog, three bamboos of scented oil, and a quantity of cloth. I returned to Matavai on the 24th, having been well received at every place I stopped at, on my way both up and down.

The work had gone on very well during my absence, and by the 30th, both sides were planked up, the ceiling in, and the beams secured. But now Norman and Hillbrant left off work and did not return to it till the middle of May. However, the heavy ironwork was done, and Coleman was now able to proceed by himself, making nails and small work. We set about collecting breadfruit gum, which we boiled into a very good substitute for pitch. With the rope that had been brought (by ourselves and the natives) from the ship, we mustered sufficient oakum to caulk the vessel all over.

We were now visited by Mottooarro, who presented us with a couple of baked hogs and some cloth. He said that he had been making presents of all he could muster or else he would have brought us more. He brought with him the dog Bacchus, which had been left with Poeno, together with a bitch called Venus, when we sailed in April '89. Although the animal had not seen us since we had been here, he knew us immediately and came fawning about us, at which the natives were much surprised.

May, 1790. The dog and bitch were separated as soon as the ship was sailed and had never been together since, by which means Mr. Bligh's intention of getting a breed of large dogs on the island was in some measure frustrated. Poeno's sister, having taken a fancy to the bitch, took her to Vyeerre, and Mottooarro, taking the dog to Morea when he was called home.

As we found it a tedious job to gather the gum or pitch, we employed a number of natives. Dressing a large hog, we made a feast for a number of the poorer sort and desired every one that partook to bring in his proportion of gum, which they did not fail to perform—according to the quantity of pork they received. As we found this answered our purpose, we repeated it till we had sufficient gum. We found that boiling it down made good pitch, and with hog's lard being mixed with it made it answer the purpose of tar.

Though the method of procuring this gum was dear, yet the hogs cost us nothing and the people were not overpaid for their labour. A hog of two hundred pounds weight would not bring fifty pounds of pitch. Their method of procuring it is this: They take a peg made of toa, and with a stone they drive through the bark in several places. Having served a number of trees in this manner, they let it stay till next morning, when the gum is run out and hardened. This they scrape off with a shell and make it up in a ball; but a man can hardly get a pound of it by himself in two days.

No other tree affords this pitch but the breadfruit, and when it first runs is as white as milk and as thin, but it soon hardens and looks like white wax. When boiled it becomes black and is in all respects like pitch extracted from pine, though this comes from the bark only and not from the tree.

17th. Norman and Hillbrant having returned to work, we got about laying the deck, which was finished by the 1st of June. In the meantime, Hillbrant set about making casks out of a white wood called by the natives fwhyfwhye, the grain of which resembles white oak. The young chestnut trees that grow in abundance in the hills made hoops. We also cut masts, boom, bowsprit, and gaffs, intending to rig her schooner fashion, and made a kellick with toa, weighting it with lead.

4th. This day we fired a volley and drank a keg of cider that had been prepared from the apples called vee on purpose for the occasion. We were also visited by Byrne and Ellison, who had come to Point Venus on their way to Tetooroa. We now set about caulking, making rope, blocks, etc. The poorow answered for the shells of the blocks, and the toa for shives and pins. The bark of the poorow being cleaned made very good rope, and a sheet of copper made a barrel for a pump, with Coleman's assistance.

In caulking the vessel we observed that an insect, called here hoohoo, had eaten into a part of the stem, which we found necessary to shift and put a new piece in its place. The rudder being fixed and the vessel caulked all over, we paid her with pitch. By the 1st of July she was ready for launching, with masts, boom, bowsprit, and gaffs complete.

We had frequent visitors while she was building who examined her inside and out and viewed each part with surprise, wondering how it was possible to make such a vessel. What seemed to draw their attention most was the method we used of twisting the plank, which sometimes proved an overmatch for us. We broke several after expending a whole week's labour on them. We were assisted by fire, water, and a good workman who understood his business—notwithstanding that we were frequently forced to throw the planks away, which with ironwork would have been of use. We lost only one pair of compasses during the time she was in hand and supposed they had been lost in the rubbish. We now put up our tools and prepared for setting her afloat.

July, 1790. With what rope we could muster, we slung the masts on the sides, making a kind of cradle under her bottom. Having finished with most of the augur shanks, we made use of them as bolts and clenched them through the keel and kelson to strengthen that department.

All being ready on the 5th we applied to Poeno, who told me that the priest must perform his prayers over her and then he would have her carried to the sea. The priest being sent for, a young pig and a plantain were given him. He began walking round and round the vessel, stopping at the stem and stern and muttering short sentences in an unknown dialect. Having a bundle of young plantain trees brought to him by Poeno's order, he now and then tossed one on her deck. He kept at this all day and night, and was hardly finished by sunrise on the 6th.

LAUNCHING THE *RESOLUTION*

When Poeno and Tew, Matte's father, came with three or four hundred men, and having each made a long oration, their men were divided in two parties. The servants of Tew having received a hog and some cloth that was provided by Poeno for the occasion, one of the priests went on board and several plantain trees were tossed to him from both sides. He then ran fore and aft and exhorted them to exert themselves. On a signal being given, they closed in, and those who could not reach by hand got long poles. A song being given, they all joined in chorus, and she soon began to move. In half an hour she reached the beach, where she was launched and called the *Resolution*. Though several trees were cut down that stood in the way, yet she received no damage, except breaking the masts in a passage of about three-quarters of a mile.

Having got the ropes from under her and a canoe afloat with her, we towed her round Point Venus into a small bay to the eastward of the Point, and moored her with the killick and a warp on shore in a good berth, and under the shelter of a point within the reef. Having the schooner afloat, we were now employed till the 12th, fixing houses and getting our things removed. When we got two houses fixed, Coleman came to live with us at the Point, which we called Cockroach Point, according to its own name.

Boiling salt took up the rest of our time this month. Having an iron pot and a copper kettle, we built a furnace of clay, fixed them in and filled them up continually. As the steam evaporated, we kept them at work night and day, dividing the night into watches of two and a half hours, which we could judge very well by the stars. But the saltwater proved so weak here, owing to the freshwater river that empties itself at the Point, we could not make more than one pound per day.

August 2nd. We now cut trees down for masts and covered the schooner over with coconut leaves, woven like mats. Employed boiling salt and making the masts. The cooper was making casks. The weather being fine, we began to kill hogs and salt them, taking out the bones and curing none but prime meat. When we cured enough to fill a cask, it was stowed away on board, putting about one hundred pounds in a cask. We had no method of weighing, but cut the meat by guess to resemble good four-pound pieces, taking care not to have any too small. This, with making rope, etc., lasted till near the end of the month, when we received from Matte about four hundred fathoms of rope; it being mostly small, we laid and made cable, etc., for shrouds and stays, and got the schooner masted and rigged.

While other matters were going on, I took in hand to repair my watch, the chain of which was broken. By the help of a pair of compasses and a nail that I filed up for a turnscrew, I took her to pieces. With much difficulty, at last I got the chain repaired, but in a rough manner. For want of tools and skill, it cost me many pains and trouble to put the work together again—which, however, I at last accomplished, and with such good success that Stewart would have me take his in hand and try what I could do. I took her to pieces and found about two inches of the inner part of the mainspring broken off. To remedy this, I softened the broken part of the spring and cut a new hole for the ketch. Having put the work together, I found that she went very well.

We also prepared a log reel and line. And by cutting a glass phial in halves with a flint, and fixing a leaden center cast for the purpose, made a tolerably good half-minute glass, counting the seconds by a musket ball slung to a thread. With this and the watch, we made it tolerably correct.

The box of the azimuth compass being too large to be conveniently kept, we got a small gourd that answered to the size of the glass and made a compass box of it, slinging it in jymbals in the binnacle, where it was intended to remain for the purpose of steering only. The spare glass answered to fix in the binnacle to keep the wet out, and a lamp made to burn oil over the compass, which answered very well. We also made some candles of goat's fat that we had saved for the purpose.

A cabouse was next wanted, and this McIntosh built of plank. Coleman cut stones square to line it inside and contain the fire. These were placed and plastered up with clay instead of mortar. Everything seemed to be had without trouble or difficulty, except sails. How to procure them we could not tell, matting being scarce and at the best very unserviceable. Though we had cut up our cloth, we had not sufficient canvas among us to make one sail that would be fit to set at sea.

September, 1790. We continued at work, preparing such things as were in our power and trusting in Providence for the rest—salting pork, boiling salt, making casks, and getting ready everything that we could think of that we might want. During this time the vessel was afloat and still continued to be tight; nor did the sun hurt her, as she was continually covered.

LOCAL WARFARE

12th. This day a messenger arrived from the Young King, desiring our immediate assistance to quell the people of the district of Tettahah. They had rebelled and made an inroad into Oparre, burning all before them. The messenger also informed us that the Oparre people had repulsed them, forcing them to leave two of their dead behind them, which were brought to the Young King's morai. They were preparing for another attack, being set on by the people of Attahooroo. He told us also that Areepaeea Waheine, the Young King's aunt who had been at Ryeatea for some years, was arrived at Oparre with a numerous fleet that was all ready for war.

As we did not know that we should ever be able to effect our purpose, though everything was getting forward, we found it necessary for our own sakes to assist them, and therefore answered that we should be at Oparre next morning, armed accordingly. On the 13th, leaving one to take care of the schooner, we marched to Oparre, where Areepaeea Waheine received us, and a dressed hog was presented to us.

Byrne and Ellison being at Tetooroa and Muspratt on a visit to Papaara with his friend Areepaeea, we were now only eight in number, but were here joined by Brown, who informed us that the Attahooroo people had made war on Tommaree. This was further confirmed by a letter from Burkett desiring our assistance. Having made our breakfast, we proceeded to Tettahah surrounded by a multitude (with Poeno and Pyeteea, two chiefs at their head) from Matavai.

Before we had proceeded half a mile, we found the marro eatooa, or signal for war (which is several fathoms of cloth in one piece, passed round several trees, crossing the path several times), and a hog tied to each tree that the marro passes round. This is generally put up with some ceremony, and the enemy is defied to take it down.

On seeing this, our party ran instantly and seized on the marro and hogs, when the enemy, who lay concealed till now, made their appearance. A fray instantly commenced and several heavy blows exchanged before we were observed by them. On our approach they fled, but this confused method of engagement prevented us from knowing our own people, who were so scattered that we were not able at a distance to tell them from the enemy. We were therefore of no use but to look on while the enemy retreated to the mountains, and our party returned with a deal of plunder and several canoes that they had not been able to remove.

We now informed the chiefs that they must alter their mode of fighting and bring their people under some command, in case they should have occasion to go to war again, which they promised to do. And having demanded mats to make sails for the schooner, we took our leave of Fatowwa, or Areepaeea Waheine, and returned to Matavai. This woman, being the first born, has the right of the sovereignty of Tahiti, but having no child, she had transferred the right to her brother during her absence and now continues it to his son—though she is not out of power herself by it when she visits Tahiti, being always honoured and respected, and always holds the reins of government when present.

She paid much regard to us and soon had sufficient mats collected to make three sails, viz mainsail, foresail, and jib. She was very active in the business and took care that we were well supplied with provisions. The Young King also sent us a double canoe forty-eight feet long, and for each a hog, a piece of cloth, and a bamboo of oil. Brown set off across the mountains to join Burkett and Sumner at Papaara, and we promised to join them as soon as the sails were made.

Coleman having made two needles, we set about making the sails, using the bark of the poorow for twine, quilting the mats and seaming them at every foot to strengthen them. Meanwhile, the Tettahah and Attahooroo people had united their forces and began to commit hostilities, both on Papaara and Oparre.

On the 20th we were demanded to assist again, which for our credit we could not refuse; nor were the sails any excuse, as we were wanted on shore. The enemy, looking on our peaceable inclination as the effects of fear, sent us word that they would come to Matavai and burn the schooner. A challenge would be sent to each of us separately by their warriors, who bid us defiance, telling us that each would have his man to carry to the morai, and much more such language. They had also entered Oparre again, burning and destroying all before them.

On the 21st early in the morning, leaving one man as before to take care of the schooner, we got into our canoes and paddled to the lower end of Oparre. Here we were met by Poeno, Tew, and Fatowwa, and almost all the men of Matavai with Pyeteea, and Mattaheyapo at their head—who were both principal men and their head warriors. We were now but eight in number, and having given the chiefs such directions as we thought necessary, they promised to observe them. Being willing to take the cool of the morning, we set forward in good order, surrounded by multitudes of all ages from both districts. The Matavai men kept close to us, claiming the preeminence and keeping the others in the rear.

On our approach the enemy retreated to a high steep eminence in the mountains that commanded a narrow pass, and was the only one by which they could be approached. As this place had resisted all former attacks, they had got all their property to the place in readiness and had formed an encampment of huts ready to dispute the pass; however, we determined to proceed, as we could not hope for peace without driving them from their stronghold; but it being some miles up in the mountains, it was noon before we got near enough to see the pass and the situation of the enemy, who we found well posted.

The heat became so intense that we should have been in a bad plight, had not our friends brought with them plenty of coconuts, which we found very refreshing. Though we had marched at a slow pace, we now stood in great need of them.

Having halted a few minutes, we proceeded to the pass, which was along a narrow ridge where two men could scarcely pass in safety. The Tahitians made a full stop when they came to the place, but seeing us proceed, they followed, and Pyeteea and Mattaheyapo came in the van to be our guides over.

In crossing the pass we found ourselves open to their stones, with which they plied us briskly from the eminence above our heads, where our muskets would not reach to do execution. Though we were forced to walk over at an easy rate for one hundred yards or more, none of us except Coleman was hurt, and he only received a blow of a stone in the leg, which did not disable him. However, his Tahitian friend received a blow between the mouth and nose that brought him down.

Having English clothes on was a mistake for one of us, and they gave us a loud shout and redoubled their volleys of stones, by which upwards of twenty more were wounded before we could fire a shot. However, we got over and, with a warm fire, advanced up the hill; they soon gave way. As soon as this was observed by our party they rushed in, and three of the enemy's head warriors having fallen by our shot, they fled. Our party pursued them down the other side of the mountains.

In the meantime, the plunder of their camp was seized by the Oparre men, the Matavai people being more intent on driving their enemies. The chief part of their houses being burnt and destroyed, we returned in the evening to Matavai. The number of hogs taken here were incredible; several of the largest died with the fatigue of coming down, their own weight and fat being more than they could support.

The party in Attahooroo being yet in arms, the Young King desired us to assist him to quell them and force them to restore the marro oora, or royal sash, together with the morai tabbootaboatea, being the movable place of sacrifice; the pehharaa, or sacred chest, wherein their images are kept with the valuables belonging to the deities; and the Effarre Attooa, or House of God, with several other things that belonged to them, which the father of the present Tetowha, chief of Attahooroo, had taken in war from Otoo, or Matte, and which had been kept in Attahooroo ever since. We found it so fatiguing that we got the sails ready in order to shorten our marches.

We had by this time between six and seven hundredweight of fine salted pork, and got it on board. Having bent the sails and gotten our ammunition on board, on the 26th we sailed for Oparre, leaving the houses in charge of the natives with the things we did not want. We left Skinner in Matavai, who was bad with sore eyes, which made our number eight. At Oparre we found Hetee-hetee, who had come from Papaara, where he had been with Burkett and Sumner. With the assistance of Muspratt, he and Brown had repulsed the Attahooroo and Tettahah people with a great slaughter. But as they would not submit to Tommaree, they had sent him to us to ask that we would keep them in play and appoint a day to let the armies of Papaara and Tepirreonoo meet in the center of Attahooroo. We kept Hetee-hetee and armed him with one of Matte's muskets.

We found at Oparre a large fleet assembled under the chiefs of Tepirreonoo, who informed us that they waited our orders, the canoes with provisions having arrived from the different districts. The morning of the 27th being calm, the canoes drew up in a line and took the schooner in tow. The line consisted of forty canoes paddling fifty or sixty hands. They had pieces of painted cloth hoisted on the sterns of each, and drums beating and flutes playing made a very warlike show.

The warriors cut a number of capers on their stages, being dressed with feathered headdresses and all in their best apparel. The smaller canoes being kept at a distance on each side, the line began to move forwards within the reef towards Attahooroo. In the meantime, multitudes went ahead by land, and the beach appeared covered all the way as we passed.

As we entered the enemy's country they fled to the mountains, and our party on shore pursued them, burning the houses and destroying the country wherever they came by rooting up the plantains and taro, notching the bark round the breadfruit trees to stop their growth, and laying all in ashes before them. About noon we anchored at Taboona, part of Attahooroo, under Pohooataya, the same known to Captain Cook by the name of Potatow. The canoes were here hauled up, and an encampment made with the roofs of the houses that had escaped the fire or that had been spared for that purpose. We were now informed that the enemy had posted themselves in a stronghold in the mountains, and could observe them with the glass, going up in large bodies to the place where they intended to stand a siege.

A council of war was now held, and finding that it would be difficult to approach them, it was agreed to send out several parties to burn the reeds on the sides of the hills to prevent them from approaching unseen, or laying in ambush for any straggling party. Hetee-hetee was appointed to this business, and in the meantime, ambassadors were sent to demand a surrender. A white flag was hung out on board the schooner and another sent to be stuck up at about two miles distant.

During the time the hills were burning, several skirmishes took place between our party and theirs. Hetee-hetee had the musket with him and always repulsed them, and they were forced to retire to their stronghold. As we did not approve of

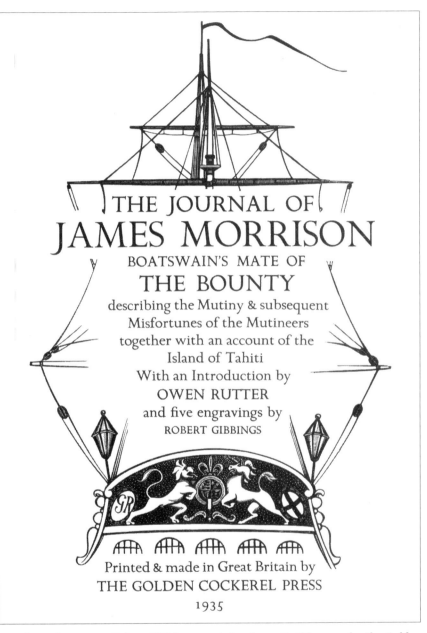

THE JOURNAL OF
JAMES MORRISON
BOATSWAIN'S MATE OF
THE BOUNTY
describing the Mutiny & subsequent
Misfortunes of the Mutineers
together with an account of the
Island of Tahiti
With an Introduction by
OWEN RUTTER
and five engravings by
ROBERT GIBBINGS

Printed & made in Great Britain by
THE GOLDEN COCKEREL PRESS
1935

Noted wood engraver Robert Gibbings created a dramatic title page for the Golden Cockerel Press edition of *The Journal of James Morrison*, published in 1935. Used by kind permission of the Golden Cockerel Press.

THE JOURNAL

PART ONE THE MUTINY AND THE SUBSEQUENT MISFORTUNES OF THE MUTINEERS

1787. On the 9th of September 1787 I entered on board His Majestys Armed Vessel Bounty, Lieut. Wm. Bligh Commander, then lying at Deptford—On the 18th October following she drop'd down to long reach & in a few days after saild for Spithead where she anchor'd on the 4th of November and after several attempts in one of which the Fore topsail Yard was carried away, (which together with a cable that was rubbd at St. Helens [were] return'd at Portsmouth Yard and new ones got in th[eir] stead) she saild on the 23rd. of December with a fresh Gale Easterly, which Increased by the 27th in which the Ships Oars a sp[are] Topsail yard & Top [Ga]llt. Yard were wash'[d] from the Quarters (one of the Eye Bolts being drawn from the side. She also ship'd a sea, which broke the Boats Chock & tore all the planks from the large Cutters Stem, and

b   17

The opening pages of parts one and two of the Golden Cockerel Press edition of *The Journal of James Morrison* are good examples of how this publisher successfully combined wood engravings and type. Used by kind permission of the Golden Cockerel Press.

PART TWO AN ACCOUNT OF THE ISLAND OF TAHITI & THE CUSTOMS OF THE ISLANDERS

Situation & Extent The Island of Taheite is better laid down by Captain Cook then I with an indifferent Quadrant could be able to assertain. Its Lattitude is between 17° 28′ and 18° South and its Longitude about 211° East. (According to Captain Cook Pt. Venus is in Latitude 17° 29′ 30″ South, Longitude 149° 32′ 30″ West.)[19]

It Consists of two Peninsulas both of which are of a Circular form with an Isthmus of Low land about 2½ or 3 Miles a Cross—the larger Peninsula is Calld Taheite Nooe or Great Taheite, and is about 80 Miles in Circumference and the Smaller, which lies to S E of Taheite Nooe, is Calld by the Names of Taheite Eete (Little Taheite) and Tyarrabboo and is about 30 Miles in Circumference according to my Computation; having no aperatus for surveying I can only give the Distance according to my own oppinion. It is in

139

A portrait of William Bligh serves as the frontispiece of his *A Voyage to the South Sea*, published in 1792. The *Bounty*'s launch and the volcanic island of Tofua are pictured in the background.

CAP? BLIGH.

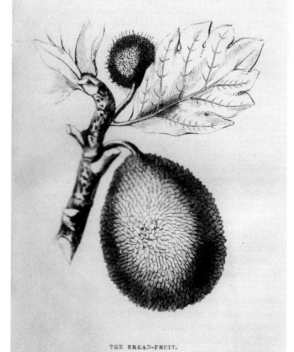

THE BREAD-FRUIT.

An engraving of the breadfruit as published in *Pitcairn: The Island, the People, and the Pastor, with a Short Account of the Mutiny of the Bounty*, by Rev. Thos. Boyles Murray, M.A., published in 1853. English merchants with plantations in the West Indies hoped that the breadfruit, transplanted from Tahiti, would serve as an inexpensive, nutritious food for their slaves.

From a navigational perspective, the first leg of the *Bounty*'s voyage was relatively uneventful, until William Bligh attempted to round Cape Horn late in the season. As James Morrison notes, "The weather continued to grow worse every day. Hail, rain, sleet and snow, or rather large flakes of half-formed ice, alternately followed each other in heavy squalls . . . the people could not stand on the deck without the assistance of a rope or something to hold." William Bligh eventually gave up the attempt and sailed toward the Cape of Good Hope to refit the battered vessel. Bounty *Rounds Cape Horn* by John Hagan. Courtesy of Pitcairn Islands Study Center.

The *Bounty* approaches the coast of Tahiti, accompanied by a native canoe. When they made landfall, the crew received a warm welcome, as recorded by James Morrison: "We were presently surrounded by the natives in their canoes, who brought off hogs, breadfruit, and coconuts in abundance, and a trade for nails, hatchets, etc., soon commenced. The sick were urged to drink plentifully of the coconuts, and this contributed so much to their recovery that in a few days there was no appearance of sickness or disorder in the ship. The plentiful provisions with which the natives supplied us soon renewed their strength." Painting by Herb Kane, © 1988.

A finely detailed drawing by Geoffrey C. Ingleton, created for the Limited Editions Club's production of William Bligh's *A Voyage to the South Sea* illustrates members of the *Bounty*'s crew loading breadfruit plants for transfer to the ship, which was equipped to serve as a floating nursery for the plants. The 1,015 breadfruit shoots collected on Tahiti were thrown overboard after the mutiny. Reprinted with permission of the Limited Editions Club.

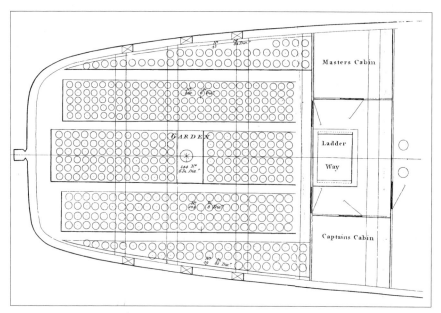

A diagram of the *Bounty*'s lower deck plan from William Bligh's *A Voyage to the South Sea* reveals how the captain's cabin was modified to serve as a garden, complete with hundreds of pots, to receive the breadfruit plants. This arrangement resulted in cramped living quarters, which may have exacerbated tensions during the voyage. Reprinted with permission of the Limited Editions Club.

Robert Gibbings's wood engraving of the *Bounty* mutiny, the frontispiece to *The Voyage of the Bounty's Launch as Related in William Bligh's Despatch to the Admiralty and the Journal of John Fryer*, published by the Golden Cockerel Press in 1934, captures the confusion and emotion of the event. Armed with a pistol, one crew member—probably Fletcher Christian—shakes his fist at William Bligh, who is bound and in his nightshirt. Other members of the crew brandish muskets and a cutlass while another one pulls a rope that lowers the *Bounty*'s launch. In the foreground, three of the crew look on, perhaps debating the pros and cons of remaining with the ship or risking their lives with William Bligh in an open boat. Used by kind permission of the Golden Cockerel Press.

The *Bounty* mutineers' first contact with the natives of Tubuai led to a brief battle at the reef-encircled island's only entrance. Native women (at left) came on board and tried to distract the crew. As James Morrison wrote, "They came on board without ceremony, being in number eighteen. Six men paddled the canoe, followed by five others. In the meantime, about fifty canoes manned with fifteen or twenty men each paddled round on the other side, closing in and blowing their conchs." Afterward, the mutineers dubbed this area Bloody Bay. Painting by Herb Kane, © 1988.

The *Bounty* mutineers constructing Fort George on Tubuai. There were some friendly natives on Tubuai who provided food to the men; James Morrison reports, "We continued at work without any interruption from the natives, who visited us in numbers every day, bringing provisions." The ship may be seen in the background. Painting by Herb Kane, © 1988.

An etching titled *View near Matavai Bay, Otaheite,* appears in Sir John Barrow's *The Eventful History of the Mutiny and Piratical Seizure of H.M.S.* Bounty: *Its Causes and Consequences*, first published in 1831. It portrays a typical Tahitian house with a thatched roof, as described by James Morrison: "The thatch reaches the ground on the back and ends, and on the front within about six feet."

Fletcher Martin's watercolor from Charles Nordhoff and James Norman Hall's novel *Mutiny on the Bounty* illustrates James Morrison and his *Bounty* shipmates constructing the schooner *Resolution*. Reprinted with permission of the Limited Editions Club.

By God, it takes resolution to build a ship without nails

A well-known engraving from Captain Cook's *Voyages*, based on a painting by John Webber, depicts Cook (third figure from right) observing a human sacrifice, with one of his Tahitian hosts explaining the ceremony. James Morrison was an eyewitness to a sacrifice during his sojourn on the island and described the ritual in his journal.

A less familiar print, *The Human Sacrifice,* appeared in *The Isles of the Sea; being an entertaining narrative of a Voyage to the Pacific and Indian Oceans,* published in 1886. Human sacrifices were relatively uncommon on Tahiti in the late eighteenth century. Morrison writes, "They never offer men unless they have committed some great crime, nor even then except on particular occasions. They offer hogs, fish, etc., without number and on every trifling affair."

Tahiti: Types of Canoes, a plate published in *Captain Cook's Journal during his first voyage round the world made in H.M. Bark 'Endeavour' 1768–71.* James Morrison describes Tahitian canoes: "Their canoes will carry from two to forty men; they have both double and single canoes equipped for sailing, with well-made rope and large sails." William Hodges painted this scene during Capt. James Cook's second voyage.

This watercolor by Fletcher Martin from Charles Nordhoff and James Norman Hall's novel *Mutiny on the Bounty,* captures the appalling conditions inside *Pandora*'s Box. This prison was constructed on the deck of *Pandora* to house the *Bounty* prisoners. James Morrison writes, "The heat of the place when it was calm was so intense that the sweat frequently ran in streams to the scuppers and produced maggots in short time." Reprinted with permission of the Limited Editions Club.

Thereafter I had a tiny window through which I had a glimpse of the bay

This engraving of the *Pandora* as it sinks on Australia's Great Barrier Reef appears in Sir John Barrow's *The Eventful History of the Mutiny and Piratical Seizure of H.M.S. Bounty: Its Causes and Consequences.* It is based on a drawing made by one of the survivors, *Bounty* midshipman Peter Heywood, who escaped the wreck with James Morrison.

HMS Pandora *Breaking Up* by John Hagan illustrates the sinking of this vessel at Australia's Great Barrier Reef and the rescue of the surviving crew and prisoners. James Morrison reports that they also rescued "a cat that he [the *Pandora*'s Master] found sitting on the crosstrees." Courtesy of Pitcairn Islands Study Center.

This engraving of the *Pandora*'s survivors on "Pandora Key" is based on a drawing made by *Bounty* midshipman Peter Heywood. It appears in *The Mutineers of the* Bounty *and Their Descendants in Pitcairn and Norfolk Islands* (1870), written by Lady Diana Belcher (Heywood's stepdaughter). Heywood and the other prisoners, including James Morrison, were refused shelter from the burning sun by Capt. Edward Edwards.

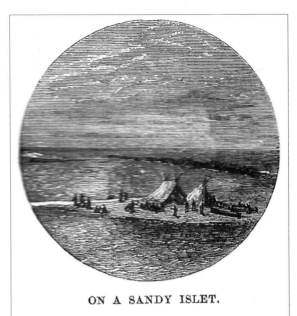

ON A SANDY ISLET,

Noon, Aug. 29th, 1791.

George Hamilton, surgeon, Royal Navy, who served on the *Pandora*. James Morrison describes Hamilton as a "very humane gentleman" who "gave us all the assistance in his power." This portrait serves as the frontispiece of Hamilton's account, *A Voyage Round the World in His Majesty's Frigate* Pandora, published in 1793.

Peter Heywood of the *Bounty*, painted in his post captain's uniform in 1822. Heywood retired in 1816, after a long, distinguished career in the Royal Navy. Along with James Morrison and other members of the *Bounty*'s crew, he lived for eighteen months in Tahiti after the mutiny. Both he and Morrison were convicted of mutiny but received royal pardons from King George III. Heywood also compiled a grammar and vocabulary of the Tahitian language that was of great service to the first South Seas missionaries. The last page of James Morrison's journal alludes to this lost work, which originally was intended to serve as an appendix to the journal. Reprinted with permission of the National Maritime Museum, Greenwich, London.

This photograph of Diana Jolliffe (Lady Diana Belcher) graced the frontispiece of *Lady Belcher and Her Friends* (1891) by the Rev. Alfred Guy Kingan L'Estrange. She inherited a manuscript copy of James Morrison's journal from her stepfather, Capt. Peter Heywood. She gave it to L'Estrange, who bequeathed it to the Mitchell Library, State Library of New South Wales, in 1915.

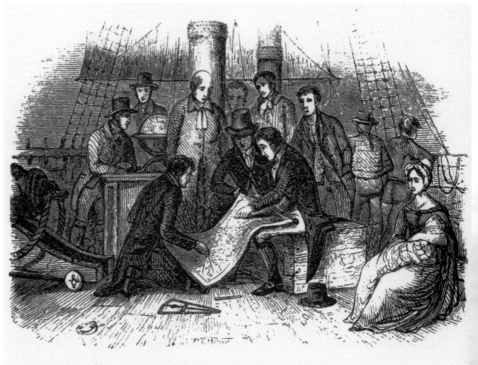

Assembly of the Missionaries previous to their distribution.

This illustration from John Campbell's *Maritime Discovery and Christian Missions*, published in 1840, depicts a group of missionaries on board a ship, preparing for their work in the South Seas. The earliest missionaries, dispatched by the London Missionary Society, studied information about Tahiti and its language contained in James Morrison's journal and Peter Heywood's Tahitian grammar/vocabulary.

The sails of a square-rigged ship, hung out to dry in a calm.

1. Flying jib
2. Jib
3. Fore topmast staysail
4. Fore staysail
5. Foresail, or course
6. Fore-topsail
7. Fore topgallant
8. Main staysail
9. Main topmast staysail
10. Middle staysail
11. Main topgallant staysail
12. Mainsail, or course
13. Main topsail
14. Main topgallant
15. Mizzen staysail
16. Mizzen topmast staysail
17. Mizzen topgallant staysail
18. Mizzen sail
19. Spanker
20. Mizzen topsail
21. Mizzen topgallant

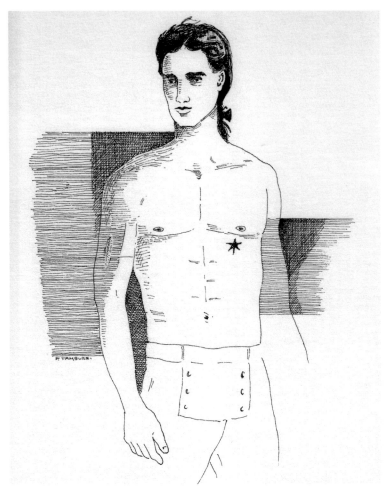

Unfortunately, no painting or drawing of James Morrison has survived, but William Bligh described his appearance following the *Bounty* mutiny:

James Morrison, Boatswain's Mate

- 28 years old
- 5 feet 8 inches high
- Sallow complexion
- Long black hair
- Slender made
- Tattooed with star under his left breast
- Has been wounded in one of his arms with a musket ball

This drawing of James Morrison is based on Bligh's description. Artwork by Pasqualino Tamburri.

their destroying the trees, the parties were called in and placed to look out. Hetee-hetee always caused one or more of his party to cry out "all's well" in the best manner they could pronounce it, every half hour. For the same purpose of giving notice on board the schooner, we fixed one of the hoops of the ship's anchor stock to serve as a bell, striking it with a hammer. This was repeated by all who happened to be awake in the camp, which together with continual fires that were kept burning all night, served to show the enemy that we were always prepared for them.

In the afternoon of the 29th we observed a white flag coming down the hill, and orders were given not to molest any who came with it. Before sunset the Chief Pohooataya with his wife, attended by a priest bearing the flag, came to the camp. A council was now held of the chiefs and principal men. It was determined that peace should be made, on condition that everything should be restored to the Young King, and that the chiefs of Attahooroo should acknowledge him as their sovereign. Pohooataya agreed to all, and with his wife came on board the schooner as hostages for the performance of his part. But as several of the things were in possession of the other chief Tetowha, messengers were sent to him to demand them, with orders to tell him that if they were not produced in twenty-four hours, he might expect no quarter.

In the night Burkett came from Papaara and told us what dispositions were made there. We informed him how we intended to proceed if Tetowha was obstinate, and having appointed the time for storming him on both sides, Burkett returned to Papaara. He informed us that Tetowha had, in their attack, been forced into the mountains and had several killed and wounded.

31st. This morning we were informed that Tetowha had passed by in the night and was gone to Oparre with the royal marro that he intended to present to the Young King in person. He hoped to get peace by it alone, without surrendering the morai, etc. As soon as we knew this, a double canoe was got ready, and Millward was sent to bring him to the schooner, which he did in the evening. On the same day Areepaeea and Muspratt, from Papaara, passed by. They called on board, and Areepaeea made each a present of a hog and a piece of cloth, and set forward to Oparre to get ready for us. When Tetowha came on board, he seemed apprehensive that we intended to kill him and made his fears known to Pohooataya, who cheered him up, telling him that he knew the English better, and that for Captain Cook's sake they would not suffer either of them to be killed. When we knew his fears, we told him that he would not be hurt, telling him that Englishmen never used those ill whom the chance of war made their prisoners. At this he seemed easy and promised that everything in his possession should be restored, and that he would submit to everything we demanded in favour of the Young King.

Tetowha's friends soon came after him to the schooner, and he gave them orders to go and bring everything that belonged to the morai, which they obeyed. He was a handsome, well-made man about twenty-two years old, about six feet high, but Pohooataya is a very corpulent old man, between sixty and seventy.

On the 1st of October the canoe bearing the morai, ark, etc., was brought and delivered into the charge of the priests of Matavai and Oparre. They proceeded with her directly to Oparre, and orders were now given for the fleet and army to return home.

They then accompanied the sacred canoe, escorting it carefully to Oparre. In the afternoon a breeze was springing up and we weighed anchor, having on board Poeno and the two Attahooroo chiefs. We ran up to Tettahah, where we anchored for the night, and weighed anchor at nine next morning, the 2nd.

Here we were joined by Burkett and Oammo, who came to assist at the peace, and worked up to Toa Roa Harbour, where we anchored in the afternoon. We landed the chiefs and went with them to the morai, where the peace was concluded. By our advice they continued in possession of their land. Paa, an old chief who was out of commission, was put into the district of Tettahah as a substitute for Mottooarro, to whom it was voted. The Attahooroo chiefs promised on their part that they would always honour the Young King as their sovereign, and by way of strengthening the peace, each of them took one of us as his friend.

Great feasting now took place. A volley of small arms was fired on the occasion, and all the chiefs of TahitiNooe, or substitutes for them, attended. On the 4th we weighed anchor and worked up to Matavai, where we arrived by noon, having carried away the head of our foremast—which being made of breadfruit, we found would not answer and therefore condemned them both.

6th. We were visited by Burkett and Oammo (the same mentioned by Captain Cook), Tommaree's father, who stayed three days and returned to Papaara.

Norman and Millward now set out in quest of masts to Heedeea, where we were informed a better sort of wood grew. In the meantime, we landed everything, cleaned the schooner's bottom, and paid it with pitch.

We were now visited by Tetowha, who stayed some time in Matavai. He died soon after of an ague and was succeeded by his nephew, a boy of the age of about four years, called by his name. He is the son of Tetowha's sister, who now takes upon her the regency or guardianship during his minority.

SAILING THE *RESOLUTION*

26th. Norman and Millward returned, having cut two masts—one of fwhyfwhye and the other of tuoy—with spars for a gaff, boom and two sweeps, and new railing. They were brought down on the next morning by two of the natives, who made a raft of them with some bamboos to help float them and sailed them down with a temporary sail made of coconut leaves. We went to work immediately to make the masts, etc., and at the same time boiled salt and salted more pork. We had the misfortune to break our iron pot when we were forced to desist, and saved the kettle to cook in. We had now nearly eight hundredweight of pork cured.

November 1st. The masts being finished, we got them in, rigged them, blacked the mastheads and rigging, and gave them a coat of grease. We found them very heavy, but did not dread carrying them away. The oars, gaff, boom, and rails with a square sail yard were now made, and everything got on board. We also got a small canoe to answer the purpose of a boat.

9th. Muspratt came to the point on his way to the islands of Tetooroa. On the 10th, having got everything on board, we got under way in order to visit Tetooroa, leaving Muspratt to follow in his own canoe. But the natives were better acquainted with the weather than us and did not come out. We stood to the northward with a fresh breeze at ESE that freshened to a gale, and forced us to heave to. The sea running very high and no anchorage near the islands forced us to keep at a distance. At four in the afternoon we wore and hove to with our head to the southward, still blowing hard and a high sea. On the morning of the 11th it moderated, and we made sail standing in for the land, having only seen the islands and not daring to venture near them. The vessel behaved remarkably well, but the sails suffered from the weather.

12th. At four in the afternoon we got inside the reef at Tettahah and ran down to Taboona, intending to sail for Morea as soon as our sails were repaired. Here we came to anchor. Pohooataya came on board, bringing two roasted hogs and some breadfruit, yams, and taro. We also met with Poeno here, who had left Matavai the same time we did, bound round the island. We got one of his men as a pilot, and having repaired our sails, in the morning we weighed anchor and ran over to Morea. We anchored in Vyeerre Harbour on the same day, the distance being little more than ten miles.

We were well received here by Fatowwa, who was here on a visit. Next morning Mottooarro sent a messenger asking us to come round to Poonoohoo, or Captain Cook's Harbour, near which place he lived, and to this we agreed. On the 14th we weighed anchor and went round, accompanied by Fatowwa in her canoe. One of Mottooarro's men piloted us into a small cove to the westward of the harbour, where we came to anchor in the afternoon.

Mottooarro and his wife Tarreredooa came on board with several of our old acquaintances, and we saluted them with six muskets. After welcoming us to the island, they enquired what our business was, to which we replied, "To see our friends." They then asked that we should not be in any hurry to leave them and ordered us to be well supplied with everything that the island afforded. Having settled matters so as to leave one on board every day to take care of the vessel, the rest went on shore to see their friends.

My principal lookout here was for mats, but these were scarce and we could hardly get sufficient to keep the sails in repair. This scarcity of mats we supposed to be owing to their unwillingness to part with us; and as they knew we could not leave them without sails, they kept the mats out of our sight. But everything else they gave us freely and loaded us with presents.

While we were here we went to see the cattle, which were about six miles distant on the west part of the island. The whole that now remained were one bull, five cows, one cow calf, and one of the cows big with calf. The bull had some time ago slipped his hip bone out on the left side, which wasted the leg and thigh. This was occasioned by a fall jumping over a ditch. Mottooarro informed us that he had got the calves since then, all very large and in good order but quite wild, being kept only as curiosities.

They have plenty of fine grass, and it is possible they may increase now, which they could not do before. The bull had been kept by himself till Mottooarro was called home, who, observing that Lieutenant Bligh had been at some trouble and expense to bring the cow and bull together at Tahiti, resolved to do the same here, to try if they would increase. He found this to work, and as we told him they were valuable and would bring a good price if a ship should come here, he promised that they should stay together while he held his authority in Morea.

As we began to think our visit long enough, and some of us thought we had been too long from home, we weighed anchor on the 25th, having on board Mottooarro, his wife Fatowwa, and several men of distinction. We worked up to Vyeerre, where we anchored the same day. Mottooarro was very desirous that we should stay some time longer, but we thought short visits best, and promised to come again. He made us each a present of hogs and cloth, and Norman having a fancy to stay a while at Morea, he took him at his word. Taking his leave of us, he set out the same night on his return homeward, and we prepared to sail the next day, having on board forty-eight hogs and a large quantity of cloth, etc.

Coleman, having gone on shore to fetch some sand for the arms, which he had found to answer the purpose of emery, about two miles from the schooner, was seized by a man (who knew that Coleman was the man who wrought iron) who threatened to kill him, having a large stone for the purpose in one hand. He said that Coleman had had his wife on board and used her ill, but some others coming up, as if by chance, prevented him and settled the matter on condition that Coleman should make him a handsome present. By this means he got off and came on board with the sand. When he told us the story, we saw that it was only a scheme to get the trade from him, and if we overlooked it, we should only encourage them to do so again. To prevent being robbed it would be necessary to go armed, and therefore we resolved to punish the offender if we could find him.

Early next morning, the 26th, Coleman, Millward, McIntosh, and Hillbrant went on shore armed and proceeded towards the place. Before they reached the house where they supposed to find him, notice was given of their approach, and those who had been concerned fled—but not so fast as to prevent the shot from overtaking and wounding two of them, one in the thigh and body and the other in the arm. Both of them acknowledged the scheme they had been concerned in and begged for quarter, but the principal one escaped. On enquiry, they found that the house belonged to him who had first seized Coleman and demanded the trade. As he was not to be found, they plundered the house and returned to the schooner with some cloth, hogs, oil, and a canoe's sail, which we wanted to repair our own with. We left the wounded to get their wounds dressed.

On their return on board, a messenger was sent to inform Mottooarro of what we had done, who sent and turned the man off his land and told us whenever they offered an insult to shoot them. He was sorry that the men who were wounded were not killed outright, which he said would deter others from such attempts. In the meantime, a peace offering came to us from the landed men of the district, desiring that we should not be angry with the whole for what one bad man had done. We accepted the offering and told them that we did not wish to hurt anyone, but that we would always punish such offenders as we were able to find out. We never wished to punish the innocent for the guilty and would therefore proceed no further in this affair. We wrote to Norman to inform him how we had settled the affair, and asked him to acquaint us if they made any further stir about it. We weighed anchor on the 27th for Tahiti.

Vyeerre is a snug little harbour on the east part of the island. The entrance is a narrow break in the reef that lies half a mile from the beach; the channel is deep and a ship may ride in seven fathoms within half a cable's length of the shore. Though the harbour's mouth lies open to the sea breeze, the swell never reaches the shore, as may be proved by the trees and grass growing close to the high-water mark. As the land breeze that blows every night affords an opportunity to get out every twenty-four hours, I should prefer this harbour to any that Tahiti affords for a single ship, as all kind of provisions are found there common to both islands, equally plentiful. Wood and water are to be had much easier at Vyeerre than at any part of Tahiti, as both may be had within hail of the ship. Captain Cook's Harbour is large and spacious, but being to leeward, is subject to heavy rains (from the clouds gathering round the tops of the mountains), while Vyeerre enjoys fine pleasant weather and is always dry except in the proper season.

The wind being light, we did not reach Taboona till the 28th, when we entered the reef and worked up inside of it to Oparre. Here we landed the hogs and sent them up by land. On the 29th Areepaeea presented us with a large baked hog and accompanied us to Matavai the same day, together with several of his friends. As soon as we could see the beach at the Point we saw it lined by the inhabitants who had flocked to the place to see us as soon as the news of our approach began to spread. When anchored, we could scarce get from the schooner to the houses of our old friends, who flocked about us and were as eager, and seemed as much rejoiced as if they had found some of their lost relations.

We now landed everything, and Coleman went to live at his friend's house, where he fell sick of a feverish complaint. As we had neither skill nor medicines, the disorder was suffered to take its course, and after having brought him nearly to the brink of the grave, it left him and he recovered.

Byrne and Ellison, being returned from Tetooroa, went to Morea to reside some time with Mottooarro.

December, 1790. Having got everything on shore by the 10th of December and expecting the wet season now to set in shortly, we got the schooner hauled up and housed over to shelter her from the weather.

Coleman declared that he would not have anything to do with the schooner, and finding that our hopes of reaching Batavia or any other place without sails— and finding that even mats could not be had—we dropped any further attempts that way and divided the pork, which on examination proved excellent meat. It was superior to any that had been salted in the ship, which we imputed to a powder cask that we had used to save the pickle in. By this means the saltpeter contained in the staves had been communicated to the whole of the pork.

23rd. This day Byrne arrived from Morea, stayed with us to keep Christmas, and then returned to Morea.

The weather being now wet, we had nothing to do but prepare for it by securing our houses and screening them in.

27th. This evening a man came into the house and, unperceived, carried off the box containing all my writing utensils, paper, etc., with the compass cards and glasses, watch, etc. The box being missed, pursuit was made, but though every means was instantly taken, no account could be heard of it till near noon the next day when it was discovered by a young man who was our neighbour. Being up on a coconut tree getting nuts, he saw the box, and getting down as fast as he could, he ran and took it from the place and returned to us with it unhurt. I was very well pleased and offered him a present, which he refused, saying he was glad he was so lucky as to find it.

About two days after, we learned that the thief was a lunatic who had come to the Point with a number of people belonging to the Ryeatea Fleet. They came over with Areepaeea Waheine, were now bound round the island, and had come to the Point on their way, intending to go to windward as soon as the weather permitted.

The thief was soon apprehended, but did not appear to be so mad as he was represented. Having seen the box open the day before, he took a fancy to the things that it contained, and as it stood on a table without any other security than its own lock, he found means to escape with it. It being instantly missed, he heard the noise that it occasioned and put it into the bush, where it was found, and made off for fear of being taken. Having informed one of our friends of the affair, he made known to us the thief. Having got him in our possession, we gave him a good smart whipping and let him go when he promised that he would never steal anymore from us or anybody else.

ISLAND NEWS

January, 1791. We had now frequent visitors from different parts and particularly from the Ryeatea people, who made much enquiry about Captain Cook, Sir Joseph Banks, etc. We were also visited by several people of note from Hooaheine, the island where Captain Cook had left O'Mai. We learned from them that O'Mai had died (of the hotatte, a disorder not much different from the fever and ague) about four years after he had landed. The New Zealand boys both died soon after. They grieved much for Poenammoo, their native country, and after O'Mai died, they gave over all hope and having now lost their chief friend, they pined themselves to death.

They also informed us that O'Mai was one of the lowest class (called mannahownes) and had been condemned to be sacrificed for blasphemy against one of the chiefs. His brother, getting wind of it, sent him out of the way, and the Adventure arriving at Tahiti at the time, he got on board and came to England. His friendship with Captain Cook afterwards made him more respected than his riches, and the meanness of his birth made him gain very little credit with his countrymen, though he kept them in awe by his arms.

His horse was killed soon after his landing by a goat that gored him in the belly, which they knew no remedy for. The only revenge he could have was to kill the goat. The mare remains yet at Hooaheine, and part of the house that Captain Cook had built for him. His goods were divided after he died, and he distributed many before his death. The muskets are in possession of a chief who was his friend (called Tennanea, brother to Tayree-tarieea, king of Hooaheine) but are of no use, being both disabled.

These accounts we also had from a very intelligent man who lived with O'Mai some time as a servant and who informed us that he was very careful of his property till he died, when it was distributed among his friends. They also informed us that his arms and the manner in which he used them made him great in war, as he bore down all before him. All who had timely notice fled at his approach, and when accoutered with his helmet and breastplate, and mounted on horseback, they thought it impossible to hurt him. For that reason they never attempted it, and victory always attended him and his party. Nor was he of less consequence at sea, for the enemy would never attempt to come near the canoe that he was in.

They informed us that his garden, having nobody to look after it, was destroyed by the hogs and goats, etc. The poultry were all dead except one goose. They were divided and kept in different parts of the island as curiosities after his death, and many were taken to Ryeatea, Tahaa, Borabora, etc.

On the 10th Eddea arrived here from Tyarrabboo, bringing with her Teano her sister, and a number of attendants. She congratulated us on the success that attended us in the war, which had proved very beneficial to her son, who was now to be invested with the royal marro—for which purpose she had now come to prepare. She made each of us a present, and next day we were entertained with a boxing match by the Ryeatea men and wrestling and dancing by the Tahitian men and women. Eddea was mistress of the ceremonies, and the number of spectators present was very great. Among them came Areepaeea Waheine, who had returned from Morea to assist at the ceremony of investing the Young King with the royal marro.

Next day, the 12th, I attended Eddea at her request to Oparre, on a visit to the Young King. At entering his bounds she was forced to change her clothes and put on those that belonged to him before she could enter his house. He asked me to waive that ceremony and received me very courteously. A hog was prepared for me, but Eddea could not partake of any provisions under her son's roof, nor could she eat in a house or canoe where he had been till all his ceremonies were performed.

He is restricted within particular bounds to prevent his rendering anything sacred that is not intended for his use, and for this reason he was never permitted to come near the ship; his presence there would have rendered everything sacred so far as to prevent not only his own family, but everybody else from either eating on board or using anything that came from the ship. All their presents would have been rendered useless to any other but himself. After we took our leave of him, I went with Eddea and aired the powder, which I found in good order, and having cleaned the arms that were here, we returned to Matavai.

14th. Burkett arrived here on a visit, with whom I set out on the 17th for Papaara, having heard much of his friend Tommaree, who I had not yet seen. We reached Papaara the next day, where we were received by Tommaree himself. He is a handsome, well made man of about twenty-seven or twenty-eight years old and about six feet high. He received me with every token of friendship and wanted me to be one of his friends. We soon became perfectly intimate, and during my stay, he feasted me every day and begged that I would be in no hurry to return home.

While I was here the Young King's flag arrived, which was received by Tommaree and conducted to his morai. They kept by the beach close down in the surf till those who carried it were abreast of the morai, when they turned short round and proceeded to the morai. As the flag passed, the inhabitants hid themselves and all fires were put out. We attended them to the morai, where Tommaree's priests, having set the flag up, made the usual peace offering of a hog and a plantain tree. The priests repeated it, and several young pigs and plantain trees were offered with long harangues. Tommaree made a long speech declaring Toonooeayeteatooa to be his chief and ordered a feast to be provided for those who bore the flag.

This flag was the Union Jack that they had got from Captain Cox. It was slung across the staff, as we sling a pendant. It was decorated with feathers, breastplates, tassels, etc. As the chief people of the district were present, we honoured the ceremony by firing our muskets. This was received as an honour, and some of those who were present interpreted this as a declaration on our part to support the flag in circumventing the island, as it was composed of English colours. They made no scruple to say that war would be instantly made on those who should attempt to stop it. It was kept one night in the morai, during which time prayers were constantly said by one or other of the priests who attended it. When it proceeded they returned to the waterside, where they had before been, and proceeded along by the edge of the surf towards Tyarrabboo.

On the 23rd I took leave of Tommaree, who gave me a pair of canoes and several hogs, cloth, etc. With Burkett accompanying me, we set off for Vyeerre, where we were received by Tootaha, Poeno's brother and Moenannoo, his brother-in-law, who entertained us civilly. We set out for the isthmus, where we hauled the canoe across. This part of the island is a low-level spot about three miles broad. It is thick of wood, but as the inhabitants frequently travel this way, there is a good road, and it is much easier to haul the canoes across than to go round the peninsula when they are bound to Towtirra.

As soon as we reached the north side we were met by messengers from Matte, asking us to come up to him at Affwhaheetdee, about six miles from the isthmus. We accepted the invitation and, leaving the canoes at a house close by, set out by land and arrived there on the same afternoon, the 25th, when a feast was prepared for us. Matte was glad to see us.

He now informed us that the people of Tyarrabboo had used him very uncivilly, although the flag had been received and passed with all the ceremonies. He said this was only for fear of us and not their regard for his son. He told us that we had a right to chastise them for killing Thompson, and said that if we made an appearance in arms in Tyarrabboo, they would never make any resistance and that his son would be sole king. He also told us that he had conversed with Tommaree, who was ready to furnish men and canoes whenever we thought proper to take it in hand.

27th. Having told him that we would consider the matter, we signified our intention to go homeward, when he ordered his canoe and went down to the isthmus with us. We launched our own and set out in company for Heedeea, and having landed at Teetoes (a man of rank) we had a dinner prepared. We then proceeded to Avye Myes, where a feast was also provided, and we remained here all night.

On the morning of the 28th, a hog and some cloth being prepared for me, I took my leave. Leaving Burkett to return to Papaara, I proceeded to Matavai, where I arrived on Saturday the 29th and found numbers assembled at Matavai and Oparre to attend the approaching ceremony. Among them were Mottooarro with Norman, Ellison, and Byrne from Morea, and all the principal men of the island. The beach was filled with canoes.

February 1st. Millward and McIntosh set out for Papaara for the purpose of seeing Tommaree and conversing with him about the war with Tyarrabboo.

10th. Eddea brought the ammunition chest with everything in it, and with a pair of pistols, delivered them into my charge, and gave me a bayonet (which she had got from Captain Cox), which I fitted to my own piece, my own being broke. Mottooarro also paid me a visit and invited me to go and live a while at Morea.

INVESTITURE OF THE YOUNG KING WITH SACRIFICES

13th. This day the ceremony of investing the Young King with the marro oora, or royal sash, took place. The sash is of fine netting on which red and yellow feathers are made fast, so as to cover the netting. It is about three yards long, and each end is divided into six tassels of red, black, and yellow feathers; for each feather they have a name of some spirit or guardian angel that watches over the Young Chief while the marro oora is in his possession. It is never worn but one day by any one king. It is then put into the sacred box with a hat or shade for the eyes made of wicker and covered with feathers of the same kind. It is never used but on the same occasion it is delivered to the priests, who put it carefully by in the sacred house on the morai, where no person may touch it.

This ceremony was performed at Oparre on the new morai that was built for the reception of the moveable morai, etc., which we had brought from Attahooroo, and where these things were now kept. The chiefs (or their substitutes) of Tiperreonoo and Morea attended, and Toonooeayeteatooa the Young King, being placed on the morai, a priest making a long prayer put the sash round his waist and the hat or bonnet on his head, and hailed him king of Tahiti.

Mottooarro then began making a long speech acknowledging him his king, when three human victims were brought in and offered for Morea. The priest of Mottooarro placed them with their heads towards the Young King, and with a long speech over each he offered three young plantain trees. He then took an eye out of each with a piece of split bamboo and, placing them on a leaf, took a young plantain tree in one hand and the eyes in the other. He made a long speech, holding them up to the Young King, who sat above him with his mouth open. After he had ended his speech and laid the plantain trees before the Young King, the bodies were removed and buried by his priests in the morai. The eyes were put up with the plantain trees on the altar.

The rest of the chiefs then brought in their sacrifices in the same manner, going through the like ceremony, some bringing one victim and some two, according to the bigness or extent of their districts. After this, large droves of hogs and an immense quantity of other provisions, such as bread, yams, taro, plantains, coconuts, etc., were brought and presented to the Young King. Several large canoes were also hauled up near the morai on the sacred ground. These were dressed with several hundred fathoms of cloth, red feathers, breastplates, etc., all which were secured by the priests and Young King's attendants.

The royal sash being now removed and taken care of by the priests, they all repaired to feasts prepared for them, which lasted some weeks. The number of hogs destroyed on this occasion was beyond all conception, besides turtles, fish, etc.

I enquired the cause of the eye being offered and was thus informed: The king is the head of the people, for which reason the head is sacred; the eye being the most valuable part is the fittest to be offered, and the reason that the king sits with his mouth open is to let the soul of the sacrifice enter into his soul, that he may be strengthened thereby, or that he may receive more strength of discernment from it.

They think that his tutelary Deity, or guardian angel, presides to receive the soul of the sacrifice. Several large hogs were placed upon the altar, and the human sacrifices offered this day were thirty, some of which had been killed nearly a month ago.

These were the first sacrifices that had been offered since our coming to the island. They never offer men unless they have committed some great crime, nor even then except on particular occasions. They offer hogs, fish, etc., without number and on every trifling affair.

20th. Millward and McIntosh arrived, who having settled the matter relative to the war, we determined to put it into execution, as none of the chiefs of Tyarrabboo had assisted at the ceremony of investing the Young King with the royal sash. Tommaree had proposed to make a grand feast, under cover of which he could have his men and canoes collected before he told them what he wanted them for. By that means he would prevent it from being blazed about. The English were to be there as partakers of the feast, and when we were ready to attack them, we could be in their country before they knew what we were at, and by this means make an easy conquest.

This appearing to us a very good plan, we agreed to prepare for it as fast as possible and began to get things in order for launching the schooner; but from the number of visitors which daily came to see us, owing to the number collected together in the two districts, we were not able to make any progress. It was the 1st of March before we got her launched. We filled the water for ballast and stowed the casks with stones and wood. We also got the pork on board, masted and rigged the vessel, but still kept our intentions a secret.

March, 1791. Among our visitors we often had the Young King, but as his presence in any house would render it useless to any of the natives, he never came inside.

Sunday, 13th. He was carried round the beach of Matavai on men's shoulders dressed in a cloak of black feathers and his head almost hid in a large garland of black and red feathers. He was attended by the principal people of the district carrying the Union Jack horizontally over their heads, but as all could not get under it, several fathoms of painted cloth were added to it. His ceremonies were not all performed yet, for which reason he could only pass by the beach and not go inland, except on sacred ground leading from the beach. He made us presents and appointed each to a portion of land, being very fond of the whole of us, and desired his subjects to treat us as his relations, calling us his uncles (or medooas).

14th. We bent the sails and got everything on board, and on the 21st weighed anchor and sailed for Oparre, leaving in Matavai Mr. Stewart, Mr. Heywood, Coleman, and Skinner. We anchored at the lower part of Oparre, where we were joined by Norman, Ellison, and Byrne, making our number now seven, being McIntosh, Millward, Hillbrant, and myself.

22nd. We weighed anchor and sailed for Papaara, but having light airs we anchored at Taboona and weighed anchor again on the 23rd. Sailing along Attahooroo, which from its white beach and the narrow border of flatland covered with trees (chiefly poorow and fwharra), we thought it much resembled the north side of Tubuai. We were invited to stop at several places where the natives were very civil, and

Pohooataya begged us to stop at his house. But the anchoring being bad at Tye tabboo (that part of Attahooroo where he now lived), we declined and stood on, the wind being still light. It was night before we reached Papaara.

We anchored for the night within a break of the reef, about a mile from Tommaree's house. Some went on shore to Tommaree's to sleep, and he came down to view the schooner as soon as he had notice of her arrival. Next morning we weighed anchor, worked up to the morai, and came to an anchor. Here we found Burkett, Sumner, Brown, and Muspratt.

THE *PANDORA* APPEARS

We went on shore to Tommaree's to breakfast, but were scarcely sat down when a friend of Hetee-hetee's arrived in haste, telling us that a ship had anchored at Matavai since we had left it. Those who we had left there were gone on board, and the boats, manned and armed, were then at Attahooroo on their way after us. Hetee-hetee, who was their pilot, had sent him to give us notice, that we might know how to act. No time was now to be lost in fixing on the best plan, and it was agreed to avoid the boats. For this reason we got on board, leaving Brown and Byrne on shore, and got under way. We stood out with a fresh breeze at ESE, standing to the southward on a wind. We hoped, by keeping out of sight of the boats, to reach the ship and go on board of our own accord—hoping thereby to have better treatment than if we stayed to be made prisoners. Hetee-hetee's messenger had given us a very unfavourable account of the treatment of those who went on board from Matavai.

When we were about a league from the land we saw two sails to leeward, but could not discern whether they were boats or canoes. As we left them apace, we thought they could be no other then fishing canoes. Soon after noon we lost sight of them, and at four o'clock we hove about and stood in. But it was Sunday the 27th before we could fetch in, owing to the contrary winds and light airs that prevailed.

When we anchored, we were informed that Mr. Hayward, formerly of the *Bounty*, was officer of one of the boats, which proved to be the same we had seen— who, finding they were not likely to come up with the chase, had returned to the ship. We also learnt that Byrne had gone to the ship and Brown, having plundered Burkett's house of all that he could, was gone on board also.

Tommaree, seeing Brown seizing on all that he could find, had sent everything back into the mountains where Burkett, Sumner, Muspratt, Hillbrant, McIntosh, and Millward went after them—leaving Norman, Ellison, and myself to take care of the vessel. In the meantime, I went on shore to get some coconuts and some provisions dressed, leaving Norman and Ellison on board. As the surf ran high on the beach, I took no arms with me when I left the vessel.

When I went to Tommaree he promised that I should have what I wanted immediately. I told him that we must go to the ship, when he said, "If you do, Hayward will kill you, for he is very angry." He ordered some hands to carry off coconuts and, in the meantime, pressed me to stay with him, saying, "If you will go into the mountains they will never be able to find you." But I still denied him, telling him that I must go to the ship. He then upbraided me with deceiving him and told me that I should not go. At the same instant I observed several of the natives on board the schooner (where they had gone by Tommaree's order, under pretence of carrying coconuts on board). They had taken the opportunity of seizing Norman and Ellison and throwing them overboard.

I then begged Tommaree to prevent them from being hurt, when he told me that there was no fear of that. A few minutes after they landed, they were conducted to me amid a thousand or more of the natives, who poured so fast on board the schooner that they bore her down on one side, and she rolled most of them overboard. However, they soon stripped her of everything that they could remove and brought the things on shore, unbending the sails and unreeving the rigging, which they brought away with them.

We asked Tommaree what was the meaning of this treatment, and seeing nothing of our companions and being unarmed ourselves, we hardly knew what to think of our situation. He told us it was because we wanted to leave him, and that we must go and secure ourselves in the mountains and keep away from the ship. We should have our arms and everything restored, and he would make good all our damages. We still refused. When he said, "Then I'll make you go," his men seized us and were proceeding inland with us when we begged of Tommaree to let us see some of our shipmates before we went—which he agreed to. A guard was placed over us till he should return.

We were conducted to the house of Tayreehamoedooa, where we had provisions prepared in abundance. We stayed here all night and next day, when we proposed to make our escape. A trusty friend who had lived with me all the time I had been on the island, being one of Poeno's men, found us out and promised to have a canoe ready by midnight to carry us to Matavai, where he said that Poeno waited with impatience to see us. As soon as it was night, he took his station on the beach, and about ten o'clock brought Brown into the house. We asked him if he had any arms, and he produced a pistol, which he said he had brought from the ship with two hatchets and a knife. These he delivered into Norman's hands and asked us what we meant to do and where the rest were—to which we answered that we had not seen the others since they landed, and that we were going to the ship.

We asked him the name of the ship and her commander, but the only account he could give was that she was an English ship of war and could inform us no further. He also produced a bottle with some Holland gin, of which he offered each a dram; but the smell proved sufficient for me, and the other two drank but sparingly. Brown told us that he had been landed at the north side of the isthmus by the ship's boat, of which Mr. Hayward had command. He was sent to Papaara with presents for Tommaree, but had not seen him. He said he had been beset near the morai and narrowly escaped being killed. His pistol, being wet, would not fire, and he was forced to shelter himself in the thick brush near the morai. He was proceeding to return to the ship when he was met on the beach by our men.

The canoe being ready, we armed: Norman and myself with a hatchet each and Ellison with the large knife. We left the pistol with Brown, who fresh primed it and set forward. Having got to the canoe without interruption, we got in and paddled to Attahooroo, landing about six miles from Papaara on a sandy beach, which being white was of some help to us in travelling. Here we left the canoe and proceeded alongshore for twelve or fourteen miles, reaching Pohooataya's house at Tye tabboo about four in the morning of the 29th.

Here we found a launch at anchor near the beach and some canoes hauled up near the house. We hailed the boat but received no answer, those on board being all fast asleep, as were those who were on shore in the canoes. On enquiry we found that the canoes belonged to Areepaeea, who was here with them. The officer commanding the boat was Mr. Robert Corner (second lieutenant of His Majesty's Ship *Pandora*, Captain Edwards). Mr. Corner was asleep in one of the canoes, and we waked him and delivered ourselves up to him, telling him who we were and delivering the hatchets to Brown when he came up; also the pistol and ammunition that he had given to Norman on the way.

Having informed Mr. Corner where the schooner was and what had happened to us, he left us in the launch with Mr. Rickards, master's mate of the ship, and six men. He set out with eighteen men as soon as daylight enabled him to proceed by land for Papaara, taking Brown with him. We remained here till two in the afternoon, when Mr. Hayward (who we found was third lieutenant of the ship) arrived with the pinnace and twenty armed men. By his orders we had our hands tied, and Mr. Rickards was ordered into the pinnace. Mr. Sevill, a midshipman, was put on board the launch and ordered to proceed to the ship, then twenty-five

Sketch Map of Pandora's Voyage

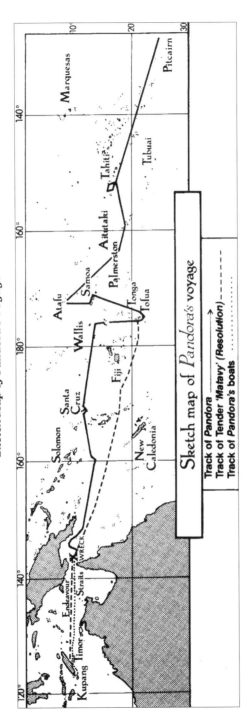

This map tracks the *Pandora's* failed search for Fletcher Christian and his party of mutineers. It also shows where contact with James Morrison's schooner *Matavy* (*Resolution*) was lost, the schooner's track, where the *Pandora* sank, and the track of *Pandora's* four boats. Reprinted with permission of Cambridge University Press.

or thirty miles distant. Mr. Hayward asked us where the others were, which we could not answer, not knowing ourselves.

We parted from the pinnace about three o'clock, and during the passage up, Mr. Sevill gave each of us half a pint of wine. From him we learnt the fate of the *Bounty*'s launch, and he also informed us that Lieutenant Bligh was made post captain. He also enquired what was become of the *Bounty* and who was in her, which we answered to the best of our knowledge. We reached the ship at nine o'clock, when we were handed on board and put in irons, under the half deck, after which our hands were cast loose. There being no marines, two seamen and a midshipman were posted over us with pistols and bayonets.

A LONG IMPRISONMENT BEGINS

Here we found in irons George Stewart, Peter Heywood, Joseph Coleman, Richard Skinner, and Michael Byrne, who informed us that handcuffs were being made by the armourer. These were put on us the next day, and orders given to the sentinels not to suffer any of the natives to speak to us, and to shoot the first man that spoke to another in the Tahitian language. We remained under the half deck some days, during which time we had full allowance of everything but grog, which we did not then want, having plenty of coconuts provided for us by our friends—who were not suffered to speak or look at us. Any who looked pitifully towards us were ordered out of the ship.

In the meantime, a hammock was given to each to spread under us, and a shirt and trousers given to each of us, but these were of no use as we could not get them on and off, our irons being clenched fast. The carpenters were now set to work to erect a kind of poop on the quarterdeck for our reception.

On the 9th of April the schooner was brought to the ship by Mr. Hayward, and in her came Thomas Burkett, John Sumner, Thomas McIntosh, William Muspratt, John Millward, and Henry Hillbrant, who were ironed hand and foot in the same manner as we were as soon as they came on board.

THE HORRORS OF "*PANDORA*'S BOX"

The poop, or roundhouse, being finished, we were conveyed into it and put in irons as before. This place we styled "*Pandora*'s Box," the entrance being a scuttle on the top, eighteen or twenty inches square, secured by a bolt on the top through the coamings; two scuttles of nine inches square in the bulkhead for air with iron grates; and the stern ports barred inside and out with iron. The sentries were placed on the top while a midshipman walked across by the bulkhead. The length of this box was eleven feet upon deck and eighteen wide at the bulkhead, and here no person was suffered to speak to us but the master at arms. His orders were not to speak to us on any score but that of our provisions.

The heat of the place when it was calm was so intense that the sweat frequently ran in streams to the scuppers and produced maggots in a short time. The hammocks, being dirty when we got them, we found stored with vermin of another kind, which we had no method of eradicating but by lying on the plank. And though our friends would have supplied us with plenty of cloth, they were not permitted to do it, and our only remedy was to lie naked. These troublesome neighbours and the two necessary tubs that were constantly kept in the place helped to render our situation truly disagreeable.

During the time we stayed, the women with whom we had cohabited on the island came frequently under the stern (bringing their children, of which there were six born, four girls and two boys; several of the women were big with child). They cut their heads till the blood discoloured the water about them, their female friends also acting their part and making bitter lamentations. They were always driven away by the captain's orders, and none of them suffered to come near the ship. Notwithstanding which, they continued to come near enough to be observed and there performed their mourning rites. On the day the ship weighed anchor, they were sufficient to evince the truth of their grief and melt the most obdurate heart.

It being customary for the officer of the watch to examine our irons before he was relieved, McIntosh, happening to have a large shackle, had got one of his legs out in the night, which was reported to the captain. A general examination took place, when the leg irons were reduced to fit close. Mr. Larkin, the first lieutenant, in trying the handcuffs, took the method of setting his foot against our breasts and hauling the handcuffs over our hands with all his might, some of which took the skin off with them. All that could be hauled off by this means were reduced and fitted so close that there was no possibility of turning the hand in them. When our wrists began to swell, he told us that "they were not intended to fit like gloves."

However, Coleman's legs being much swelled, he was let out of irons, as were Norman and Byrne on their falling sick, but they were always handcuffed at night. McIntosh's and Ellison's arms, being much galled by their irons, had them taken off till they should get well, but their legs were still kept fast.

May, 1791. The schooner being fitted and the water complete, we sailed from Tahiti on the 19th of May and on the 20th had our grog served in full allowance.

We stood to the NW and next day made Hooaheine and Ryeatea, Tahaa, etc., and laid off and on here several days, sending the schooner close to the land. Heteehetee was landed here, having come from Tahiti in the ship. We next proceeded to Wytootache and Palmerston's Isles, and in the examination of them, the jolly boat with Mr. Sevill and four hands (one of which was the son of the boatswain of the *Pandora*) was lost by being blown off when going to the schooner, which lay at anchor near the reef. The ship and schooner both ran to leeward in quest of her, but to no purpose. On these islands was found part of the *Bounty*'s driver yard, which was in the raft that went adrift from Tubuai.

THE *RESOLUTION* VANISHES

June, 1791. Standing to the northward, several islands were discovered. At one of them, called Chatham Island, the schooner was missed and given over for lost. We cruised some time in search of her but without success, and stood for the Friendly Isles, where we met with wet weather. The roughness of the work made our habitation very leaky, and when any rain fell, we were always wet. We applied to the first lieutenant to have something done to remedy it, to which he replied, "I am wet too, and everybody on deck, and it will dry when the weather clears up."

Our miserable situation soon brought sickness on among us, and the surgeon (Mr. Hamilton), a very humane gentleman, gave us all the assistance in his power. [George Hamilton described his experience in *A Voyage Round the World,* first printed at Berwick in 1793 and edited and reprinted by Sir Basil Thomson in *Voyage of H.M.S. 'Pandora,' Despatched to Arrest the Mutineers of the 'Bounty' in the South Seas, 1790–91* (London: Francis Edwards, 1915).] At the same time he informed us that Captain Edwards had given such orders that it was out of his power to be of any service to us in our present circumstances. However, between him and the second lieutenant, a copper kettle was provided to boil our cocoa, which was served with sugar in lieu of butter and cheese. This and Divine Providence kept us alive.

As the place was washed twice a week, we were washed with it, there being no room to shift us from place to place. We had no other alternative but standing up till the deck dried (which we could but very badly do when the ship had any motion) or lying down in the wet. When the roughness of the weather gave the ship any motion, we were not able to keep ourselves fast, to remedy which we were threatened to be stapled down by the captain; but Mr. Corner gave us some short boards to check ourselves with, which he made the carpenters secure, and thereby prevented us from maiming each other and ourselves.

We anchored at Annamooka, where we wooded and watered and returned to the northward again in quest of the schooner. We left a letter with one of the chiefs for her if she should come in our absence, and it is possible that if she had come here that she would have been plundered by the natives. They behaved very indifferently, even to the ship. The second lieutenant was knocked down on shore by some of them, and some of the men were stripped stark naked. Some of them, having gotten into the cabin, jumped out of the windows with several of the captain's books, etc. Being pursued, they left the things and escaped. One of their canoes was seized for the captain and brought on board.

July, 1791. At Chatham Island the natives were also very dexterous at thieving. One of them made a shift to get out of the port in the lieutenant's berth under the half deck, with a new uniform jacket belonging to Mr. Hayward. He put it on as soon as he was astern of the ship and paddled off with it.

We cruised ten or twelve days and returned to Annamooka without hearing any tidings of the schooner, and she and her crew were both given over as lost.

The natives of the newly discovered isles seem to differ very little from the Friendly Islanders. Their language seems to be the same and the construction of their canoes is very near alike. They have hogs, but they are remarkably small. These islands are high, but do not appear to be very fruitful, and are about a two days' run to the NEN of Annamooka.

Yams were now purchased by the purser to issue in lieu of bread, which were served at the rate of three pounds of yams for one of bread while they lasted. Having completed the water, the ship sailed from Annamooka about the 1st of August, steering to the NW. It was now known that her destination was the island of Timor.

August, 1791. Several islands were discovered on this passage. On the 22nd we made the reef that crosses the straits in the latitude of 9°, having narrowly escaped running on a patch about a mile long, which lay by itself but a few days before. This was called Well's Reef, from its being discovered in the night by a young man of that name. [This may be a copyist's error for Willis, the name Edwards gives. This dangerous reef is now called Indispensable Reef, after the name of the ship whose commander discovered it. The straits mentioned by Morrison are the Torres Straits, between Australia and New Guinea.]

DISASTER ON THE GREAT BARRIER REEF

Finding no opening in the reef we hauled to the southward, working to windward some days. On Sunday the 28th of August, the second lieutenant was sent to find an opening in the reef with the yaul, and the ship hove to. On Monday the 29th at seven p.m. the ship went on the reef, just at the time the boat returned within hail and warned them of the danger; it was now too late. The current running fast towards the reef caused a heavy surf, in which the ship was forced onto the reef with violent and repeated strokes. We expected at every surge that the masts would go by the board.

Seeing the ship in this situation, we judged she would not hold together for long. As we were in danger at every stroke of killing each other with our irons, we broke them so we might be ready to assist ourselves and keep from killing each other. We informed the officers of what we had done. When Mr. Corner was acquainted with it he came aft, and we told him we should attempt nothing further, as we only wanted a chance for our lives—which he promised we should have, telling us not to fear. In the meantime, the ship lost her rudder and with it part of the sternpost. Having beat over between eleven and twelve, she was brought up in fifteen fathoms with both anchors, and the first news was nine feet of water in the hold!

Coleman, Norman, and McIntosh were ordered out to the pumps, and the boats got out. As soon as Captain Edwards was informed that we had broken our irons, he ordered us to be handcuffed and legs ironed again, with all the irons that could be mustered. We begged for mercy and desired leave to go to the pumps, but to no purpose. His orders were put into execution, though the water in the hold had increased to eleven feet, and one of the chain pumps broke. The master at arms and corporal were now armed, each with a brace of pistols and placed as additional sentinels over us, with orders to fire among us if we made any motion. The master at arms told us that the captain had said he would either shoot or hang to the yardarms those who should make any further attempt to break the irons.

We found there was no remedy but prayer, as we expected never to see daylight. Having recommended ourselves to the Almighty's protection, we lay down and seemed for a while to forget our miserable situation. We could hear the officers busy getting their things into the boats, which were hauled under the stern on purpose, and heard some of the men on deck say, "I'll be damned if they shall go without us." This made some of us start, and moving the irons, the master at arms said, "Fire upon the rascals." As he was then just over the scuttle, I spoke to him and said, "For God's sake, don't fire, what's the matter, there is none here moving." A few minutes after, one of the boats broke adrift and having but two men in her, she could not reach the ship again till another was sent with hands to bring her back.

Now we began to think they would set off together, as it was but natural to suppose that everyone would think of himself first. However, the boats returned and were secured with better warps. Now we learned that the booms were being cut loose for the purpose of making a raft, and one of the topmasts fell into the waist and killed a man who was busy heaving the guns overboard.

Everything seemed to be in great confusion. At daylight in the morning the boats were hauled up, and most of the officers being aft on the top of the box, we observed that they were armed and preparing to go into the boats by the stern ladders. We begged that we might not be forgotten, when by Captain Edwards's order Joseph Hodges, the armourer's mate of the *Pandora*, was sent down to take the irons off Muspratt and Skinner, and send them and Byrne (who was then out of irons) up. But Skinner, being too eager to get out, got hauled up with his handcuffs on, and the other two followed him closely.

The scuttle was shut and barred before Hodges could get to it, and he, in the meantime, knocked off my hand irons and Stewart's. I begged of the master at arms to leave the scuttle open when he answered, "Never fear, my boys, we'll all go to hell together." The words were scarcely out of his mouth when the ship took a sally, and a general cry of "there she goes" was heard. The master at arms and corporal, with the other sentinels, rolled overboard and at the same instant we saw through the stern ports Captain Edwards astern, swimming to the pinnace. It was some distance astern, as were all the boats that had shoved off on the first appearance of a motion in the ship.

ESCAPING FROM *PANDORA*'S BOX

Burkett and Hillbrant were yet handcuffed, and the ship under water as far as the main mast. It was beginning to flow in upon us when the Divine Providence directed William Moulter (boatswain's mate) to the place. He was scrambling up on the box and, hearing our cries, took out the bolt and threw it and the scuttle overboard. Such was his presence of mind, though, he was forced to follow instantly himself. On this, we all got out, except Hillbrant, and were rejoiced even in this trying scene to think that we had escaped from our prison—though it was full as much as I could do to clear myself of the driver boom before the ship sunk.

The boats were now so far off that we could not distinguish one from the other. However, observing one of the gangways come up, I swam to it and had scarcely reached it before I perceived Muspratt on the other end. It had brought him up, but it fell on the heads of several others, sending them to the bottom. Here I began to get ready for swimming. The top of our prison had floated and I observed on it Mr. Peter Heywood, Burkett, and Coleman, and the first lieutenant of the ship.

Seeing Mr. Heywood take a short plank and set off to one of the boats, I resolved to follow him. I threw away my trousers; bound my loins up in a sash, or marro, after the Tahitian manner; got a short plank; and followed.

After having been about an hour and a half in the water, I reached the blue yaul and was taken up by Mr. Bowling, master's mate, who had also taken up Mr. Heywood. After taking up several others, we were landed on a small sandy key on the reef, about two or three miles from the ship. Here we soon found that four of our fellow prisoners were drowned, two of them, Skinner and Hillbrant, with their handcuffs on. Stewart and Sumner were struck by the gangway. Burkett being landed with his handcuffs on, the captain ordered them to be taken off. We also learned that thirty-one of the *Pandora*'s ship's company were lost, among whom were the master at arms and ship's corporal—but all the officers were saved.

TORTURE ON A TINY ISLAND

A tent was now pitched for the officers and another for the men, but we were not suffered to come near either, though the captain had told us that we should be used as well as the ship's company. We found that was not the case, for on asking Captain Edwards for a spare boat's sail to shelter us from the sun, being mostly naked, it was refused, though no use was made of it. We were ordered to keep on a part of the island by ourselves, to windward of the tents, not being suffered to speak to any person but each other.

The provision saved being very small, this day's allowance was only a mouthful of bread and a glass of wine; the water being but a small quantity, none could be afforded. We stayed here till Wednesday morning the 31st fitting the boats, during which time the sun took such an effect on us—who had been cooped up for these five months—that we had our skin flayed off from head to foot, though we kept ourselves covered in the sand during the heat of the day.

This was all the shelter that the island affords, the whole of it being no more than a small bank washed up on the reef, which with a change of wind might disappear. It is scarcely 150 yards in circuit and not more than six feet from the level at high water. There are two more of the same kind, of which this is in the middle. Between it and the one to the southward is a deep channel, through which a ship might pass in safety. These keys were laid down by Captain Edwards, and their latitude is between 10° and 11° south, about one day's run from the north cape of New Holland.

During the night we found the air very chilly and having no covering, we threw up a bank of sand to sleep under the lee of, which proved but an indifferent barrier.

We had frequent flying showers of rain sufficient to make our lodging miserable, though not sufficient to allay our thirst, which was very great. We tried for water but found none. Mr. Corner made a fire and got a copper kettle, which he filled with salt water, making it boil. He attended it all night, saving the drops that the steam causes in the cover, which he put into a cup till a spoonful was mustered. One of the *Pandora*'s people (named Connell) went out of his senses drinking salt water.

On the 30th the master went with a boat to the wreck to see if anything had come up. The topmast heads being out of the water, the topgallant masts struck. He returned with part of one of the topgallant masts, which he sawed off to get clear of the cap, and a cat that he found sitting on the crosstrees. One of the ship's buoys drifted past, but was not thought worth going after, though we had no vessel to contain water when we should find it.

The boats being ready, on the 31st at ten a.m. we embarked in the following manner: McIntosh, Ellison, and myself in the pinnace with Captain Edwards, Lieutenant Hayward, and nineteen officers and men, making her complement twenty-four; in the red yaul went Burkett and Millward, with Lieutenant Larkin and nineteen officers and men, making her complement twenty-two; in the launch, Peter Heywood, Joseph Coleman, and Michael Byrne, with Lieutenant Corner and twenty-seven officers and men, her complement thirty-one; and in the blue yaul Norman and Muspratt, with the master and nineteen officers and men, making ninety-nine souls in all.

In this situation we had a passage of between four and five hundred leagues to run before we could reach the Dutch settlement on Timor, with the scanty allowance of two musket balls' weight of bread and hardly a gill of water and wine together for twenty-four hours—in a scorching hot sun, now nearly vertical.

A LONG, AGONIZING VOYAGE TO SAFETY

We left the key (which was named Wreck Island) and proceeded to the NW. Next morning, the 1st of September, we made land, which we supposed to be part of New Holland. The two yauls were sent in with the land while we stood on towards an island, where we hoped to get water. In the afternoon we were joined by the yauls, which had got water, and having filled their vessels followed us. They joined us, and we stood into a bay to search for water. Approaching the beach, we found that there were some inhabitants on it, though it was but small and did not appear very fruitful.

The natives appeared on the beach to the amount of eighteen or nineteen men, women and children, who appeared to be all of one family. They came off freely to the boats, and we found that the colour of their skins was heightened to a jet black by means of either soot or charcoal. They were quite naked and their hair long and curling, but matted like a mop, and some had holes in their ears that were stretched to such a size as to receive a man's arm.

We made signs that we wanted water, which they soon understood. A half-anker was given to one of them, along with some trifles by way of encouragement, and he soon returned with it almost full, which being started into a brecco and gave it to him again. He then called a young woman who stood near him and sent her for the water. She soon returned, and with her was a man with a bundle of spears. When she came to the beach, the man who had sent her went and received it, and standing up to the waist in the water, made signs for the boats to come in. We declined and he kept retreating.

Meanwhile, two of the men began to prepare their weapons. A javelin was thrown that struck the pinnace, and an arrow fired that fell close alongside. Both were taken up and several muskets were fired, at which they dropped. The man who had the keg let it fall and fled, but finding himself not hurt, he returned and took it with him. They soon disappeared and Captain Edwards ordered the boats to follow him, putting off and standing to the westward to some other islands then in sight. At this the first lieutenant seemed displeased and spoke his mind so loud that Captain Edwards heard him and desired him to be silent, obey his orders, and at his peril to say no more about the matter.

We reached the islands and examined them, but they afforded neither water nor anything eatable, except a sort of plum that contains a glutinous gum, which sticks in the mouth, teeth, throat, etc. They were by no means a delicacy, but they were eaten. We could not touch the shellfish that we had brought from the key, for want of water. Among the shellfish found on the key were two large cockles of the gigantic sort; the shell measured about a foot long.

Finding no water here, we bore away to the westward, and at three the next morning made an island where we hoped to get water. Standing in, we came to an anchor till daylight when we weighed anchor and got close in, seeing no natives. A party was sent on shore to search for water, which at last they found by digging, and every vessel was filled. The kettle was boiled with portable soup, and a pint served to each man with as much water as we could drink.

We were reduced to many shifts to collect water, having made canvas bags. A pair of boots and everything that would contain water if only for a day was filled, and then the whole did not amount to two hundred gallons—a scanty allowance for ninety-nine men to subsist on, who did not expect to reach Timor in less than fourteen days. We knew of no place where we could find more till we reached it, and though we had got an additional stock of water, it was no addition to our allowance as we knew not how long the passage would be.

Having filled our water we sailed to the westward, and for fear of parting company in the night, the pinnace took the other boats in tow all night, which was the case every night through the passage.

The heat of the weather made our thirst insupportable, and as the canvas bags soon leaked out, no addition of allowance could take place. To such extremity did thirst increase that several of the men drank their own urine. A booby being caught in the pinnace, the blood was eagerly sucked, and the body divided and eagerly devoured. Two others were caught by the other boats, which shared the same fate, as the distress was general. We kept a line constantly towing, but never caught any fish, though we saw several.

On the 9th, as I was laying on the oars talking to McIntosh, Captain Edwards ordered me aft, and without assigning any cause ordered me to be pinioned with a cord and lashed down in the boat's bottom. Ellison, who was then asleep in the boat's bottom, was ordered to the same punishment. I attempted to reason and enquire what I had now done to be thus cruelly treated, urging the distressed situation of the whole, but received for answer, "Silence, you murdering villain, are you not a prisoner? You piratical dog, what better treatment do you expect?" I then told him that it was a disgrace for the captain of a British Man-of-War to treat a prisoner in such an inhumane manner, upon which he started up in a violent rage and, snatching a pistol that lay in the stern sheets, threatened to shoot me. I still attempted to speak, when he swore, "By God, if you speak another word I'll heave the log with you." Finding that he would hear no reason and my mouth being parched so that I could not move my tongue, I was forced to be silent and submit, and was tied down so that I could not move.

In this miserable situation Ellison and I remained for the rest of the passage, nor was McIntosh suffered to come near or speak to either of us; however, we made ourselves as easy as we could, and on the 15th we made the island of Timor. The boats separated and stood in for the land, having had a fine breeze and fair weather all the way. We tried for water at several places, but could find none till the 16th in the morning, when we found a well near the beach. Here the launch joined us again when we proceeded in company to Coupang, which we reached at midnight and came to a grapnel off the fort till morning. We found a ship in the road and a number of small craft, and at eight in the morning, the captain went on shore to the governor.

About ten we were landed and conducted by a guard to the governor's house, and from thence to the castle. Notwithstanding our weak condition, we were put into stocks. On the 19th the yauls arrived and we were joined by our fellow prisoners, whose treatment had been better, but their fare the same. Immediately upon our landing provisions were procured, which now began to move our bodies, and we were forced to ease nature where we lay, which we had not done during the passage. Some were now so bad as to require repeated clysters [enemas], but the surgeon of the place who visited us could not enter the place till it had been washed by the slaves.

We had laid six days in this situation when the Dutch officer commanding the fort, being informed of our distress, came to visit us. Taking compassion on us, he ordered irons to be procured and linked us two and two, giving us liberty to walk about the cell. A guard of the *Pandora*'s men was placed before the door in addition to the Dutch soldiers.

As we were yet mostly naked, we got some of the leaves of the brab tree [a species of palm] and set to work to make hats, which we sold to procure us clothing; but every article being dear, we could purchase nothing here. With thread and needles being very dear, we made but little progress. However, we made shift to supply ourselves with tobacco and some little refreshments.

We found that there were prisoners in the fort—seven men, a woman, and two children—who had escaped in a boat from Sydney (or Port Jackson, Botany Bay). [Then a penal settlement. As they confessed after the arrival of Captain Edwards, these people were escaped convicts, and having stolen a ship's gig had reached Timor after an adventurous voyage of ten weeks.] They had passed for part of the crew of the ship *Neptune* and they reported to have been castaway, but not being able to keep within bounds, they were discovered to be cheats and confined in the castle till they should pay the debt they had contracted.

October, 1791. We remained here till the 5th of October, when we were removed to the *Rembang*, a Dutch ship then in the road. Mr. Larkin, being the officer on this duty, came to the prison with a guard and cords to pinion us with his own hands. He set his foot against our backs and braced our arms together as almost to haul them out of their sockets. We were tied two and two by the elbows and, having our irons knocked off, were conducted to the beach and put on board a longboat to proceed to the ship. Before we reached her some of us had fainted, owing to the circulation of the blood being stopped by the lashings. When we got on board we were put both legs in irons and our lashings taken off.

Reconstructed Route of the Matavy; June 22–August 1, 1791

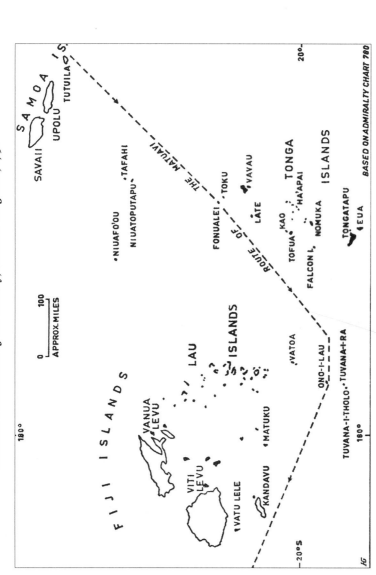

The *Matavy*, a seaworthy schooner constructed by James Morrison on Tahiti (originally named the *Resolution*), became separated from the *Pandora* during its search for Fletcher Christian and the *Bounty* mutineers. The crew of this small vessel became the first Europeans to make contact with the people of Fiji. Reproduced with the kind permission of the Honourable Editor of *The Mariner's Mirror*.

The Botany Bay men were now brought on board by a party of Dutch soldiers and put in irons with us, in the same manner. The ship weighed anchor in the evening for Batavia, and the next day McIntosh, Coleman, and Norman were let out of irons, with liberty to walk the deck. Our hands being now at liberty, we expected now to find some little ease and prepared to go to work on hats, having brought our stuff on board with us; but happiness is not to be always found where it is expected and is ever of a short duration.

The ship was very leaky, and we were ordered out of irons two at a time, for two hours in the forenoon and two hours in the afternoon to work the pumps, with sentinels over us. This new liberty (as we thought it) we gladly embraced, but soon found our strength unequal to the task. One day I told Mr. Larkin that I was not able to work at the pump without a break (the ship requiring the pump continually at work), to which he replied tauntingly, "You damned villain, you have brought it on yourself, and I'll make you stand it; if it was not for you we should not have been here nor have met with this trouble," to which I replied, "Trouble often comes unsought," and he then ordered me to be silent.

However, this work was soon at an end. The deck where we lay being constantly wet, and having no clothing under or over us, soon put us past labour. We were then kept below, the pumps being now left to the Dutch seamen and Malay slaves.

This ship was badly found and worse managed, and if Captain Edwards had not taken the command and set his men to work, she would never have reached Batavia. Having split most of her sails in passing the Strait of Bally and having none to bend in their stead, she very narrowly escaped going on shore.

THE *RESOLUTION* IS FOUND
However, we reached Samarang, a Dutch settlement on the island of Java by the 30th of October, where we came to an anchor. Here we found the schooner, which had arrived at this island six weeks before, with all her crew, consisting of a master's mate, midshipman, quartermaster, and six men, one of whom had died since their arrival. They were joyfully received by their shipmates, and the schooner, being brought out of harbour, accompanied us to Batavia, where we anchored on the 7th of November.

November, 1791. We were now put on board an old hulk in the road with the *Pandora*'s officers and men. Here, McIntosh, Coleman, and Norman had the liberty of the deck as before, and here we received 10 shillings per man for short allowance in the boats, with which we purchased some few refreshments in addition to the ship's allowance—being still victualled by the purser of the *Pandora*. The schooner being put up for sale, the captain purchased her and sent her as a present to the governor of Timor, and divided the money among the ship's company.

Nankin cloth was here purchased and served to the ship's company, and as we had now recovered our health, we commenced being tailors as well as hatmakers, and by working for the ship's company got some clothes for ourselves, which we stood in much need of. But this was prohibited by Captain Edwards as soon as he knew it. We remained here till the 23rd of December, during which time we were not permitted to come on deck but twice, each for about half an hour at a time to wash ourselves. Here we enjoyed our health, though the *Pandora*'s people fell sick and died apace.

A HELLISH PORT

With respect to the city of Batavia I can say nothing, not having had a view of it, but it makes no show from the road, the church and some storehouses being the only buildings that can be seen from the shipping. It is situated at the bottom of a deep bay or inlet and surrounded by low and, to all appearance, swampy land that has no appearance of cultivation. The small river by which its canals are filled empties itself into the bay and teems with such filth that the road where the large ships lie is little better than a stagnant pool. During the night the dew falls very heavy and the morning is generally darkened by a thick, stinking fog that continues till it is exhaled by the heat of the sun.

As the sea breeze seldom reaches the road till afternoon, and sometimes not during the day, the weather is close and sultry. The land wind coming off in the evenings brings with it a sickly, disagreeable smell, sufficient to breed distempers among Europeans. To prevent being infected by this, we applied for liberty to smoke tobacco, which being granted, all our leisure time was thus employed—particularly in the mornings and evenings, which we found very beneficial and freed us from headaches, etc., which we supposed to be occasioned by the pestilential vapours.

The climate of Batavia is by no means calculated for Europeans and, together with the new arrack (a most pernicious liquor), carries off great numbers daily. Death made such a havoc within the last six months that the fleet now in the road was forced to send to Holland for hands to navigate them. Even now they were not half manned, though the crews of the outward bound ships were put on board as fast as they came to an anchor.

It was said that 2,500 officers and seamen had been carried off this season exclusive of the inhabitants. The Chinese and natives of the island do all the labour in loading and unloading the ships, as the Dutch seamen are mostly removed as soon as the ship is made fast. Provisions here are neither cheap nor good, the beef being all small and lean. Rice is the only substitute for bread, at least all that can be the fare of the ship's company. Clothing of all kinds, and especially the manufactures of Europe, is dear also, and in fact I could find nothing cheap but arrack, which is as bad as poison. Nevertheless, it is plentifully used by the Dutch, and it cost the *Pandora*'s officers some trouble to keep their men from using it also.

November 20th. The first lieutenant, Mr. Larkin, sailed in a Dutch ship for Europe with part of the ship's company, and on the 23rd of December, the remainder were divided—Lieutenants Corner and Hayward taking each a party, and with them the Botany Bay men. We were put on board the *Vreedenbergh*, in which ship was Captain Edwards with twenty-three officers and men. On the 24th she weighed anchor and dropped down to a small island in the entrance of the bay called Onrest, where the dockyard is. To this place they send their convicts, where they are employed making rope and careening the ships.

We weighed anchor from this place on the 25th, tiding it out through the straits. It was the afternoon before we got any provisions, having been victualled no longer than the 22nd by the purser of the *Pandora*. When we got it, it was served after the Dutch method, which was thus: two drams of arrack per day, equal to one-third of a pint; three pounds of flesh (beef and pork); one and a half of fish; ditto of sugar, ditto of tamarinds; half a pint of gee; half a pint of oil; and a pint of vinegar with rice in lieu of bread to serve each man for a fortnight. The rice was little better than grains, most of it having the husks on it, and the oil and tamarinds were fit for no use that we could put them to.

Such was our food, and two quarts of water a day gave us plenty to drink, but our lodgings were none of the best, as we lay on rough logs of timber. Some of them lay some inches above the rest and which our small portion of clothing would not bring to a level. The deck over us was very leaky, by which means we were continually wet, being alternately drenched with salt water, the urine of the hogs, or the rain that happened to fall.

We passed the Strait of Sunda on the 1st of January, 1792, and met with nothing material during our passage to the Cape except burying two of the *Pandora*'s men and several of the Dutch seamen. This and the method of issuing the provisions was the only thing that occurred worth notice. As it shows the true character of

Dutchmen, it deserves notice that they made a fortnight's allowance to serve us sixteen days, and by the time we reached the Cape, they had gained upon us nearly a fortnight's allowance.

March 14th. This day we were let out of irons two at a time to walk the deck for two hours each, but were scarce able to stand on our feet. We got this weak by living, or rather existing, on our miserable allowance. This was the first and last indulgence of the kind we had during the passage, except one or two who had been let out for a few hours in a day by the intercession of the Dutch surgeon. We now found the weather sharp and cutting.

RETURNING HOME ON AN ENGLISH SHIP

15th. Made the Cape of Good Hope, and on the 18th came to an anchor in Table Bay, where to our inexpressible joy we found an English Man-of-War. We were soon informed that it was His Majesty's Ship *Gorgon* from Port Jackson, and on the 19th we were sent on board her, where our treatment became less rigourous and two-thirds allowance of provisions now seemed a feast.

Shortly after, the other ships arrived with the rest of the *Pandora*'s men. We learnt here that the first lieutenant of the *Pandora* had sailed some time, and having left one of his men behind, he was sent on board this ship by Captain Edwards. McIntosh, Coleman, and Norman were here at liberty as before and the rest of us only one leg in irons. Every indulgence was given, and Lieutenant Gardner of this ship, in the absence of Captain Parker, very humanely gave us a sail to lay on—which by us was thought a luxury indeed, as we had not enjoyed such for the last twelve months.

Here being supplied with shirts and trousers, we laid what trifle of cash we had out in refreshments. We began to get our health and strength very fast, having the benefit of the fresh air, which for some time before we had been strangers to, being removed from between decks to sit on the forecastle for six or eight hours every day.

On the 4th of April Captain Edwards came on board in order to take his passage in the *Gorgon*, and on the 5th she weighed anchor for England. On the 10th we were ordered full allowance.

18th. Made the island of St. Helena, which we passed near enough to show our colours and see two ships in the road, who returned the compliment by hoisting theirs.

22nd. Made Ascension and anchored the same day. We found riding here an American schooner belonging to New Providence and, having got on board twenty-eight fine turtles, sailed on the 24th. After crossing the line we spoke an American brig bound to Bengal and an English brig, the *Prince William Henry,* bound to the South Fishery.

June 19th. Anchored at Spithead. On the 21st we were removed to His Majesty's Ship *Hector,* where we were treated in a manner that renders the humanity of her captain and officers much honour. Beds were given us and every indulgence that our circumstances would admit of allowed.

On the 12th of September our trial commenced on board His Majesty's Ship *Duke* in Portsmouth Harbour, and to the minutes of the court-martial I refer the reader for a more particular account of that transaction. Meanwhile, I shall endeavour to give some account of the island of Tahiti, or King George's Island, and of the manners and customs of the Society Isles in general—with an account of their language such as I was able to procure during my stay on shore there of nineteen months—exclusive of nearly five months that elapsed while the *Bounty* lay there under Lieutenant Bligh's command—and five months more that we expended after the taking of the ship before we landed, most part of which time we were conversant with the natives.

Part Two

AN ACCOUNT OF THE ISLAND OF TAHITI
AND THE CUSTOMS OF THE ISLANDERS

An Account of the Island of Tahiti
and the Customs of the Islanders

SITUATION AND EXTENT

The island of Tahiti was better laid down by Captain Cook than I am able to ascertain with an indifferent quadrant. Its latitude is between 17° 28' and 18° south, and its longitude about 211° east. (According to Captain Cook, Point Venus is in latitude 17° 29' 30" south, longitude 149° 32' 30" west.)

It consists of two peninsulas, both of which are of a circular form with an isthmus of lowland about two or three miles across. The larger peninsula is called TahitiNooe, or Great Tahiti, and is about eighty miles in circumference. The smaller, which lies southeast of TahitiNooe, is called by the names of TahitiEete (Little Tahiti) and Tyarrabboo, and is about thirty miles in circumference according to my computation. Having no apparatus for surveying, I can only give the distance according to my own opinion. It is in most parts defended by a reef of coral, in some places a mile or a mile and a half from the shore, within which are several small keys. The beach in some places is black and others white.

FACE OF THE COUNTRY

Both peninsulas are mountainous and covered with trees of different sorts—having each a border of flat land (except where it is separated by mountains rising out of the sea), which is likewise covered with trees, chiefly the breadfruit and coconut. Several of the mountains rising out of the sea rise gradually till they form one great or general pile in the center of the island, which may be seen at twenty leagues distant. They are intersected by innumerable valleys, all of which are clothed with verdure. The ridges are covered with reeds that at a distance resemble grass while they are green, and the tops of the hills are for the most part covered with large trees.

The highest mountains teem with innumerable cascades, forming a delightful prospect. Thirty of these may be counted pouring from a high mountain lying behind Matavai called Ora fwhanna, which water the neighbouring valleys. Before it reaches the sea, it forms many small rivers and brooks, all of which are excellent water, being produced by springs, some of which issue from the solid rock.

AIR AND CLIMATE
The climate of the Society Isles differs very little from that of the Leeward Islands and may be called (after changing the seasons, one being in north and the other south latitude) the same. During the six months that the sun is to the southward of the equator, the weather is unsettled and the wind variable, and when the sun draws nearly overhead, the rainy season begins. It continues with intermissions while it is passing to the south and repassing to the northward, which is generally from October till April. In this season the westerly wind is the most prevailing, and it sometimes blows very hard and brings with it a heavy sea.

When the north or south wind happens to prevail, it generally brings much thunder and lightning with it, and the rain falls in deluges, swelling the rivers so as to overflow the lowland in a few hours—bringing large trees from the mountains and tumbling huge rocks before it. Frequently it carries away the houses of the natives into the sea. However, the loss they sustain is not great, and they are generally supplied with plenty of timber for fuel without the trouble of going to the hills for it.

The westerly winds bring a heavy sea with them, and this season of the year is the worst that a ship could choose to visit Tahiti, as the bay of Matavai is by no means a safe road. It is entirely open to these winds, nor is there any place about the island that affords a good harbour except Oparre, where the *Bounty* lay. The entrance of this being narrow and rocky, it is necessary to have buoys placed to steer in by. The advantage of a calm must be taken to tow out, as the trade wind blows right in and the westerly winds always bring bad weather.

Oparre Harbour is the only one that Tahiti affords where a ship may ride in safety at any season of the year (Matavai Bay cannot be counted safe more than six or seven months in the year). The anchorage is good in eight to sixteen fathoms, black sand. To the westward of the reef that defends Point Venus, about a cable's length, lies a bank of coral that is called the Dolphin Bank. The shallowest part of it is barely thirteen feet, but between it and the reef is a good passage with twenty-two fathoms of water. This passage I would recommend before going to leeward and by keeping the reef aboard and coming no nearer than ten fathoms.

You may run in and anchor in safety, but by going to the westward, you are liable to meet with sudden puffs thrown off in a southerly direction from One Tree Hill (a bluff commanding the bay), which is sometimes followed by a few minutes' calm before the true wind recovers its force. A ship may be baffled and, if weakly manned, as is often the case after a long voyage, forced to bring up in foul ground or be driven out and obliged to work to windward again. But this is not always the case, and with a fresh sea breeze there is no fear; by keeping to the eastward of the bank all trouble may be avoided. There is another rock in the bay, but it is in sight and close to the east part of the beach.

Water is plentiful all over the island but wood for fuel is not, as there are few other trees in the lowland except the breadfruit and coconut, with which it is covered. Every tree has its owner and must be either purchased or permission to cut obtained from the natives. While the sun is to the north of the equator, the air is clear and the weather fine. The southeast wind blows regularly, and the lowland, being covered with trees, affords an agreeable shade. The heat is not felt to any excess, and during this season the natives pass through the mountains from one side of the island to the other, which they cannot do in the rains. They are then forced to keep to the seaside if they have occasion to travel.

The seasons differ much on the opposite sides of this island, partly owing to the island of Morea or Eymayo lying in a north and south direction across the western part of it. While the trade wind blows on the north side, the west wind blows fresh on the south; but when the wind gets to the southward of SE, it prevails against the west wind. Then the south side is deluged with rain from the clouds that settle on the mountains of Tyarrabboo, while the north side enjoys fine, pleasant weather with scarce a shower of rain for six months. This makes a material difference in the breadfruit harvest, which generally begins on the north side about November and is over by January. On the south side it is sometimes over by November at one season and does not begin till January at another.

The tides in this, as in other tropical countries, are not great, and the highest tide that I observed at Point Venus was eighteen inches, and the time nearly two o'clock at full and change.

SOIL AND PRODUCE

The soil of the country is rich and fertile, and in the valleys and lowland is a fine black mould. Near the isthmus on both sides it is coral and sand, and rather barren, producing little else but fwharra (or palm) trees. The hills consist of several strata of red, white, black, yellow, and bluish colours, with several kinds of stones. The red is a kind of clay, and in it is found a stone something like the cornelian, which will strike fire, but is full of veins and joints and will not stand a second stroke. The white is a kind of pipe clay without stones, the black a fine fat mould, and the yellow of a gravelly nature with large stones. The blue is a strong, tough loam.

All of these are found in a depth of ten or twelve feet from the surface. Under that is a soft, sandy rock of a brownish colour intermixed with some that is hard and black. There are also large cliffs of a black stone in the mountains, which runs in squares from two to eight or ten inches, and several feet in length, of which the natives make their adzes.

The mountains are rocky to the tops but covered in most places with earth to a good depth that produces a number of large trees. The cliffs in the mountains bear evident marks of having been burnt by fire, though there is no account among the natives that ever a volcano subsisted here. In one place in the mountains of Fwhassyeano a whole hill appears to have been overturned, but the natives say it was done by thunder; it was more probably by an earthquake. The beds of the rivers are gravel and large stones, part of which appear to have been washed from the hills. Some are hard pebbles, others contain a glassy substance and will melt in a hot fire, and many appear full of holes, like the pumice stone but heavier.

The valleys are fruitful and run for some miles, but far up the mountains are inaccessible, being very steep and frequently drenched with rain. The only road to ascend the mountains is from the seaside along the ridges, by which route those who travel them must proceed.

The produce of these islands in general are hogs, which are large and plenty and their flesh excellent; goats that are also plentiful and good food; and dogs, which are here esteemed a delicacy and are allowed by former voyagers to equal an English lamb. These are all the quadrupeds that they esteem good food. They have also cats and rats but eat neither. What black cattle had been left there they hold in no esteem. Fowl are plenty and good and, if killed young, are equal to those of Europe, either for taste, tenderness, or flavour. They have a number of birds and fish that shall be described in their places. Their vegetable productions are fruits and roots of different sorts and are these—

ROOTS

Yams, called here oowhi, grow wild in the mountains and are from one to six feet in length, but not more than five or six inches round. They are very good, but as it takes much trouble to dig them out, they are seldom sought after. Except when the breadfruit is scarce, they never take the pains to cultivate them.

Taro, another root that they cultivate, grows in water. The ground must be leveled for that purpose and banked up to keep the water constantly on it. They grow to twelve or fourteen inches long, as much round, and are little inferior to yams. The root, when dressed, is mottled inside with green, blue, and white. The leaves make excellent greens, having a taste something like our asparagus; but if they are not sufficiently dressed, they cause an itching in the fundament for several hours after they are eaten.

Oomarra, a kind of sweet potato, differs from those of America or the West Indies. They are of an orange colour, somewhat near the size of those in England, and are plentiful. They are produced by planting slips from the stalks, which take root and produce the potatoes.

Yappe are large mountain roots, something in shape like the taro but much larger. They are also coarser and more insipid, and if eaten without being properly dressed, cause a disagreeable itching in the mouth and throat that does not suddenly go off. To remedy this, they are kept all night in the oven, which takes away the itching and biting quality.

Mapoora is a kind of small taro that grows in the mountains. It is hot and biting, but made eatable in the same manner as the yappe; with this they make paste for their cloth.

Dewe is another hot, biting root, like a large turnip radish, that grows in all parts of the island and must be dressed in the same manner.

Peea is a root resembling a potato, but is bitter to the taste and cannot be eaten till it has been grated down and steeped in water. It answers best for paste by roasting and beating it up with a little water. The method of preparing it for food is thus: Having gathered as many of the roots as they want, they get a rough stone that they wash clean. They grate the peea into a trough filled with clear water, mixing it up. When it settles, the water is poured off and more applied for five or six days, when the water is strained off and the peea dried for use. It is then like fine flour and makes excellent puddings or pancakes.

E'huoy is a kind of fern root growing in the mountains only. It is good eating when dressed. Many other roots found in the mountains are good food but seldom sought for, except when breadfruit is scarce.

Ginger and turmeric grow in abundance all over the islands, as does also tobacco, sugar cane, Indian corn, pumpkins, red peppers, etc.

FRUITS

Among the fruits the breadfruit, of which there are near thirty sorts, deservedly takes the lead. This tree (called by the inhabitants ooroo) grows to the size of an oak and affords food, raiment, timber for houses and canoes, and pitch for their seams. The leaves also are of use, serving to wrap up their provisions when they dress them. The leaves are of different sizes, some of them not more than nine inches and others two feet long; they are broad and of as much substance as a cabbage leaf, notched on the edges with four or five notches of about six inches deep and the colour a dark green. It never sheds all its leaves and appears constantly in bloom, as the leaves that fall are forced off by young ones making their way out.

The branches are large and spreading, and on the ends of them the fruit grows, singly or in pairs, but seldom more. Some of them are round and others long, and are from three to six inches in diameter. The fruit while unripe is a bright green, and the rind is rough. As it ripens, the rind becomes smoother and the colour changes to brownish with a yellow tinge and appears spotted with white from the gum, which forces its way through the rind and dries on it. The fruit is then fit for use, and if it stays but a few days on the tree after the gum has made its appearance, it grows mellow and falls.

The taste becomes sweet and is too luscious to eat till it is mixed with some that has been made into mahee, but if gathered before it falls, its colour inside when baked is yellowish, and its consistency like that of a potato—though the taste is not like anything that I recollect in Europe, America, or India. It is nevertheless pleasant and agreeable. When dressed it will not keep good more than two days, yet it is so plenty as to answer every purpose of bread and is here the staff of life. The method of making it into mahee for store shall be described in its place.

The heare, or coconut, is the next fruit and is a very serviceable tree. The nuts when young are excellent drink, and when old make oil, sauce for fish puddings, etc. The shells make cups for eating and drinking, the husk makes lashings for their canoes, and with the leaves they make temporary huts, screens for their houses, baskets, etc. The trunk when past bearing makes fuel, though they stand many years, except when they chance to lose their top by lightning—which they often do, more than any other trees. They are always green and shed some of their leaves, or rather branches, every year, growing taller still as they grow older.

The vee, or yellow apple, is fine, delicious fruit, growing to the size of an English apple but different in smell, taste, and substance. The pulp is contained in a stringy substance round the seed. It has a thin, tough rind like a plum, and its colour when ripe is a fine gold, its flavour superior to the pine. It has no bad quality unless eaten to excess. It grows on a fine, stately tree, which sheds its leaves regularly. The leaves begin to fall in September, and by Christmas the fruit and leaves appear. The fruit is full ripe in June. Some of these trees are nine feet round, but the wood is soft and spongy and fit for no use but fuel. It will either grow from the seed or by lopping of a branch, which when stuck in the ground takes root and soon bears fruit.

The eheyya is another kind of an apple, more like the English, but the taste is more watery and insipid. When ripe it is of a fine red and white, and the tree is about the size of a common cherry tree. It sheds its leaves in the same manner, but the fruit is not ripe till October. These two trees, and another bearing a red flower like a honeysuckle, are the only trees on the island that shed all their leaves at one time or before any others appear.

The rataa, or ihhe, is a kind of horse chestnut shaped like a broad bean about two inches over. The trees are large and serve for fuel, etc.

The shaddock, called here ooroo pappaa (or English Bread), is a tree that was planted here in Captain Cook's time, but the fruit has never arrived at any perfection. The trees have been planted in different parts of the island by the natives, merely as curiosities.

The mayya, which is the general name of plantains, grows here in abundance and in the highest perfection. The large horse plantain, called here papparrooa, grows to nine inches in length and as much round and, with taro and coconuts, makes excellent pudding.

The oraya, or maiden plantain, is the best of all the small kinds, of which these islands produce twelve different sorts, not named here—but no bananas.

The payee, or mountain plantain, is different from all the others and is called mountain from its growing chiefly there. As I never saw any of them in the East or West Indies, I suppose they are peculiar to these and the other islands in the South Seas. The stalk or tree is of a dark purple or blackish colour, the leaves much longer and the colour much darker than the common plantain's. The fruit does not hang down but grows erect, and clustering thick round the stalk from a kind of pyramid. If gathered green they make a substitute for bread, and if cut while raw they smell like a cucumber. When ripe they smell like yellow paint, and the inside of them when bruised is something like it in colour and appearance. The skin is then of a reddish brown. When baked and made into a pudding, they are as good as custard. The root also when dressed is equal to a yam. As they grow in great plenty in the mountains, they want no labour but that of bringing home.

Among their forest trees are the following, with shrubs, plants, etc. The toa, or casurina, is a very hard wood with which they make their war spears and clubs, beetles for making cloth, etc. With its bark they make a fine brown dye. This wood is too hard for any tools that we had, but the natives work it with stone tools, which costs them a deal of labour.

Tummannoo, or calophyllum mophylum, is a very large spreading tree, which they use for building the large canoes, making stools for sitting on, pillows, and pudding stools, with dishes and trays. Some of these are six feet long, intended to hold a large hog when dressed. These are wrought out of the solid wood and neatly finished. The wood, being something like walnut, receives a fine polish, and the nut, which grows to the size of a walnut and as plentiful, makes a very sweet perfume for their clothes.

Marra is a large tree, the wood of which is hard and white, and the grain close. When it grows old the colour grows brown. This is chiefly used for building the war canoes and making cloth beams and long steering paddles. It makes good axe and adze handles.

Fwhyfwhye is a tree as large as an oak and in grain something like white oak. It answers for several purposes, such as building canoes, making large chests, etc.

Amai is a hard, close wood of a reddish colour that they also use in building their canoes, making axe and adze handles, etc. With this tree they generally plant their morais, or places of worship, and the leaves of this tree are always used in religious rites. Tuoy is another large tree, of which the wood is white and hard, used for building both war and common canoes, planks for scraping the cloth plant on, etc.

Poorow, or hibiscus tiliaceus, is somewhat like an elm bearing a yellow flower. The body of the tree serves for building canoes and making paddles. We found it to answer very well for timbers and knees while building the schooner. Some of the young shoots run straight for a good length, and of them they chiefly make the rafters of their houses, sprits for their canoes, bows, etc. The cleaned bark makes neat washing mats of a fine texture for wet weather. It also makes rope and line, and we found it of much use in making our rigging.

Eyto is another large tree, the wood a reddish brown and nearly as hard as toa. It answers several purposes in their canoes: With the bark they dye or tan their cloth nets and lines, which, though only done by steeping in cold water, gives it a strong colour that will not wash out. The bark of the toa has the same property.

Torrotaya is a hard, tough white wood used for outriggers for their sailing canoes. Being durable, it is preferred for the purpose of railing their houses.

Hootdoo is a large tree that answers the purpose of building canoes, but is not durable. It bears a nut about the size of a sheep's heart, of a black colour that has the property, when put into the holes in the reef where the fish resort, to stupefy them—so that they never attempt to escape but suffer themselves to be taken. It is not much used for either purpose.

Toodooe, or candlenut tree, grows to the size of a walnut tree, bearing a fruit exactly like a walnut but of an oily nature. If eaten, it causes almost an immediate vomiting. The kernels, after being roasted till the shells come off, make a good substitute for candles by being strung on the stem of the coconut leaf, burning with a strong blaze. The bark of the root makes a fine, light brown dye, and the trunk is used as fuel.

Tow, or cordia sebestina orientalis, the wood of this tree is soft and white, and of this they make scoops for bailing their canoes. The leaves, mixed with the berries of the mattde, make a beautiful red for painting their cloth.

Mattde is a species of fig about the size of a common cherry tree. The figs or berries are about the size of a small cherry and are of a brownish colour. Squeezing them on the leaves of the tow produces a fine scarlet dye. The bark makes excellent fishing lines, twine for nets, and a fine matting for sashes, or marros. It also makes a good, strong cloth.

Nonno, or morinda citrifolia, is a small tree bearing a fruit like a small soursop [annona muricata], but not so pleasant to the taste, and is seldom eaten. The bark of the root makes a fine, light yellow dye for their cloth.

Eawwa is a kind of wild fig or sloe tree, the bark of which makes an excellent grey cloth called oraa, which is the most durable of any they have, and is therefore highly esteemed.

Booa is a handsome tree called by Captain Byron the Barringtonia; it bears odoriferous flowers of a yellowish hue, with which they make garlands for their heads. The teary, a tree bearing white flowers of a fine smell, answers the same purpose.

Evyavye, or the silk cotton tree, grows in abundance all over the country, but no use is made of it.

Roaa (urtica argentea) is a shrub, the bark of which answers the purpose of hemp, and is used for their best lines and fishing tackle. It grows as high as hemp, and the leaves are not unlike each other.

There are two sorts of the youte (morus papyrifera), or Chinese paper mulberry tree, which are here called myeree and poorow. They use the bark of these to make their finest white cloth, and they cultivate large plantations of it for that purpose. In these plantations the goats are destructive animals, eating the bark off and spoiling the young plants. They cannot be kept out by the ditches and fences encompassing them, and for this reason, the goats about the plantations are either kept tied fast or driven back into the hills, where they run wild—as they are not esteemed of great value.

Ohhe, or bamboo, grows here in abundance, some of which are sixty feet long, but their substance is not very strong. However, when cut into lengths they serve to hold oil and, for those who dwell far from the beach, to carry their salt water, which serves every purpose of salt in this country. It also serves for making fences, fishing rods, knives, etc.—and of a small, hard sort they make their arrows, while the large makes quivers.

Aeeho, or reeds, grow in abundance on the hills and are serviceable for many uses, such as fixing the thatch on for their houses, making fences, and burning at night when fishing. They frequently burn them to clear the ground.

Oporro, or the chili peppers, were planted here in Captain Cook's time, and with the tobacco, may now be found in all the islands, being carried about as curiosities.

Eowtay is a shrub about the size of a rose tree, bearing a red flower with which they dress their heads. It is also used as a medicine for sore eyes, which is common among children. It is in no way disagreeable and is taken in their food.

Fwharra, or prickly palm, called in India pandanes, grows here in abundance, generally near the beach in barren ground. The roots of the tree grow aboveground and support it like shores standing round to the height of five or six feet. The outside of the tree is hard, and with it they point their javelins, but the inside is soft, spongy, and fibrous. The leaves grow in a special manner round the branches and are about six feet long and four inches wide with long prickles on their edges and center. With these they make their thatch by sewing the leaves on reeds. They also make mats for their sails and for performing their heivas, or dances, on, some of which are of a large size. The blossom is a large bunch of flowers of a buff colour, yielding a fragrant smell. With this they scent their oil and cloth. The seed is composed of a number of nuts that grow upon a round core and have the appearance when ripe of a pineapple. Their taste is sweet and pleasant, and they are frequently put into the earth with plantains. When they are put to ripen, it gives them a fine flavour.

Paapa is a kind of palmetto, the leaves something like the fwharra but without prickles; of this they make their mats for sleeping on and for wear in wet weather. This grows chiefly in the mountains, and here also is found the ohi, or sandalwood, which has a smell like cedar; with this they scent their oil, etc.

Hooerro toomoo, or cabbage tree, grows also in the mountains, but is small and not very plentiful. They seldom exceed thirty feet in height. The bark is rough and hard, pointing over like scales from the earth to the top of the tree, where the cabbage grows singly, and the leaves or branches look like fern, forming a circle horizontally. They seldom eat the cabbages, as it is some trouble to get them.

Pirreepirree is a small shrub growing to the size of heath, and with the bark they make a very fine matting for sashes, or marros. Eayeeay is a kind of running shrub or vine of which they make fish pots and other wickerwork. It is used in the construction of their houses, answering better than line for securing those parts that are exposed to the weather.

Toe, or sugar cane, grows here without cultivation, to as large a size as any in the East or West Indies. I have no doubt that if cultivated it would be much larger. The natives make no use of it except to chew as they pass where it grows. When it becomes too thick, they clear the ground by setting it on fire.

Toepappaa, or Indian corn, was first introduced by the *Bounty* and is now to be found in all the islands. It grows here luxuriantly, and we have produced three crops from the same seed, and a fourth well on, in twelve months. It may be produced in any of the islands with little trouble, as the soil of the whole is, in general, good from the beach to the top of the mountains. But the natives, though they are fond of it, never take the pains to cultivate it in any quantity, alleging that they have plenty of food, and it is therefore no use to labour for what nature has abundantly supplied them. Such is their opinion respecting every other article of food introduced among them by European ships, which are either destroyed by shifting from place to place as curiosities or suffered to run wild for want of being cultivated and taken care of. Some of the cobs of corn that we produced were twelve inches long and well filled.

They have several sweet herbs for scenting their oil and cloth, and a kind of cress that makes excellent salad, to be found in all parts of the country. All the English garden seeds planted on our first arrival were nearly gone to decay and destroyed as before described, though with care they might be had in tolerable perfection.

Yava, or intoxicating pepper, is cultivated here with much care and pains; with the root of this, they intoxicate themselves. They always drink it before they eat, and it is prepared thus: Several hands have each a proportion of the root given them to chew, which, when they have done sufficiently, they spit it into a large platter. Some of the leaves are then infused and squeezed to pieces in it. In the meantime another prepares a strainer from the stems of coarse grass called mo'oo, something like hemp, and the whole, being well mixed, is wrung through the strainer, and the leaves and chewings thrown away.

The juice is then divided, according to the number who is to drink it, by dipping the strainer into the platter and wringing into each man's cup his share. They now drink their dose, which, as it is of a tolerable thick consistency and smells something like a mixture of rhubarb and jalap, can be little better to take. Almost immediately it deprives them of the use of their limbs and speech, but does not touch the mental faculty. They appear in a thoughtful mood and frequently fall backwards before they have finished eating. Some of their attendants then attend to chafe their limbs all over till they fall asleep. The rest retire, and no noise is suffered to be made near them. After a few hours they are as fresh as if nothing had happened and are ready for another dose. A gill of this juice is a sufficient dose, but if they eat anything immediately before it, it has no effect.

After about a fortnight's constant use, the skin comes all over with a white scurf like the land scurvy, the eyes grow red and fiery, and the body lean and meager. But on being left off for a few days, the scales fall off the skin, which becomes clear and smooth. They soon grow fat and wholesome to view. This gives me reason to think that this nauseous draught must be very wholesome, as those who use it are seldom afflicted with disorders of any kind, and those who use it regularly are some of the oldest men in the country. It is common to all but is more used by the chiefs and their families, servants, etc., than by the common people. They prefer the method of chewing it to any other. It is in much request among people of rank, but even some of them never taste it.

Tee is a plant growing in the mountains, the root of which is sweet; this they roast and eat. The leaves are about fourteen or sixteen inches long and five or six wide, and serve for thatching temporary huts and lining their pits for mahee. They make a temporary garment for fishing in, etc., by plaiting all the stems together to reach round the waist and splitting the leaves, which depend to the knees.

All these grow in the lowlands, but the largest timber grows far back in the mountains. The breadfruit is to be had at all seasons, but it is most plentiful at the harvest when they gather it in and lay it up in store, making it into a sour paste, by fermentation, called mahee, which shall be described in its place. The coconuts, plantains, and almost every sort of food are plentiful at all seasons.

Their cultivation does not extend to any great degree. The chief articles of it are the cloth plant, yava, taro, and sweet potatoes. Sometimes they plant coconuts and plantains, but these plantations are generally the labour of the chiefs, and if they make one in their lifetime, they sufficiently do their duty. They seldom plant any breadfruit trees, as they grow up wherever the root is separated by the hogs or otherwise, and they often have to root the young ones out to clear the ground of them. But the plantains want planting sometimes after the westerly winds, which, if they are not secured, are often blown down. These are the only things they take any pains with, nor can this be said to cost them either labour or toil.

As every part of the island produces food without the help of man, it may of this country be said that the curse of Eden has not reached it, no man having his bread to get by the sweat of his brow, nor has he thorns in his path.

BIRDS, ETC.

They have many birds for which we could find no names, but among those we knew were these: herons, blue and white; wild ducks; parakeets (green, blue, and white); fly flappers; woodpeckers; doves; wild pigeons; a chattering bird like a jay; sand larks; plover; martin; man-o'-war birds; and tropic birds, with several other aquatic birds. The mountains produce birds of different kinds unknown to us, among them a large bird nearly the size of a goose, which is good food. They are never seen near the sea or in the lowlands.

They have no venomous reptiles or insects except the centipedes and scorpion. The former are large and plenty, but the latter small and scarce and I never heard of any harm being done by them. The natives think nothing of them and will handle them with as little ceremony as we do earthworms, etc. The lizards are of two sorts—one a fine bright shining colour and an innocent harmless look, the other of a black or dirty brown and of a most forbidding appearance. They are both harmless and are seldom more than six inches long.

Butterflies, moths, and common flies are like those of Europe. They have also a fly that differs very little from the common black fly, which bites very sharp and is sometimes very troublesome. They say these were first brought here by the Lima Ships. [Two Spanish ships had visited the island in 1774 and had left two priests, who had been taken back on the return of the vessels a year later.] The mosquitoes are not very troublesome. The other insects, such as grasshoppers, crickets, beetles, etc., are the same as in other countries.

FISH AND FISHERIES

These islands abound with the greatest variety of beautiful and delicious fish, besides the fish common to other countries within the tropics. The reeds afford of the most beautiful colours that can be conceived, and those with rich colours are always fine fish. Among those found near these islands are the grampus, a young whale; porpoise; swordfish; shark; turtle; albacore; dolphin; bonita; skipjack; white salmon; and cavally old wife. There are white and red snappers; garfish; barracuda; ballihoo leather jacket; yellowtail; ray, sting and common; parrot or rainbow fish; flying fish; squid; sprat; sea and river eels; hedgehog fish; sea cat; white and red mullet; stone brass; blochan flounder or sand dab; warrior fish;

doctor dogfish; miller's-thumb; sea chub; sea roach; sea gudgeon; and innumerable others for which we could find no names.

Among these the whale, turtle, porpoise, shark, albacore, and dolphin are sacred, and the women must not eat them. The turtle is either presented to the king or eaten on the morai, as they are not caught in great numbers. Besides these they have shellfish, with which the reefs abound, among which are small conchs; pearl and small common oysters; crabs; crayfish; prawns and shrimps; common and horse cockles; periwinkles of different sorts; clams, mussels; and sea eggs, with a thousand other shells for which we could find no names. They have also land crabs, but few eat them. I never found in those islands the grouper, kingfish, or jewfish, which are common in the West Indies.

Their fishing tackle consists of seines of large dimension, lines and hooks of all sizes, spears, snares, pots, etc. Every fisherman makes his own hooks, lines, twines, and every article of his gear, which are not to be equaled by anything but their skill in using them. They make their lines from the bark of the roaa (and others already described), twisting it (in either two or three strands as is found to answer best) on their naked thigh, and make them with great judgment and regularity. They are not half the size in proportion to the fish for which it is intended that ours are.

Their hooks are made of pearl shell, bone, wood, etc., of different construction for the different fish, some being made to answer the double purpose of hook and bait. They make their hooks by grinding them into form on a stone with water and sand. With a drill made of a shark's tooth they make a hole, into which they introduce a sprig of the coral as a file and work out the inside part. As they have no beard, they make the point to round in towards the back of the hook, inclining downward, and seldom lose a fish after they get it hooked.

They have a number of methods of fishing and are expert at all. The first is with seines, from five fathoms long and one deep to sixty fathoms long and twelve deep. These large ones have a bag or cod in the middle. When they haul them in deep bays, they never land them till they are done fishing. They cast off the cod on the outside of the surf and bring the fish on shore in their canoes. Then they haul the seine into the canoe, and having laced on the cod, shoot it afresh; in this manner they catch a great number of fine fish and some turtle. While they are fishing in this manner the net is always surrounded by swimmers who dive down and secure such fish as are like to escape.

Though the sharks often attend them, they seldom interrupt their work, and if they catch the sharks in the surf, they surround them and force them on shore, which is so far from being deemed dangerous that it is counted fine sport. The sharks here are not very large, seldom exceeding five or six feet in length.

With their small seines they catch the flying fish, having small canoes that will carry two men for that purpose. The seines for this purpose are fifteen or twenty fathoms long and nine feet deep. These they shoot among the fish, and splashing the water about with their paddles, frighten the fish till they dart into the net and mash themselves. They then haul in their net and take out the fish, and following the school, shoot it afresh.

As they fish for them for bait for the dolphin, they frequently take the night for it and choose the dark in preference to the moonlight, when the fish cannot see to avoid the nets. In calm weather they follow the school with a number of canoes and surround them with their nets in a circle. Having drawn them into a small compass, they make the canoes fast to the nets and jump overboard, diving under the nets and seizing what fish they can by hand. They frequently bring up one in each hand, besides what get mashed in the nets, the fish being prevented from rising by the sight of the canoes. Keeping close together, the fish never attempt to escape till the men come among them.

They have cast nets also for small fry, both square and circular, and throw them with great dexterity. When the fish comes into the shallow water to spawn, they get a quantity of coconut leaves, from which they take the stems; tying them together, they twist them, the inside forming a kind of rope with the leaves all round it. This they call row, and with this they sweep the reefs and shallow water, bringing whole schools of fish to the beach, where they apply their small seines and laden nets to land them.

They also sweep the beaches with those small seines with a man at each end. They wade out till they are up to their necks together, and then separating to the length of the net, walk in and often (especially in the night), and at the mouths of the rivers, have good hauls.

They catch plenty of fine rockfish in pots and wares and are excellent hands at diving after them. I have seen a diver in clear water and calm weather pursue a fish from one hole in the rocks to another without coming up to breathe. In rough weather they cannot see to follow them, the bottom being darkened by the ripple on the surface. The most curious part of this fishery is that of taking the hedgehog fish and sea cat—the one being so full of prickles that they can take hold of it only by the eyes, which is the method by which they get them—very few are caught any other way. The others adhere so close to the rocks that it is as much as two men can do at times to haul them off. I have seen them in three or four fathoms forced to quit them and come up several times before they could accomplish their end; if a stone lies handy below they kill the fish there, and then they get it off easy.

This may seem an odd method of fishing, but I have seen it attended with good success, and the divers return in a few hours with large strings of fine fish. In the night they fish in canoes and on the reefs for different sorts of fish, which they draw round them by lighting bundles of reeds; they have nets made to scoop them up and put into their baskets.

In the rainy season they catch large quantities of small fry at the mouths of the rivers by means of a large bag made of the membranous stratums of the coconut tree, sewed together. The mouth of the bag is made with two wings, to spread the river water. They place it and lay stones on the lower part to keep it down; they then sweep the river with a row and bring all the fry into the bag. In this manner they get several bushels at a haul.

In the meantime the women have their part of the fishery. Each is equipped with a bag and a basket, and they form themselves into three or four lines across the river, up to their middle. Keeping the lower part down with their feet, they hold the upper part in their hands, alternately searching it and putting the fish into their baskets till they are either tired or satisfied, when they leave off and go home to dress them. It is no disgrace for any woman to be thus employed, and if the queen is present, she generally makes one herself. They are generally paid for their labour with good sport and plenty of fish.

Another method is used when the rains are over and the waters subside. They dam the river up with stones and grass, leaving several sluices to which they fix their bags or nets. Going some distance up along the bank, they all plunge in together and drive the fish before them, which fly to the sluices and fall into the nets. This method is not used till the fish grow scarce.

When they angle in the sea, they generally use baked breadfruit for bait and stand up to their necks in water, having a long bamboo for a rod and a basket hung round their necks to put the fish in. They catch in this manner several fine fish. The white mullet they catch with hand lines and the red in small nets; these latter, though delicate fish, are here used as bait for the albacore and bonita, which are caught thus: They have a double canoe carrying six or eight men, and in the bow is fixed a long pole, like a crane, to lower and haul up on a crosspiece, or roller at the heel, by means of a back rope. On the head of this they fix two pieces spreading like horns, to which they bend the lines. On the top of the crane they fix a bunch of long black feathers from cock's tails, the motion of which, when lowered near the water, attracts the fish and draws them round the canoe.

Between the canoes they sling a kind of basket with their bait, which admits the water, keeping the fish alive till they are wanted. When they see any fish, they paddle towards them till they come round the canoe, and then they keep the stern of the canoe to windward and paddle from them.

A man is then placed to throw water with a scoop and make a continual spray like rain. The hooks being baited, the crane is lowered so as to let them just under the surface. The man on the bow who baits the hooks keeps throwing now and then a small fish, while the other with the scoop keeps a constant shower about the hooks. The fish soon fly at their prey and get hooked when the men who attend the crane rope, having notice given them, haul up. The fish swings in to the man who attends to receive them and bait the hooks afresh.

Some of these fish are very large and often run the canoes under water when they do not haul up briskly. This is attended with no evil except if the line should break; when they lose the hook, which if it chance to be an iron one, is as great a loss to them as we should think an anchor. The skipjack is caught by a hook made to resemble a small fish, with some hog's bristles fixed for a tail. It is drawn after the canoe in the same manner but caught by a long bamboo for a rod, which the fisherman works with the heel in the bottom of the canoe and plays it by hand while another paddles the canoe.

The canoes for this fishery are mostly single, with some one-man and some two-man. Those with one man can do nothing if there is any wind but let their hooks tow, while they paddle to windward. They always lose ground while they stop to unhook a fish and put their hook over again, by which time the school has gone a long distance. Those canoes that have two men always keep up with them.

They catch the skipjack, as well as the albacore and bonita, in great numbers. They also catch the cavally and white salmon in their small canoes, but without rods. These fish are forced to play, and the canoes being light, when they have hooked a fish they steer after it till it is tired. Drawing their line in gradually, they get it alongside and watch for an opportunity to seize the small part near the tail in their hand and whip it into the canoe—seldom trusting the strength of the line to haul them in. The lines used for these fish are in general not bigger than what we use for mackerel. Nevertheless, they seldom lose any. In this manner they also catch the shark and other large fish with small lines. Their canoes being extremely light, they soon weary the fish and, by this method, easily take them.

They always fish for dolphins four or five leagues from the land in sailing canoes, plying to windward. When they reach their distance, they bait with flying fish and are very fond of iron hooks. Their lines for these fish are generally two strands and of a good length, some of them measuring one hundred fathoms. They choose the two-strand lines, as they are less apt to get foul by twisting than those of three strands, and as the dolphin jumps and twists about when hooked, they are not so ready to break and easier cleared after running out.

They never wet their lines till they see a fish, and then they make sure of it, though they are often deceived. The fish will sometimes leave part of their jaws behind them if too suddenly stopped in their career. They are forced to play them some time before they haul them alongside to get them in, which they always do by laying hold of the tail part with one hand and the line in the other. The canoe is low for that purpose. These fish follow the sun and are therefore most plentiful when the sun is to the southward of the equator, during which season there are not less than sixty sail of canoes from Matavai employed in the fishery. The fish spawn about March, after which they seldom look for them but get ready for the albacore and bonita fishery that commences. The sailing canoes ply between Tahiti and Tetooroa for these fish, which are caught in great quantities about the reefs of Tetooroa.

While the dolphin season continues, they catch a number of flying fish of an extraordinary size. These they catch with bait in this manner: They get a number of wands of six or eight feet long, from which they strip the bark and balance by slinging a stone to one end, so they swim upright with one half their length out of the water. To the lower end they fix a hook (made of fish bones and baited with coconut), with about a fathom of line. These being all prepared (they generally have as many as they can conveniently stow in the stern of the canoe), they stand off to their proper distance and throw the wands overboard at a distance from each other.

Standing in, they pick them up again, when they frequently find fish at each, so that if they have no luck of dolphin they seldom return empty. They often take sharks and other fish on which the shark preys, which, flying to the canoe for shelter, are often taken by hand. The shark they often catch in a noose prepared for that purpose, seldom having occasion to bait a hook for them. When they get the shark fast, they haul his head out of water and beat it till they see no signs of life in it, with heavy toa bludgeons that they carry for the purpose. When he is dead they get him into the canoe.

They frequently meet with the swordfish while they are out, who never fails to attack the canoe. If the bottom or side is not of very hard wood, he strikes the sword into her in several places before it sticks fast enough to hold him. As soon as he sticks, they are overboard and secure him with the noose. Having freed him from the canoe, they kill him with their bludgeons and get him in. Frequently, they are forced to steer homewards to stop the leaks that he causes. Their day's sport is then over, as they are sometimes closely put to it to reach the shore, seldom carrying anything with them that is fit to stop a leak; their only recourse is to bail.

Besides other methods of fishing, they have spears that they throw with great exactness. These are fourteen or sixteen feet long, pointed with two prongs of toa. They use no line, but if they strike a fish, they swim after it. They have others with several prongs that they throw at random among the schools and frequently kill two or three at a time.

They seldom kill any whales but young ones that get entangled among the reefs and thrown over by the surf into shallow water. When they find one in this situation, they attack him with their war spears and kill him, though they sometimes get their canoes dashed to pieces by him.

Among the fish there is a kind of conger eel of a brownish colour, with a green border round the fins from head to tail. They are caught about the reefs and are of different sizes, from one to six feet long. These fish are of a poisonous nature to some and if eaten gives the most excruciating pain. Others who eat of it feel no effects, nor do the natives know who will be affected by it till they have eaten it. As they have a remedy for it they take no account of the matter and eat them at a venture.

I partook of one of these fish without feeling the smallest effects from its poison, while another who ate of the same fish was almost raving mad. His body and limbs swelled to a very extraordinary degree and were covered with red blotches. At the same time, the hands and feet were itching in such a manner as to be insufferable and burning as if on fire. The eyes swelled and were fiery and to appearance fit to start from the sockets.

This continued with short intermissions for eight days, but in the course of a week more, by the assistance of some of the priests who procured medicines, he got quite well—but often found a great itching in the palms of the hands and hollow of the feet.

These fish are called by the natives puhhe pirrerowtee. As they don't know the good from the bad, they are loath to throw them away and therefore eat them to make sure of them. They have also a small red crab, not bigger than a small horse bean, which they say will kill a man instantly if he eats it. These are the only poisonous things we ever heard of except the hootdoo or hootnut mentioned before, but this, though it stupefies the fish, will not affect a man.

MINERALS
As to minerals, there are few in these islands but iron, and that is scarce; in fact, few of us were sufficient judges to know any other.

MANUFACTURES AND TRAFFIC

It is on all hands allowed that necessity is the mother of invention, and though the divine bounty has rendered art almost useless for procuring the necessaries of life in this country, yet the ingenuity of these people is highly conspicuous in every article of their manufacture. Their cloth matting and oil are particular articles of their traffic, if it may be so called—but this is generally carried on by making presents rather than by exchange of commodities.

Their cloth, of which the general name is ahhoo, is of different sorts and made from the bark of different trees, but the process for all is the same.

The best and finest white cloth, called hoboo or parrawye, is made from the youte, or cloth plant, and is made thus: The plants, having grown to their proper length (ten or twelve feet), are cut by the men and brought in by them, which is their part of the work. The women then strip off the bark by entering a pointed stick between the bark and the plant. By ripping it the whole length on one side, the bark peels off.

After they have stripped all the plants, they take the bark to the water, where they wash it and, spreading it on a board for the purpose, scrape it clean, taking off the outside rind with a large cockleshell. Having freed it from the sap and slime, it is wrapped in plantain leaves and covered with grass, where it remains for two, three, or four days, when it becomes clammy and glutinous. It is then fit for working.

It is then spread to a regular thickness of several strips, forming a band of seven or eight inches broad and of what length the piece is intended to be. The ground where they intend to work is spread with plantain leaves to keep it from the dirt. The beams are then placed at equal distances, about six feet asunder, and at each of them two women work. Having the piece between them, they beat it with square beetles to its proper breadth. [Beams and beetles are tools and equipment for making cloth.] This they perform by a song given by one and chorused by the rest, and keep regular time, shifting the piece backwards and forwards till it is all beat out to a regular breadth and thickness.

It is then spread in the sun to dry for one day, after which it is bleached in the morning dew till it is perfectly white. It is kept from the sun till it is sufficiently bleached, and then it is spread for one or two days in the sun to dry and put up for storage or use.

Sometimes they notch the outward bark with a stone and wrap the plants in leaves for two or three days before they strip them, which makes the cloth beautifully clouded with several shades of brown. They also mix the cloth plant with breadfruit bark, but this is of a coarser kind and does not bleach so well, though the cloth is equally strong. Some of this cloth is very fine, and neck cloths made of it might be mistaken at a small distance for the labour of the loom.

If a landed man wants a large quantity of cloth made at once, he informs his tenants when he means to cut his plants. On the day appointed, all the women attend, each with their beam and beetle. A proportion of breadfruit being prepared, they bring the work together and, sometimes to the number of two hundred, strike off together, making as much noise as so many coopers. The piece is finished in one day and is sometimes forty or fifty fathoms long and four fathoms wide.

They make another sort of several thicknesses that are not placed regular or above half beaten; this is called marro. Of this they make their upper garments by stripping from one part and pasting on to another till they bring it to a regular breadth and thickness. They trim the fragments off with a piece of split bamboo, which answers the purpose of a knife. These they paint with mattde, a beautiful red extracted from berries of that name, and leaves before described, which they prepare thus:

The berries and leaves being gathered, several hands begin and nip them till they emit a drop of yellow juice that they put on a leaf, and so proceed till all are done. The leaves, with the juice on them, are then put into a platter and sprinkled with water, when they are wrought up by squeezing till they become red. After they are sufficiently squeezed, they are thrown out and the juice put into a shell for use. A bunch of the fibers of the mo'oo is then procured to dip in the paint and wet the leaves and sprigs they mean to imprint on the cloth—which being placed on it and pressed by the hand, leaves the print behind. In this manner they paint it in many fanciful forms.

Besides this method of painting they dye the hoboo, of several colors—as brown of several shades from the bark of several trees, scraped off and infused in cold water, into which they dip the cloth. The sun heightens the colour. Twice dipping and six or eight days' sun are sufficient to produce the highest shade, which never fades till the cloth is worn out.

The black is produced from the sap of the mountain plantain, or payee—or by soaking the cloth under the root of some particular coconut trees that grow in swampy ground—where in a night's time, or three or four separate dippings, it becomes jet black. The brown is called heere or poowhirri, and after it has been worn some time makes a good black, being then better than clean white for receiving the colour. The black they call oowerre.

The yellow they extract from turmeric and the roots of the nonno. With the latter, being a pale light colour, they dye the lining of their brown cloth, which they paste in very curiously and paint the border with red, giving it a very showy appearance. This is now called hapaa. They also take of red, black, yellow, and white a piece of equal dimensions and paste them together, cutting them in curious forms so as to show all the colors.

Another method is taking old brown cloth, which they tear in pieces and mix with some new bark, beating the whole into one piece. When finished, it is spotted all over. This they dip in the yellow dye and line it in the same manner, infusing sweet scents in their dye. This is called opottapotta.

The oraa is a grey, strong cloth made of the bark of the sloe tree. Large quantities of these trees grow in the mountains, particularly near Vyeooreedee, where there is a great lake that they call Vye Heereea. They say it produces a large kind of eel that is as big around as a man. To the banks of this lake resort numbers of the Areeuoy, who are generally good cloth makers, though it is chiefly women's employment to make the cloth, it being held in great esteem as the strongest and best for wear. They generally stay some months on the banks of this lake, where they have plenty of provisions. Some few inhabitants live constantly there and are mostly employed making cloth. The lake empties itself into the valley of Vyeooreedee, and they say that they have never yet found its bottom. On it they waft themselves from side to side, on rafts made of the trunk of the mountain plantain.

They make cloth of several different trees but these are the most common. It is chiefly the work of the women, though the Areeuoys are very excellent hands in every branch of the work, especially at dyeing and painting. The only tools requisite for making the cloth, after the plants are stripped, are a shell to scrape the bark; a board about a foot wide and two feet long to scrape it on; a beam of eight inches square and ten or twelve feet long to beat it on; and a beetle of two or three inches square and fourteen or sixteen inches long to beat it with. The beam is made of marra, a hardwood, and the beetle of toa, having grooves on each square of four different sizes for the different kinds of cloth they are intended to work. The beam is called tdootdooa, and the beetle ayyey.

The cloth serves them for dry weather, and they can wash and dress it as often as they please, scenting it with the tummannoo nuts, which are bitter to the taste but of an agreeable smell. They infuse them (when pounded) into water and dip the cloth into it. The smell will remain for several weeks and generally till the cloth wants dressing afresh.

Matting is no inconsiderable branch of their manufacture. Of this they make sails for their canoes, bed mats, clothing for wet weather, sashes for dress, and carpets for acting their heiva or plays upon. Those for sails, carpets, and bedding are made from the leaves of the palm and palmetto; the former is called moya and the latter evanne. Some of these are ten, twelve, and fourteen fathoms long, and two fathoms wide. They are wrought with great regularity and are as coarse or fine as the makers fancy, being from two to sixteen parts to an inch.

Those for dress are known by the name of ahhoo, with the name of the bark, etc., of which they are made. They are made of different sizes for the different parts of dress, and from the bark of the poorow, mattde, roaa, coconut leaves, etc. Some are very fine and have from twenty to thirty parts to an inch. They are all made by the women, who work them by hand without the assistance of any machine except a mussel shell to split the stuff.

The women also make mat bags or baskets, with black and white, neatly disposed and of many different patterns.

The wicker baskets are made by the men, from a running vine called eayeeay, and are equal in workmanship to those of Europe. Their platters, stools, chests, etc., are all neatly made and well finished and even more admirable when we consider their tools, which are no other than stone adzes of different sizes; shells; shark's tooth; bones; sand to scour; and fish skins to polish. With these tools they build their houses and canoes.

Their toil and pains have been much lessened since they learned the use of iron, and they esteem nothing more valuable. They work the pearl shells into many forms for fishhooks, having a differently shaped hook for every different fish. With this they compose the ornaments of their mourning dress, which are neatly disposed. It is surprising to see with what exactness and dispatch they put it into form and drill holes with a shark's tooth (fixed in a long stick, which they work between their hands) that will scarce admit the point of a common pin.

Their lines for fishing, etc., are made from the bark of several shrubs, but the best is made of the roaa, and are equal if not superior to any in the world. They twist them on their thigh in two or three strands for their different purposes and ball them up as they make them.

The rope for their canoes, fishing seines, etc., is chiefly made of the poorow, which when stripped of its outside rind and laid in water to steep for three days, to take off the slime, is then dried and twisted by hand, making two strands first and then laying in the third. They make the strands as they lay them by supplying them with more bark as they twist up, and when it is finished, is smooth and as regular as if spun on hooks in a rope ground. With the help of tar it would be good rope and is nearly as strong as common hemp. They seldom make any larger than three inch, but to any length they have occasion for; for particular occasions they lay three of these together.

Their method of making oil is this: The coconuts, being full grown, are gathered in and freed from the husk. They are then broken in halves, and the milk, which is then sour, is thrown away. The inside of the nut is grated into a trough made for the purpose. A piece of coral tied on a kind of horse, on which they sit to steady it, serves for a grater. The nuts being all grated, the trough is hung up or fixed on a stand, and the stuff left to dissolve. In a few days the oil begins to run. Then they grate into it sandalwood and mix into it the dust from the palm blossoms and other sweet flowers, herbs, etc. When all is dissolved, they strain it off and put it into bamboos for use, the oil retaining the scent while it is kept close stopped.

This process of making it takes up nearly three weeks, during which time they mostly turn it over and mix it every day. Another method is by placing the nuts in the sun to melt, which is done in a few days, but the oil thus made is always rank. The coconut is the only oil they make, and the chief use of it is for dressing their hair or anointing their bodies where they chance to be sun burnt—it is called monnoe.

Their manner of traffic, which they call tarahow and eho, is this: If a man has occasion for more cloth than he can procure from his neighbours, he takes a large hog or two to the house of some of the people who inhabit the valleys, and whose chief employment it is, and agree with him to make the cloth by such a time and in such quantity as shall be deemed the value of the hogs. This being settled, the undertaker calls his neighbours together and tells them he wants so much cloth made by such a day, and those who choose to be concerned signify it to him.

The hogs are then killed and a feast made, after which each furnish their proportion and the women meet and put it together. When finished it is delivered to the purchaser—but should the undertaker not fulfill his agreement, or delay the time through negligence, the other may, if he is able, plunder his house as for a theft.

If a man wants a house or a canoe built, he employs one or more carpenters, paying them beforehand one-half of what shall be judged the value of the work they are to perform in hogs, cloth, oil, matting, etc. He also finds them provisions all the time they are at work. When the work is complete, he pays the remainder according to agreement, but should he refuse or neglect, and the neighbours think the labour worth the stipulated agreement, then they may plunder him of all that he is worth.

If a man wants to be constantly supplied with fish, he takes a hog to a fisherman and, according to its size, agrees with the fisherman to supply him with fish for one or more months—which they seldom fail to perform, weather permitting, for the stated time. What they look upon as fulfilling the agreement is bringing as much fish every day as the family can eat, and for failure of promise they may be plundered, as said before. Sometimes they agree for a supply every other day, and when the fisherman fulfils his promise well, they make him a feast. The fish they bring are sometimes equal to ten times the price at a fair exchange.

Such is the method they use in trade. If a man wants help to cultivate a piece of ground for cloth, yava, taro, etc., he employs his labourers in the same manner, always paying them the whole or one-half of their hire beforehand. But their principal method is by gifts and presents to each other, and it is not common to refuse the greatest stranger anything he stands in need of, whether food, raiment, or anything else.

DIVISION, GOVERNMENT, ETC.

The island of Tahiti is divided into seventeen districts called Venooa (or Lands), with the name of the head chief of each annexed. These are again divided into the chief's shares (or patdoo), and these again into lesser divisions called bahooe, which are the squire's shares. The lord of the manor holds three bahooe.

The names of the districts of TahitiNooe are:

1st Oparre, 2nd Matavai, 3rd Fwhapyeano, 4th Yunnowheaa, 5th Teearey, 6th Heedeea. These six are always in alliance and are called by the general name of Tepirreonoo and Teeahhoroa. They extend from the isthmus along the north side of the island westward to Tettahah.

7th Vyeerre, 8th Vyeooreedee, 9th Papaara. These three extend from the isthmus westward on the south side to Attahooroo, and are known by the name of Tedevvaeuta. They are always in alliance with Tepirreonoo.

10th Attahooroo, 11th Tettahah—these two districts lie on the west side of the island and were ever rebellious to the reigning king till they were reduced in our time into subjection.

TahitiEete contains six districts that are:

1st Affwhaheetdee, 2nd Towtirra (called by Captain Cook Oheitepeha), 3rd Teparre, 4th Vyeowtaya, 5th Matowwye, 6th Vyeooroo—the first beginning at the isthmus on the north side and the last ending at the isthmus on the south side. These six were also rebellious and never suffered the king's flag to pass till our time—for a list of the present chiefs of Tahiti see the vocabulary. [The vocabulary to which Morrison refers here and elsewhere was compiled by Midshipman Peter Heywood during his imprisonment on HMS *Hector*. Morrison was composing his journal at the same time, and they must have seen that their projects were complementary. See "Introduction," pages 4 and 6.]

The chiefs of Tahiti are of two houses, which are Tepirreonoo and Tedevvaeuta. Each one is absolute in its own dominions, but only one can be earee nooe, or king, and the other lives in friendship with him till death or war dispossesses him of his honours and title—which then devolves on the other. They are supported by voluntary contributions and free gifts; however, the people must not refuse to make them if they have wherewithal to supply the demand. If they have not, it is not expected.

The present earee nooe (or king) is the son of Matte, or Otoo. His name is Toonooeayeteatooa, which may be thus translated: "Too, the Great begotten of God," and his title Eatooa Raa, or Sacred God. This sacrilegious name and title he obtained by his mother, declaring that the Deity (Taane) cohabited with her in her sleep, and proving pregnant soon after, the child was declared to be the offspring of the Deity and is revered as something supernatural. The only male of the House of Tedevvaeuta is Tommaree, son of Pbooraya (called Oberea by Captain Cook), deceased, and Oammo.

Should both lines become extinct, the royal marro becomes elective and every chief in the Society Isles becomes a candidate. The chiefs are numerous and every district has two or three, besides others who reside as private gentlemen on their own estates. While out of employment, they still are regarded as chiefs, though they reside as squires under other chiefs. When they are called into office, they leave their estates to the care of their friends, who have no rent to pay except supplying such demands as are made by the chiefs in common, as if the land belonged to any other person.

Before I proceed any further, it may be requisite to the better explanation of their manners and customs to describe the different classes into which they are divided, which are four:

1st Earee rahi or nooe, or king.

2nd Earee, chief of a district, who is greater or less according to his possessions, and towha, which answers to the lord of the manor.

3rd Ratirra—esquire, and

4th Mannahownes or mattaeyna—tenants. Among each of these classes are some raa, or sacred, and some noa, unhallowed or common. Servants are called tewtew in general, but those who wait on women are called tewty by way of derision—though it is not uncommon to find young men of the first families and the younger brothers of chiefs in the service of the fair sex; by debasing themselves thus, they are rendered incapable of assisting at any religious ceremony.

The chiefs each have personal estates and when in office have either a district or part of one called a patdoo, which maintains them by contributions. Under them are the towha and ratirra, each holding his land independent of the other. Any ratirra can put a rahooe on his own division (which is so named from their power to prohibit the expenditure of any species of provisions on his own land), the chief on his patdoo, and the king on the whole, or any number of districts. But if the chiefs should not act up to the dignity of their office, they may be divested of their office. They remain chiefs, and though the king may be stripped of his government, he still retains his royalty, and none but one of the two families can ever enjoy that dignity while they are in being—so that it is no more than a change in the ministry. With the other chiefs it is the same and they often change stations.

When a king is invested with the marro oora, or red sash of royalty, he sends two flags round the island by different routes. Those who acknowledge his supremacy pass them with ceremony and attend his coronation. With every chief comes a human sacrifice, but if they refuse to acknowledge him, they break the staff and trample on the flag as soon as it enters their territory—upon which war is declared against them, and if they cannot reduce them by war, they enjoy their independence, but the king is still king.

While these flags are passing, no fire is made near the beach, nor must any canoe be launched for any purpose. The bearers of the flag pass close to the surf the whole way; any breach of this would be punished with death and forfeiture of estate, the beach being made sacred by the royal flags. It would be a crime of the highest nature to launch a canoe over it or make a smoke nearer than two or three miles of it.

When a chief is present in any company, the men strip their bodies to the waist, not suffering any covering on their head or shoulders in his presence. All the women present uncover their shoulders, tucking their cloth under their armpits to cover their breasts, in token of obedience and respect in his presence. The men are not always particular in this point except upon the chief's hereditary land or that of his adopted friend, where any neglect would be deemed an insult and punished accordingly. But in presence of the king the chiefs themselves must strip—nor do they stop to see him first if they have notice of his approach, either by land or in a canoe. Nor must any person pass his land by walking over it or sailing by it without paying the compliment.

If a chief takes a liking to anything in the possession of any person, and they don't like to part with it immediately, he then curses it or calls it by his own name or any of his relations. It is then sanctified so far that the owner cannot again make use of it upon pain of death or forfeiture of their land, though they may keep it if they will. This, however, is seldom the case, nor is the chief often obliged to make use of this alternative—as they make it their study to anticipate the wishes of their chiefs and leave them nothing to ask for—giving them whatever he seems inclined to have.

When the chiefs do ask for anything, it is given freely at the first word. If a chief should enter or even touch the house of any female of a lower class, it is rendered sacred by his presence, and she can never eat in it any more (but any man may) and she must provide herself with a new house and new furniture. For this reason, if the chief should be caught in the rain, he must not take shelter till he comes to a man's house or one of his own (of which he has several for that and such like purposes), though he should be a mile from one.

For this reason also, no woman except of equal rank can eat on board a ship after the chief has been on board, under pain of severe punishment. This accounts for the women calling the provisions on board maa raa (sacred food), everything on board being made sacred by his presence. Nevertheless, when they were very hungry, they would eat in private, though even then they will hardly ever eat in company with other women, unless they are well acquainted.

The chiefs are in general taller, stouter, and of a different appearance from the common people, and their women are also larger and fairer than the lower classes. They have in general a more serious and thoughtful turn and are more accomplished. They are always superior to them at all things, either labour or diversion, and the earee women are by far the best cloth makers. In labour they are always first, it being no disgrace to know how, but a great disgrace not to know how—and they always bear a part in cooking provisions for their guests. They are company for their meanest subject or servants, who nevertheless pay them due reverence and respect, and their poverty never renders them despicable, as they never lose their rank—nor can any who are not born a chief ever arrive at that dignity. When a child is born, the titles and honours of the father immediately fall to it, yet the father is still a chief and is always regarded as such, though out of office by the birth of a child—to which he is sometimes a guardian or regent.

Their only pride is cleanliness and generosity, for which they are remarkable, and I may say they have no equals in these points. Their retinue costs them nothing, as they pay their attendants no wages and change them often, no man staying in their service longer than he pleases—though they have some who stay their whole lives in the service of the same family. These old servants are always considered as one of the family, and by them the household is managed. They, like other courtiers, have as much to do in the government as their masters.

Few of the chiefs are shorter than six feet, but many of them exceed that height by some inches. For this reason they readily believed that Captain Cook and his tall, stout officers were chiefs; they have no conception that a short man can be a chief. If any person speaks disrespectfully of a chief, he is sure to suffer death, and should one chief speak ill of another, it would instantly bring on a war. This has been the occasion of several bloody battles and is at present the subject of the animosity between Tyarrabboo and TahitiNooe—the late chief of Tyarrabboo having refused to acknowledge Toonooeayeteatooa, who he said was not the son of the Deity nor of Otoo, but of a favourite minion; and that his mother had only raised that story out of her own head, that her son might not be disinherited if he did not attain his proper size.

PERSONS

The people in general are of the common size of Europeans. The men are strong, well limbed, and finely shaped. Their gait is easy and genteel, and their countenance free, open, and lively, never sullied by a sullen or suspicious look. Their motions are vigorous, active, and graceful. Their behaviour to strangers is such that at first sight, their humane disposition—which is as candid as their countenances seem to indicate, and their courteous, affable, and friendly behaviour to each other—shows that they have no tincture of barbarity, cruelty, suspicion, or revenge. They are ever of an even, unruffled temper; slow to anger; and soon appeased. As they have no suspicion so they ought not to be suspected, and an hour's acquaintance is sufficient to repose an entire confidence in them.

The men wear their hair in different forms and their beards neatly picked, which they do with a fish scale. Here, a painter might make an excellent copy of a Hector or an Achilles. Some have their hair cut short, and others wear it long and flowing over their shoulders in waves, and others tied in a bunch on the top of their heads. The women are finely shaped, and the natural colour is a brunette, though some who are more exposed to the sun are very dark—especially those who are fishermen and constantly exposed to its rays. But those who are not exposed are of fine, bright colour, and a blush may be seen in their faces. Their skin is as tender as Europeans', and they scorch as soon in the sun.

They are in general handsome and engaging, their eyes full, sparkling, and black almost without exception. Their noses are of different descriptions, their mouths small, lips thin and red, and their teeth white. Even their breath is sweet and perfectly free from taint. The hair of both sexes is mostly black or dark brown, in some coarse and others fine, which the women wear short and neatly cut in waves in their neck. They take much pride in keeping it in exact order and decorate their head with sweet flowers. They are careful to keep it free from vermin. For that purpose they were exceedingly fond of our combs, as they also were of scissors to trim it, a shark's tooth being the only instrument they have for cutting hair. Though the women hate to have vermin in their heads as much as we do, the men are not so delicate, and many eat them.

Though the fashion in which the women wear their hair is contrary to the inhabitants of other countries, it is no way injurious to their beauty. Neither sex wear anything on their heads but garlands of flowers, nor dress their hair in any other manner than by combing and oiling. All are particular to have it regularly trimmed; some trim their eyelids and brows and pick them into form. Their limbs in general are neat and delicate, and though they go barefooted, their feet do not spread like the inhabitants' of Africa and other hot climates, and many, with the help of a fashionable dress, would pass for handsome women, even in England.

The number of inhabitants in Tahiti is near thirty thousand, of which their warriors may be reckoned at nearly one-third of that number. Their chief strength consisted formerly in their naval force. At present it is being trimmed, their navy being on a very indifferent footing—Otoo thinks it better to keep peace than make war. At present his whole naval force does not exceed twenty sail-of-war canoes, and for most of these, he is beholden to his sister Areepaeea Waheine, who brought them from Ryeataya. But he stands in no need at present of large canoes, as Morea is now under him—Mottooarro having adopted his son to be heir to Morea.

At the time the island was discovered by Captain Wallis, Tommaree, the son of Pbooraya (since deceased) and Oammo, was earee nooe. Oammo, being an Areeuoy, had left her, but not till the boy was born. Then Pbooraya, who was a stirring, active woman and regent for her son, got him declared king and invested at Oparre with the royal marro. Matte, or Otoo, who was then about seven years old, was forced to fly to his father's estate at Papaara, where he lived privately, though the marro was his right. But soon after Captain Wallis sailed, Matte made a party in Attahooroo and soon forced Tommaree to exchange stations, and take his own possessions.

Tetowha and Pohooataya, chiefs of Attahooroo at the head of their men, seized on the morai, carrying it and the marro to Attahooroo, where they forced Matte to come to have his ceremony performed. At the same time, they laid him under restrictions that made him more a dependent to them than their king. All the religious rites were now to be performed at their morai, where all the other chiefs were under the necessity of bringing their offerings and were often plundered of them before they reached the morai. Of this they were afraid to complain, fearing the Attahooroo people who, being mostly renegades supported by Tetowha, had gained themselves a great name in the war. They at last became very troublesome neighbours, keeping both Matte and Tommaree in awe of them.

TahitiEete, taking the advantage of this situation of affairs, revolted, and as they looked upon themselves separated from TahitiNooe by the isthmus, they declared for Vay-heeadooa and made him their king. But they could not obtain the marro, being forced to retire to their own country. Tommaree and Matte, having united to keep their right in their own families, repulsed Tyarrabboo with great slaughter but could never reduce them to subjection by reason of the many strongholds that they possess.

About the same time, Morea revolted, and Maheine (the uncle of Mottooarro, proper king of that island) seized on the government. He forced Mottooarro to fly to Matte for refuge, together with his sisters Eddea and Teano, where they were on Captain Cook's arrival at the island. At that time a truce was made.

This may in some measure account for the situation in which Captain Cook found the island and for his finding Pbooraya living retired with her husband, with whom she then lived; they had parted before on account of a quarrel but had now made matters up. Tommaree is the same Captain Cook calls Teridiri—probably T'aree rahe, or head chief, which title he assumes everywhere but in the presence of Toonooeayeteatooa—he being called earee nooe, or the great chief. The young woman Toematta was his cousin and sister to his present wife, Teereetahi; Pbooraya had no other child but Tommaree, having killed all that came before him.

Otoo, or Matte, is the eldest son of Tew, or Whappai, who is also mentioned by Captain Cook. These two are now on friendly terms, and Tommaree, having no children, adopted a daughter of Otoo's; she died young, but it is probable he may have issue by his present wife. If not, the right falls to the present king, who is a boy of about ten or twelve years old.

On or about the time of Captain Cook's arrival at Tahiti the last time, Otoo was engaged in a war with Morea. With the assistance of Tommaree and Tetowha and Pohooataya, who joined their forces to his, Otoo would have reduced Maheine to obedience or forced him to relinquish his claim to the island to Mottooarro, the proper heir. But Tetowha began to grow jealous of Otoo's growing power and of his enjoying the rich presents made him by Captain Cook. Tetowha determined to lessen it if possible and for that purpose kept back his supplies. After Captain Cook sailed, he turned his force against Otoo and joined with Maheine, who between them destroyed Otoo's fleet and plundered him of everything. They killed and destroyed most part of the cattle and stock that Captain Cook had left and carried off the rest.

Maheine was now suffered to remain in quiet possession of Morea. Mottooarro and his sisters were forced to remain at Tahiti, where Otoo took Eddea, Mottooarro's sister, to be his wife. Mottooarro took Otoo's sister, Tirrayraydooa, to be his wife. Maheine, who was against these matches and supposed they would at one time be the means of driving him from the possessions he had seized upon, was determined to set them to work, if he could not separate them.

Finding that he could make nothing of them, though he set Tyarrabboo and Tommaree by the ears, Maheine now declared war against Otoo, who was forced to make an effort with the small fleet he had left. These he put under the command of Moana, Tootaha's brother, and Wyetooa, Otoo's own brother. A bloody fight took place in Matavai Bay when Maheine brought his fleet.

He was killed by Wyetooa, and the fleet was mostly destroyed. His men fled home, where they placed his adopted son, Tayreehamoedooa, on the throne of Morea, where he remained till after the *Bounty* sailed in April 1789. Having made a party in the island, he got possession, and by the help of the arms left with Otoo, he obtained his right and forced Tayreehamoedooa—with his aunt and mother—to fly to Tahiti for refuge, where he now resides privately.

WAR

Their genius and temper being described, I shall now describe their manner of making war.

War in this country often happens due to mere trifles; however, what we may think a trifle may seem to them of great consequence. The districts all have a parting or boundary line, frequently a river, which separates their lands from each other. If any dispute happens, the party who happens to be the occasion of it is called upon to make good any damage or deficiency.

If it refuses to do it, war is declared in this manner: The priests and the head men of the contending party assemble near their bounds and the priests are consulted. If they give a favourable answer, war is then the word, and the party who thinks itself most injured sends out a slinger to the boundary line. Having charged the sling, he discharges it over the heads of the opposite party, crying out, "W'affwa te Vye ay O," which signifies that war is declared, but literally, "The water has borne down its banks."

This is answered by a slinger from the other side, who slings a stone and calls out in the same manner. They then cry out to each other, "Yowrye t'Eatooa te Tamye ra" (God save you in your war). They then return home, seemingly in peace, and make a war feast, killing a number of hogs for the warriors; they sometimes make a human sacrifice.

Next morning they repair to the appointed ground. They are always attended by inspired priests, who, before they come to the charge, encourage them to fight manfully and spirit them up by blowing their conch shells that they always use on these occasions, having a bamboo tube that they blow through like a trumpet. They always send or offer conditions of peace to those who are deemed the weakest party. If they refuse and are worsted, they are driven from their possessions.

The conquering chief puts a subordinate chief of his own in to command the conquered country. If the vanquished people promise to pay obedience to the new chief, they are permitted to remain and enjoy their lands as before. But this they seldom will do, having so great an affection for their chiefs that they had rather partake of his disgrace and lose their estates than enjoy their property under another. Should they act otherwise they would be very meanly looked on, be made a byword among their countrymen, and their lives be a torment to them afterwards.

They take no captives nor give any quarter, unless a man falls in with one who has formerly been his adopted friend, a breach of which they were never known to make. They are not forced to fight any longer than they please. A man never obtains the name of a warrior, though he kills his man, should he receive any wound himself, as they think that a man who suffers himself to be wounded does not know how to defend himself. They believe it is more honour to return with whole bones than broken ones. Though they are not immediately under the authority of the chief in battle, yet they fight furiously, knowing that in case of being vanquished they lose all their possessions.

Though this seems of small account, yet they all prefer having to give than being forced to receive. When they make a present, it is so freely done and so graceful that Christianity may blush at the action and be ashamed to be surpassed by those whom we call savages. This is the chief reason that a Tahitian has to fight for. In some of their sea actions, much blood has been shed, as they frequently lash bow to bow and fight it out. The strongest party generally gets the day and the weaker are forced to save themselves by jumping overboard.

Their weapons are spears of twelve or fourteen feet long, pointed with the stings of the stingray; clubs of seven or eight feet, both of which are made of toa, a hard, heavy wood; and slings made of the plaited fibers of the coconut. They have bows and javelins for sport, but never use them in war.

Some of their war canoes are very large and carry from one to three hundred men. They often have one hundred paddlers, all of which have heaps of stones. Each man has a sling besides spears and clubs; and when one party becomes too strong for the others, they are forced to fly, and the conquerors carry off their prize in triumph. Such was mostly the fate of Otoo's fleet after Captain Cook left him. Since that time his navy has gone almost to ruin, though he has still been lucky and often conquers; but he always prefers peace to war.

They always bring off the dead, if they can, by any means, as all that they leave is carried to the morai, where the body is offered as a sacrifice. The lower jawbone is cut out and placed in the morai as a trophy, and the body is interred in the morai. The man who killed him now takes his name. This being the only method by which they attain to the character of a warrior, they must bring off their dead, which is often severely disputed by the living—and especially by the friends of the fallen warrior, who fight more furiously to protect the body when dead than they did to assist him while living. If the conqueror should prevail and maintain his conquest, he takes the name of his adversary as a title of honour.

After the peace is made, the relations of the deceased warriors soon find out the men who killed them, and each family sends a present to the man by whom their friend or relation was killed. They hire a set of urre heiva, a sort of people somewhat similar to our morris dancers. A principal part is acted by the daughter or nearest female relation of the deceased warrior in a dance at the house of the man who killed him. The dance being finished, the cloth, matting, and dresses are all presented to him, and he now entertains all the deceased's relations sumptuously for several days.

They declare that they do not owe him any grudge or animosity for killing their relation, and their sorrow is now turned to joy. Everything is most amicably settled, and the conqueror, to make the friendship more firm on his part, adopts the nearest relation of the deceased as his friend. By bearing his name, he becomes one of the family, is ever after treated as such, and is as much beloved in the family as if he had been born in it.

RELIGION
Their religion is without form or regularity, and though in many respects peculiar to themselves, yet it may be, in many respects, compared to that of some of the ancient Jewish tribes. Their traditions, which are numerous, may be compared to theirs and, in many respects, correspond with our books of the Old Testament. They have images, but they offer them no kind of adoration. Their deities are three, which are called by the general name of Eatooa, but worshipped as three distinct persons and spoken of separately. They are called:

Taane, the first or Father of Gods, sometimes called Eatooa Nooe (Great God) and sometimes Eatooa Munna, Tremendous or Awful God, Maker of the World, and all things and the cause of all things: light, darkness, thunder, lightning, and rain, etc.

Oromattowtooa, or the Son, who presides over war and peace, who punishes chiefs with sickness and death for any neglect of their duty.

Teepahooamannoo—the hoa, or friend, of both and their messenger to earth— these they style eatooa fwhanow, po, or po roa, who are gods born of, or brought forth from, darkness or eternal night. To these they never apply but in time of war or when any sickness befalls their chiefs. They deem them too great to interest themselves in any trivial or insignificant affairs, and are very cautious how they attempt anything that may offend them—for fear they should destroy the world entirely. They were near doing that when they were offended, having overset the world and broke it to pieces, which is the account they give of the cause of the many islands they are acquainted with.

Besides these, they have a number of inferior deities. Every man and woman has a guardian angel whom they suppose to be the souls of their departed relatives who have been deified for their good works and whose business is to watch and protect them while on earth. And as they believe that every man shall be rewarded with happiness in the next world, they take leave of this one without any anxiety. When they die, they take leave of their friends with as much composure as if they were going on a journey.

As they believe in a future state, so they also believe that those who have been good men and have been liberal to the gods shall have the highest place. They think of no place worse than earth, say when they dream that the soul is absent; and talking of dreams, they say, "My soul saw such a soul, etc." When anyone dies, they say their soul is fled and that it flies to the Deity who (as they express it) eats it—that it then comes out through him, and partaking of his divinity, is sent to take care of some other mortal who may be born at the same time—or suffered to roam, at large, through the Heavenly Mansions, where it wants for nothing.

They also believe that there is an evil demon whom they call Tee, but that his power extends no further than being able to punish them on earth by getting into them and causing madness, fits, etc. He cannot enter without the leave of their angel, the only one who can drive him out. For this reason, as soon as they fall sick, they instantly apply to the Deity to remove the cause by prayer and offerings and apply to the priests for their assistance. Enquiring of themselves, they endeavour to rectify any little affair that may have caused a misunderstanding by sending a peace offering to those whom they think they have offended.

When they have given all they have away to the priests and deities, and cannot appease their anger, they call their friends about them and recommend them to the care of their guardian angels. They ask them to be careful not to offend them and to be mindful to make much of their chiefs and be generous and good to strangers. They frequently die without a groan, though reduced to the last by pain and suffering.

They believe that the sun and moon are the original parents of all the stars. When they are in eclipse, they say they are in the act of generation; that everything on earth is produced in the same manner; and that everything made by the deities at first is dissolved and dropped away, that others are produced in their rooms, and that the whole system of nature keeps constantly changing. In support of these arguments, they say, "Don't we see some die, and some born every day, the rivers run to the sea, the trees rot, and the rocks fall from the mountains? All this has continued from the beginning of the world, and yet they are not diminished, but others supply their places."

Their traditions respecting the Creation are in many respects the same as we find in the Bible; they do not limit the time but say that God produced all things from nothing and set everything in motion by his command. Some of their accounts of the stars may be said to correspond with the Greek fables. They have names for most of them, into which men and women have been transformed for good and evil works. They say that a girl called Tow-rooa, of great beauty but a great whore, was, for cursing Taane, sent into the planet Venus, where she must remain for her punishment—along with several others of the same and suchlike descriptions.

Castor and Pollux they say were two brothers who begged of Taane to be taken away from their parents, who had refused to give them some fine fish. They went away from home, and praying to Taane, a white cloud came and took them away. They are called Beebirre Maa or the Beebirres.

As they are superstitious in all their customs and think that every transgression against God or man is attended with punishment, they have but few that may be called real crimes among a people who have no other law but that of nature. They firmly believe what they are taught by their priests and forefathers, and which they suppose to be the command of God. They know that from him all their blessings proceed, and when they approach their places of worship, it is with a reverential awe that would be an honour to Christianity. When in the act of praying they always behave with due decorum.

Although they maintain that their method is right as they are taught, they allow that another is as good and are charitable enough to allow that every man—if he worships his god as he is taught—is in a fair way to happiness and will meet such reward as he deserves. Believing that this world is the only place of punishment, they all hold and think it impossible that there can be another.

Their women bear no part in their religious rites, and neither they nor their male servants ever partake of these ceremonies. They have no place of worship for themselves, nor do they ever enter one but at their birth, but any priest may officiate for them when anything ails them. They are no less in the eyes of the Deity than those who are admitted to be partakers of religious rites.

Their ceremonies consist of innumerable sacrifices, prayers, feasts, etc., held on the morai, at which their priests always preside; but before I proceed to the ceremonies it is necessary to give some little account of the morai and priests.

The morai, or places of worship, are oblong, square pieces of ground planted thick with trees and enclosed by a wall of stone some four, five, or six feet high and as much thick. Some are piles of stone rising in large steps and are built solid and firm. The largest in Tahiti is at Papaara. See Captain Cook's *Voyage*; he having given an account, I need not here further describe it. [The description of this morai is given in Captain Cook's *First Voyage*, under the date of June 27, 1767. It consisted of "an enormous pile of stone work, raised in the form of a pyramid, with a flight of steps on each side, and was nearly 270 feet long, about one third as wide and between 40 and 50 feet high. . . . In the centre was the representation of a bird, carved in wood; close to this was the figure of a fish, which was in stone. This pyramid made part of one side of a wide court or square, the sides of which were nearly equal; the whole was walled in, and paved with flat stones."] They are of different dimensions and are built without mortar. In the center is a table or altar, on which they make their offerings, and on one end is a house for the reception of the priests when they come to offer sacrifice and feast on the morai.

In one of these morais, which is their grand and principal one, in the district of Oparre, they keep a movable one somewhat similar to the Ark of the Jews. This is the occasion of as many quarrels as the Ark formerly was. This morai is called tabbootaboatea, thus translated, "sacrifice the white hog." It is the place to which every chief on the island, and those who are subject to them on other islands, must repair to offer their sacrifices, as they think it the only residence of the Deity on earth.

This movable morai is a box about three feet long, two feet wide, and one deep, in which are kept the three deities—or rather the images to represent them, as they are only for the purpose of remembrances and are not worshipped. Nevertheless, they bear the names of the deities. On the top of this box are raised several pieces of rude carved work, on the tops of which are represented birds with extended wings, as the Deity is fond of birds and makes use of them to come to earth in. The whole is decorated with bunches of red and yellow feathers, which to them are as valuable as gold.

This, with a movable house that is part of the morai and fixed on a stand together, is called Effarre Attooa, or the House of God. They are screened in and kept covered with the best cloth the island produces, painted in different colours. Here also is kept the royal marro, etc., and none must approach but the priests, on pain of death; even they are obliged to divest themselves of their clothes to the waist whenever they enter a morai. When they enter the Effarre Attooa, they strip naked, leaving their own clothes outside, and while there they cover their nakedness with clothing belonging to the sacred place that they pull off at their return, leaving them there, and resume their own.

This morai is their principal place of worship, and here only they offer human sacrifices. It has ever been the object of dispute, all desiring to have it in their own possession. It was seized from Otoo, about twenty years before our coming to the island, by Tetowha, chief of Attahooroo, who had assisted him to recover it from

Tommaree. Tetowha, finding himself of some consequence, insisted on having possession of the morai, etc., keeping them in Attahooroo, which he had done till our time. Having in our time made war with Otoo and refusing to acknowledge his son, Otoo demanded our assistance.

By our help, Tetowha was reduced as before described, and the morai brought to Oparre, where a new stone was built for its reception. There were made the first and last human sacrifices that they made during our stay on the island, and these we were informed had been found guilty of blasphemy against God or the king. These were not burnt, nor do they burn any.

The walls of the morais are, as said before, built without cement. Though some stones appear round and some exactly squared, no tools except stones are used in the construction of them.

When a morai is to be built, the chief gives notice thereof by sending a piece of coconut leaf to every man under him, with orders that at the time and place appointed he shall appear with a stone of the dimensions that he shall find described by the priests; they accordingly attend. If the stones are not judged sufficient, the order is renewed. These leaves are generally made up by the priests with knots, tied in a manner peculiar to themselves, and contain the dimensions of the stones that each man may work without the assistance of another.

When the stones are all collected, the priests give notice that they are ready, and a part of each day is set aside for the work. A sacrifice is then made, and they proceed in their work, during which time no fire must be lighted in the district till they leave off work each day. After the work is finished and the altar erected, they expend two or three days in the consecration of it, which is done by making many sacrifices, human and common, with prayers and feasts. During the time religious parts of the rites are being performed, no fire must be lighted. This is observed in all rites wherein the generality of the people are concerned.

The priests are of two classes and are formed out of all ranks of people, according to the ability they possess. They are the only people who have any knowledge, and it is their business to keep the lower classes in ignorance. Though some are of the lowest class themselves, yet they gain esteem according to their knowledge—or rather from their being lucky in the business they profess.

The first of these are called totowa moray, and their business is to make offerings at the morai and have the charge of the holy place. Their prayers or hymns they chant out in an unknown tongue. The natives, or at least such as are not of their profession, do not understand it, nor do many of the chiefs, though they are all considered priests. The chiefs seldom officiate except on particular occasions when they are forced to assist for want of priests; but as they are plentiful, the chiefs are seldom under such necessity.

The others are called tawra tooa and pretend to divine inspiration. They are consulted on all occasions, whether in war, sickness, or otherwise, and through them the will and pleasure of the Deity are known. Few of them pretend to be inspired by the same deity, and those who claim the superior ones are men of great art and address. From their skill in their art they make themselves of great consequence.

They never attempt to apply to their deity unless a chief is taken sick, or to know the result of any war that they may have a hand in. As they are well acquainted with most of the circumstances, before they begin they can tell events of this kind to a certainty. If their skill proves ineffectual in sickness, they never fail to accuse the friends and relations of the sick for their want of religion and neglect of their duty in the performance of it. But should he recover while under their care, their characters are firmly established, and though of the lowest class, become the bosom friends of the chief or party on whose behalf they used their skill. They are sent for on all occasions and caressed, even if their skills should afterwards fail.

When they are consulted with respect to the event of war, etc., they dress themselves in a fantastical form. They decorate themselves with red and black feathers, of which they suppose the Deity to be immoderately fond, as he always makes use of birds when he descends on earth. Having his head bound with rowavva, one goes into a close place, screened in near the morai for that purpose, or into some thick bush where he remains a few minutes.

He comes out sneezing two or three times, when he begins to look wild, his eyes staring, and his body distorted into many forms. In a moment he seems to have undergone a most amazing change. These postures he attributes to the contest between his own soul and that of the Deity endeavouring to take its habitation, which it at last effects. He appears as if stupid and does not know any person. His colleague, who is generally a tahowwa, then compliments him by the name of the Deity, which he professes to be inspired with, and asks him such questions as he, or the party concerned, wishes to have answered.

He returns him answers in a low, squeaking tone of voice and makes large demands of the party concerned; but should he be questioned while struggling with the Deity, he sometimes utters half sentences in a curious manner, as if both souls endeavoured to speak at the same time. He sometimes speaks with his natural, and sometimes in a squeaking, voice. When the spirit leaves him, he begins to gape and yawn and often falls backward with a loud shriek and lays speechless some minutes.

When he awakes, as if from a sleep, and his body being reoccupied by his own soul, he resumes his own voice and seems to know nothing of what has passed. He generally times it at the flight of one of the birds from the morai, and his colleague does not forget to inform him of what demands the Deity has made. Those concerned seldom fail to furnish him with everything he requires, if they have it or can by any means get it.

This is the method by which they always proceed. Several women pretend to the same office and make their enquiries for their own sex in sickness and childbirth. Such is their belief in them that they think if one of them is present and not applied to, that the mother would never be delivered. Instead of one they have sometimes half a dozen who facilitate the birth of the child by their prayers and offerings, and in return strip them of half they possess, without giving them any other assistance.

When priests or priestesses enter a house for this purpose, they always bring with them a young plantain tree. Having taken one of the leaves from it, they throw the tree on the top of the house and then enter, making several short prayers in different parts of it, and stick the leaf up over the door or entrance. They then proceed to enquire into the particulars of the business and are always perfectly acquainted with every circumstance before they proceed in anything—by which means they know what answers to make, whether there is any hope of success or fear of disappointment, before they begin.

RELIGIOUS AND OTHER CUSTOMS

When they make an offering to the Deity, the hog is brought to the morai, where it is killed and cleaned as if for eating. It is then besmeared with its own blood and placed on the altar to rot. They suppose the Deity is gratified by eating the soul of the victim, as he also does of those who die, whether man or beast; but those who are killed on purpose for him have always the effect of procuring favours for the maker of the sacrifice. The priests then dress the entrails with breadfruit and roots, and eat them on the morai. As they observe the birds often eat the plantains, they frequently lay a bunch or two of the best sort on the altar, together with fish, fowl, etc. They are scarce ever without something on them.

The first fruits of all kinds are offered to the Deity, next to the chief and to the lord of the manor before they eat any themselves, and the fish in like manner. If a man has a fishing seine to wet or a new canoe to launch, he makes a feast on the morai for the priests, who offer up plantain trees and prayers for his success. The first fish always goes to the morai, where the priest offers it with prayers; the next to the priests; the third to the chief; and the fourth to the lord of the manor or landlord; and till all these are served, they never taste the fruits of their labour.

The first pig is always offered at eight or ten days old, and a chicken of the brood is also offered. For their children they always make an offering according to their ability, either a pig or a fowl.

If anything touches the altar, or even the sacred ground about the morai, let the value be ever so great, it is deemed sacred. For that reason it can never be brought into unhallowed ground or touched but by the priests. And should a hog or dog, etc., run into any of the sacred grounds, it is killed for sacrifice.

When a feast is made on any morai, it is always from a freewill offering (of which they have many), and the whole of the victuals must be eaten there and not removed from the sacred ground, let the quantity be what it will. The breast and one shoulder of every hog is the chief's share, but in his absence they fall to the priests with the head and entrails, which is their own share. Nevertheless, if any person at hand is entitled to eat on the morai and has not been served, they invite him or them to partake.

When the priest or priests (as before said) attend these feasts, they and all who enter on the morai must be naked to the waist. When they attend any ceremony off the morai, they have their shoulders covered and their head anointed with oil; a kind of turban bound on with sacred leaves; a breastplate (called tawmee) on their breast; and their clothes bound on with a sash or girdle of braided hair or coconut fibers, neatly plaited of a great length, and made up in bights or doubles, with a tassel at each end. The provisions brought to the morai must be dressed on it, and near the house where baskets are kept for keeping them in, should they last three or four days.

They always wash themselves before and after they eat, and should a dead lizard, mouse, or rat touch them, they would wash before they handled any food. Should they happen to find one in or near their oven or touch any of their culinary utensils, they would use them no more. Notwithstanding which, they will eat a hog that has died if they know of no disorder which might be the occasion of his death.

Any person who touches a dead body, except of those killed by war or for sacrifice, is rendered unclean and can touch no provisions with their hands for one month—during which time they must be fed by another. If a man killed in war is touched by a relation, he must undergo the like, but otherwise washing is sufficient. If any person has a running sore or large ulcers, he is touched by no person else, and if he dies, the house wherein he lived is burnt with everything belonging to it.

When mourning for the death of any relation, they shave the forepart of their heads and sometimes the hindpart, together with their eyebrows and beards, and cut their heads with shark's teeth in excess of grief or joy. See "Mourning Rites," pages 218–20.

They always venerate the grey heads and are kind to strangers, and protect the fatherless and the widow.

A child may curse its father, mother, uncle, or aunt, but it would be blasphemy for them to curse it. The child may not curse its grandfather, grandmother, brothers, or sisters, but the grandfather and grandmother may curse their grandchildren with impunity; but it is death for any man to blaspheme or revile the gods or the king.

When they marry they never join with their blood relations, but a man may take two sisters and a woman two brothers at the same time if they are all agreeable. It is looked upon as a piece of great friendship for a man to cohabit with the wife of his adopted friend if she is agreeable. The adopted friend is always accounted as a brother.

If a woman has a husband and he dies without issue, the husband's brother takes her; if he has no wife and should he have issue by her, the children are called by the former brother's name and take his estate; but should he have a wife, he keeps her at his house till she gets a husband, and she is still acknowledged as one of the family.

If a man has a reason to part with his wife, he informs her of it, to which she mostly agrees, deeming it reproachful to remain after such notice. He then divides all his goods and chattels with her; she leaves him and takes the female children with her, leaving him the males. If she lives single, she always claims the rights of a wife, and though they do not cohabit, always look on each other as friends. They apply to each other for any little property, that at any future period of their separation they may stand in need of.

Each enjoys his or her own estate, but should they choose to live together after such separation it lies at their own option; they may return to each other at any time. If the woman takes another husband, she relinquishes all claim to her rights in her first husband and can demand no more of him but her own estate and her part of the goods as before described.

If a man finds his neighbour or one who is not his adopted friend in the act of adultery with his wife, he has the law in his own hands. He may, if he thinks proper, put one or both of them to death with impunity or punish his wife with stripes and plunder the house of the offender. The latter is the most common, but I have known two men killed who were taken in the fact. No further enquiry was made than the acknowledgement of the parties present to certify the fact.

Their marriages are no more than an agreement between the parties and their friends, and though the young are uncontrolled, they generally take the advice of their parents and friends. This being settled, they join and are called man and wife without ceremony except the greeting of their friends, who present them with hogs, cloth, and sundry necessary articles.

If the woman is a virgin, her friends must perform an amoa (a ceremony to be hereafter described) to their new son-in-law before the males of her family can eat any provisions with him or that he has touched. The young man exchanges names with his father-in-law and the woman with her mother-in-law. If she has had a husband before, the exchange of names and presents is the only necessary ceremony. The husband then claims his wife's possessions, which are delivered to him without reserve. And they, having houses on each, live where they think proper (but should they part, then the wife's property returns to herself as before said). If they have children they proceed thus:

When a child is born, whether male or female, it is taken to the family morai (of which every family has one) by a person who is employed to attend it while the mother goes into a warm bath. The father and priests repair to the morai and offer a young pig or a fowl or two to the Deity, and a priest, who is well paid for his trouble, cuts off the child's navel string within six or eight inches of the belly with a piece of split bamboo. While the others are praying, he buries it in the morai.

A temporary hut is then prepared near the morai to which the mother repairs. The child is brought to her by the servant appointed to attend it and who must remain there with the mother and child till the rest of the navel string drops off. This may be either kept in a house sacred to the child or buried in the morai. If the child is male, they may bury the navel string as soon as it comes off, which may be six or eight days. If female, it is sometimes kept a fortnight or three weeks, during which time the mother touches no kind of provisions herself but is fed by another person.

Whosoever else touches the child must undergo the same restriction till an amoa is performed to take it off, previous to which an offering must be made of a plantain tree and a young pig or a fowl or two for the mother. This is done as soon as the navel string is buried, or the time fulfilled for the removal of the child from the morai nearer the father's house, which is built for and sacred to the child's use. But they still cannot enter that house nor touch the child with the same clothes on that they wear when they eat their own provisions—to take off which from the father and uncles, a second amoa must be performed; and from the mother and aunts, a third; before the child may come into a house where its father and uncles eat, a fourth; and for the mother and aunts, a fifth.

If the child is male, there is one more that is performed when he adopts a friend, which is the whole required to make his head free. Everything he touches, being in his minority or sacred state, is made sacred by his touch and rendered useless to any other. If the child is female, there are two others—one when she gets a husband, that her male relations may eat of the provisions that he has touched, and another that they may eat out of the same dish. Then her head becomes free also, but she is generally free before these two, unless her head should touch anything.

These ceremonies when performed for the males are called amoa only, but for the females, they add fwhatoe, signifying something more, as they have one more than the males. For the males, hogs or fowl and cloth are always presented. For the females, if they cannot raise them, a fish will do. However, this is seldom the case, and they are in no way sparing in the performance of these rights. Much feasting then takes place.

Everything the children happen to touch before these rites are all performed is rendered sacred and thrown in a place adjoining the house in which they live, railed in for that purpose. They are always careful how they go about, and should a child's head touch a tree by the carelessness of the attendant, the tree, though ever so valuable, is cut down and destroyed root and branch. If it should break a limb of another or bruise the bark in its fall, that tree must be destroyed also; nor must they use the timber for fuel.

Some of the women are sixteen or seventeen years old before all their rites are performed, which makes them very cautious what house they go into or what things they touch. The men are generally made free as fast as the father can get it done, which is sometimes by six years old and sometimes not till twelve. The children of people of rank take generally longer before they have all their rites performed than the lower sort, as it has a grander appearance by taking long. They always make large feasts on these occasions.

The reason for all these ceremonies is that as soon as a child is born, it being the fruit of the father and mother, is superior to either—as much as the fruit is to the tree for food. For this reason the child is, as soon as born, the head of the family. The honour and dignity of the father are transferred to the first-born child, whether male or female. Before all these rites are performed, the parents are not thought worthy to partake of the child's food. But as they have always a sufficient provision for themselves and have the ruling for their children, those of high rank defer the performance, under colour of it being grand to have their children longer in a sacred state. In fact, it is that they may continue longer in power. Those of low degree have no interest in it and, therefore, get it done sooner; and as soon as the child's head is free, it then becomes perfectly its own master and may act for itself.

Where this uncommon custom, so contrary to nature, took its rise we could never learn, it having been with them from time immemorial. It may in some measure account for the difference in stature between the higher and lower classes of people. The latter class, having sooner their liberty, have earlier connections with each other than the higher. The chiefs in particular are mostly arrived at years of maturity and manhood before they cohabit with their women.

The amoa we saw thus performed at a marriage ceremony and differs very little from that performed through the different degrees of childhood. The friends of both parties being assembled at the morai, the young man and his wife were placed on a large quantity of cloth spread for the purpose near the morai, alongside of each other, the man on the right of his wife. Opposite them at the distance of thirty or forty yards and at the other end of the cloth, sat the father, mother, uncles, and aunts of the bride.

A priest then having furnished the mother with several pieces of sugar cane and some leaves from the rowavva (or sacred tree), she takes a shark's tooth. Cutting her head on the forepart, she lets a drop of blood fall on each piece of the sugar cane. She places a piece on a leaf, gives two to the father and each of the uncles and aunts, and keeps two for herself. These they place on the palms of their hands and, holding them up to their foreheads, rise up and proceed slowly along the cloth till they arrive where the young couple sits, keeping their bodies half bent all the way. Having deposited the leaves and sugar cane at the feet of the young pair, they retire without speaking in the same manner to their seats.

The priest then advances with a branch of the rowavva in his hand and makes a long prayer. Having finished, he goes to the young couple, and bidding them, "God bless them in their Union" (or as they express it, in their sleeping together), he takes up the leaves and pieces of sugar cane and proceeds to the morai, where he buries them with prayers and makes an offering to the deity of a hog, etc.

In the meantime, the couple rises and goes to their parents, embraces them, and bestows their blessings on them. The cloth is then gathered up and presented to the son-in-law, who generally throws part of it out for the young people present to scramble for. They are proud if they can get a narrow strip of it to put on in honour of the rite and wear it till it is expended, telling all they know how they obtained it.

The company then returns to the bridegroom's house, and he sends three or four hogs to his father-in-law, who has them immediately killed. A feast is made, of which all the males of both families partake. A feast is also prepared for the women, and all partake of the festivity. The father of the bride then delivers her portion to her husband as before described, and an exchange of names takes place.

When a man adopts a friend for his son, the ceremony is the same, only placing the boy in the place of the woman. The ceremony is ratified, and the boy and his friends exchange names and are ever after looked as one of the family—the new friend becoming the adopted son of the boy's father. This friendship is most religiously kept and never dissolves till death. Though they may separate and make temporary friends while absent, when they meet they always acknowledge each other.

Should a brother or one who is an adopted friend become poor or lose his land in war, he has nothing more to do but go to his brother, or friend, and live with him, partaking of all he possesses as long as he lives—and his wife and family with him, if he has any. If any relation or friend, though not in immediate want, comes to the house of his friend, he is always fed while he stays, and is not only welcome to take away what he pleases but is loaded with presents.

They are ever courteous to the stranger and hospitable to the wayfaring man, and what they have is always at the service of their visitors. When a stranger enters a house he is saluted by the master and perhaps all the family with "mannowa" (welcome), "Yowrye t'Eatooa te' Narria mye" (God save you in your coming), and "Yowrrana te Tirre raa" (God save you in your journey), and the like compliments at parting.

When they meet each other after but a short absence, they embrace each other as we do, but instead of kissing each other, they join noses and draw in each other's breath through the nostrils. Sometimes in token of great love they almost suffocate each other by their long continuance of their embrace. This method is common to both sexes, but if they have been long absent, the women weep and cut their heads with a shark's tooth till the blood flows copiously, which is always the case in either excess, whether of grief or joy, to show their love. They always perform this ceremony on the slightest accident happening to their children, and every woman is provided with one or two shark's teeth as soon as she is married, as they never cut their heads before and have them wrapped in cloth. They are fastened with the pitch of the breadfruit, so that the points stick out about a quarter of an inch like lancets.

People of note always travel by water about their own island, and as there are a number of houses built by the chiefs of each district for the reception of strangers, they are never at a loss for an inn. Some of these houses are 150 feet long, 50 or 60 wide, and 30 or 35 high.

As soon as they land, they haul up their canoes near their inn and send notice to the nearest of the same rank, who repair to the place immediately with provisions for them. If they stay long enough, everyone of the same class in the district supplies them with one day's provisions for all their company. In fine weather they put up anywhere and erect temporary sheds in the most convenient place.

If any person of whatever class he may be should be travelling by land and meets none who invite him, or should happen to be unacquainted in the district he is passing through and has occasion for provisions, he enquires the name of the first ratirra [squire] and repairs to his house. On his entering he receives the usual compliments, and having made known his business, the master of the house immediately orders provisions to be got ready for him. The mistress entertains his wife in the same manner, and they enjoy a secret pleasure at having had the good fortune to have the strangers come to their house. They are forever after deemed friends, though they had never seen each other before.

When a chief or stranger of rank from other islands visits them, they perform a ceremony called ootdoo, a peace offering, which is done thus: The chief or stranger having taken up his residence in one of the houses built for the reception of strangers (of which there are several at convenient places in every district), the chiefs and people of the district assemble near the spot with their presents, each chief being attended by a priest with young plantain trees and pigs.

They then take their places opposite the stranger, about thirty or forty yards from him, and the priest of the first chief begins by tying a young pig and a small bunch of red feathers to a young plantain tree. He makes a long speech, welcomes the stranger in the name of his master and the people, and then lays the plantain and pig down at the stranger's feet, who takes the red feathers and sticks them in his ear or hair.

A number of hogs, cloth, etc., are then brought in and presented to him by the chief's men. The inferior chiefs and landed men go through the same ceremony, each presenting him with a pig or fowl with a plantain tree, which is the emblem of peace on all occasions and used in all civil and religious ceremonies with their present of hogs and cloth.

When the whole have made their offering and presents, the stranger is invited to a feast prepared for him of baked hogs, breadfruit, etc.—of which none but himself and his retinue partakes. I have seen at one of these feasts fifty hogs baked and as much provisions as one hundred men could carry, prepared for a stranger of quality for one day—and repeated for several days in the same district, each person of the same rank providing one day's food.

Nevertheless, it is better to visit a private gentleman of quality than a chief; though both fare sumptuously, yet the gentlemen are the most numerous, and they may expend more time in one district in a continual feast. Sometimes they make a month's stay in one district, but seldom hurry when they are on a visit.

The lower classes always entertain those of their class or society in the same manner, according to their abilities. But they mostly prefer the method of visiting in the retinue of chiefs and gentlemen. This method of living draws many young people into the roving society of the Areeuoy, which shall be described in turn. As they always find plenty of food and raiment without much trouble, they never think of settling till they arrive at a man's estate, if they do then.

When people of equal rank visit each other in their own or other districts, they are always made welcome by greetings as soon as they enter the house as before described. As soon as they are seated, the master of the house orders a feast to be prepared for them and enquires the cause of their visit, what they want, etc.—to all of which they answer without hesitation or preface. Their wants being made known, they are instantly promised to be supplied if the other has it in his power.

In the meantime, they are presented with a piece or two of cloth and one or more live hogs, by way of earnest of their being supplied. If the man of the house has not what his visitors want, he begs them to stay at his house till he can procure [goods] sufficient to supply their wants among his neighbours.

All the provisions dressed for the visitors they must take with them, it being accounted no treat if any of the family partake with them. Nor do they call anything a present that nature produces, unless accompanied by something that is procured by the assistance of labour or the art of man; for which reason they always give cloth or something else with their gifts, provisions being held of no value, being produced by nature; and they think it not proper to store them.

They never return thanks but by deed, having no word in their language expressive of it, and when they part, they always use compliments. They always beg their visitors to remain with them till they are perfectly well satisfied with their treatment, for should any depart unsatisfied they would get a bad name. Those who are not well treated never fail to declare how they have been used. In this manner, they frequently make a visit of several months, getting a little from one and a little from another, till they get what they want and return home.

The tenants (or mattaeyna) hold their lands from the towha (lord of the manor) or ratirra (squire), to whom they pay their rent by making cloth when they want it or supplying his demands in hogs—if they have them. If they have none, he requires none and never forces them to find what they have not.

It is no disgrace for a man to be poor and he is no less regarded on that account, but to be rich and covetous is a disgrace to human nature. Should a man betray such a sign and not freely part with what he has, his neighbours would soon put him on a level with the poorest of themselves by laying his possessions waste and hardly leaving him a house to live in. A man of such a description would be accounted a hateful person, and before they would incur such a name as that of covetous or stingy, they would part with the cloth off their back and go naked till they got more.

If any man is caught in the act of theft and is immediately put to death, the person who killed him is brought to no account for it. But if the thief escapes and the property is afterwards found on him, the person whose property it is may plunder him of his goods and chattels, which the thief always submits to. The owner leaves with him the property that he stole, taking all the rest. Should he absent himself and take his goods off his land, the person injured may oblige the thief's landlord to deliver to him the house and land that the thief did possess till the damage is made good—or ransom it with hogs, to the full satisfaction of the injured party.

This latter mode is mostly practiced. If the land was once put into possession, the party so holding it could never be removed, except by war or the commission of some crime against the chief. After such ransom is paid, the squire may, if he pleases, compromise matters with the thief and let him return, on condition that he pays the ransom or gets friends to do it for him—or give it to some other who has been distressed by war—then the thief must go and live on his friends.

They have carved wooden images of men that they call etee set up as boundaries of their estates not to pay devotion to, but to remind passengers below and of equal rank to the possessor and owner of that land to strip the clothes off their shoulders and heads as they pass by—in compliment to the owner. All ranks of people must pay this homage as they pass the land belonging to the earee da hye, or king. The etee or image denoting the king's land is remarkably larger than the common size, and the towha's or ratirra's land is known by a number of little white flags being fixed in different parts beside the etee.

Any neglect or refusal of these honours is the occasion of disputes, and often is the occasion of wars or household quarrels between the parties. If the owner is a minor, the affront is the greater; the mother instantly applies the shark's tooth to her head in grief that her child should be insulted, and the father flies to strip by force those who have offended. If the offender makes a concession by offering a plantation leaf and declaring his ignorance, the matter is settled; if he continues, obstinate blows ensue that increase as the friends of each party become acquainted with the affair and repair armed to the place. The battle becomes general and often ends with the loss of some lives and often involves whole districts in a war with each other.

A chief and his people may be driven from the land through the means of a quarrel arising from the neglect, or refusing to pay the proper compliment, to a poor man's child, though the father might have been beaten with impunity by one who might quarrel with him. But no man must presume to treat the heirs of large estates with such contempt or neglect on pain of death, and such insults often end in the total extirpation of one of the families concerned, it being deemed blasphemy to call it by a wrong name.

Their chiefs are accounted the head not only of the people but also of the priests and every other society that is instituted among them. They are accounted more than merely their superiors. None refuse to pay them the proper homage, and they are always particular in performing their part strictly where it is due—every chief paying that homage to the child of another.

They have few law disputes. Private disputes between men relative to themselves only seldom produce a blow, and I cannot say that ever I saw a blow given in consequence of a quarrel that did not arise from such grounds as before described.

If any dispute should happen about the boundaries of their land, as they have neither records nor any deeds of gift, they always refer to the neighbours for a decision. They newly mark the bounds of each man's land, and none disapproves of such decisions, as they are very superstitious in religious rites. They would rather submit to let the whole be common to both than either one undertake to mark his own bounds, fearing that he should be punished with sickness or disease if he encroached on the property of his neighbour.

This and all other disputes are settled by the neighbours, and the party who is declared to be in the wrong almost always submits at the first word, making a peace offering to the man offended. He declares himself at fault and desires he may think no more of it. No man ever claims a right to any land but his own or his adopted friend's, which he may use during his friend's life. Should his friend die without any other heir, the adopted friend is always considered as the right owner, and no man disputes his right.

If a man bequeaths the whole or a part of his land or property to any person before his death, and there are witnesses to prove such bequest, none objects to it— even if the heir himself should be absent and know nothing of it till the witnesses inform him of the right he has and call him home to take possession.

These rules are handed down from the father to the son, and they want no law to keep them in force. Nature has taught them to use all men as they would be used by them, which is their common standard. Though there are some exceptions, yet I may assert with no more than truth that this is their general character.

They have a ceremony called rahooe, which is a kind of jubilee, but have no fixed time allotted for keeping it. It is a prohibition or embargo laid on the provisions and stock, in whole or in part, in any one or more districts. It is intended to prevent a decrease by consuming the provisions or stock or transporting them out of the districts so rahooed, which they are forced to observe, under pain of being driven from their land.

The chiefs, towhas, and ratirras may at their will and pleasure rahooe the whole or any particular species of provisions, stock, fish, etc., within their own limits. When they think it necessary to prevent a great decrease of hogs, they can rahooe them through the whole district.

The king can at his own discretion rahooe several districts and sends his orders accordingly to the chiefs, towhas, and ratirras to prohibit the expenditure or removal of such provisions as he shall name within their several districts and estates for the time specified by him. He generally takes the advice of the inferior chiefs, priests, etc., and they always have timely notice before it takes place and know the reason why it is to take place.

On the day fixed, proclamation is made by criers for that purpose. A large bundle of bamboo leaves is hung up on the first tree at each end of the district, or part rahooed, to give notice to all passengers that all within the limits are under such circumstances and to inform them what treatment they may expect in them.

A hog and part of such provisions as are rahooed are hung up near the road in some conspicuous place, the hog being killed and hung up by the heels. When the rahooe is taken off, the leaves are taken down, and a feast of the jubilee takes place after an offering has been made at the chief's morai, which lasts three weeks or a month.

The chiefs and people are all entertained by contributions made by the people of the district or districts that have been rahooed. Each of them gets ready daily by two o'clock or thereabouts one hog, with a proper proportion of vegetables, which is brought to the place of rendezvous and there divided into seventeen proportions, one for each district. Being delivered to the chief of each district, it is taken to their separate rendezvous and divided by the servants, giving each towha and ratirra their share. They again divide it among their people, and everything is carried on with the greatest harmony, no quarrels ever ensuing at these feasts.

The feast is called towrooa aree (the chiefs' feast). After dinner they amuse themselves with wrestling, dancing, throwing the javelin, running for hogs, scrambling for cloth, etc., which are given by the chiefs or holder of the feasts.

Many of the Areeuoys always attend these feasts, and as they are mostly young men who are active and lively, they help the sport. The things put up for the scramble are canoes, hogs, cloth, bamboos of oil, etc. They are brought into an open space by the servants of the chiefs, who keep the hogs fast till the time appointed; they are always the wildest they can pick out, that they may make the better sport.

The canoes have masts fixed to hang up the oil and, being placed at equal distance from each other, have the cloth hung up by the ends between them. A priest then advances and makes a long prayer, at the end of which he throws a young plantain tree into one of the canoes. The hogs being turned loose, the scramble is begun by all ages and sexes, and as they are frequently numerous, they afford some sport before they are all taken.

The canoes, unless they happen to be seized by a whole family, are generally torn to pieces. The cloth is generally torn in ribbons that are worn as trophies, and preferred to whole pieces obtained any other way. The fowl are frequently torn in pieces, and the hogs and goats often get killed in the scramble. If a man takes a hog fairly, it is his own, and none will attempt to wrest it from him unless two or more happen to lay hold at the same time. Should a man receive a bruise or break a limb by being thrown, he never blames any person, as they never willingly hurt each other.

Though the chiefs or ratirras have power to put on these rahooes on their land without the consent or approbation of each other, they seldom do except to prevent a scarcity. Hogs are the principal objects of it, though it frequently extends to several other kinds of provisions when the king sees it necessary to prevent a scarcity—such as when large numbers of people are collected in one district for the arrival of a ship or fleet of canoes. After the first feasting is over, he puts on a rahooe till they shall return home or the concourse of people lessens and the visitors be distributed; otherwise, they would destroy the whole stock and breed a famine there.

At such times the reefs are rahooed to prevent the shell and other fish from being destroyed, as people flock from all parts of the island to view the strangers, without bringing provisions for their own use. They generally give to the strangers all they bring with them, trusting to the district they come to for food—which the owners are ashamed to refuse while they have any for themselves. When the people return homewards, the rahooe is taken off so the strangers may be supplied—who are nevertheless plentifully fed from the neighbouring districts where the rahooe has not been put on.

The rahooe on the reefs is signified by placing bushes along the part rahooed, with bits of white cloth tied to them. After they appear there, no person dare fish there on pain of forfeiting their lands, but they may fish with nets, hooks, etc., in their canoes, by which means they procure good supplies. If the beach is rahooed, they must not launch a canoe off to fish or any other purpose. This happens only when the king's flag is passing.

Besides the feast of the jubilee, or rahooe, they make a feast on the morai, at which none can be present but raa, or sacred, men. This always consists of one or more hogs and other provisions, with plenty of yava. These are mostly held on family morais belonging to the ratirras and are called oboo nooe.

At them the chief of the Padtoo and all the ratirra and priests attend. When the provisions are taken out of the oven, the priests make a long prayer by way of grace and, taking a piece of bamboo for a knife (if they have knives they must not be brought there, else they could not carry them away again) and taking a part of each sort with a bit of yava, put them on a plantain leaf. With a prayer they offer them on the altar or on top of the house.

In the meantime, some of the rest cut up the hog or hogs and distribute them as before described, and they begin. Should a stranger pass at the time, they send to invite him, and if he is not known to any present, they enquire if he is a raa or noa man, to which he answers truly. If he be raa, or sacred, he partakes of the feast; if noa, or unhallowed, he refuses, none ever attempting to impose on strangers in such matters; they are liable to be found out afterwards, when death would be the result of the fraud.

The women have also their feasts, which are called oehvimoo; they are generally of fish. Of these their male servants may partake, and so may any other man. They are held on the common ground in such place as they find convenient.

BUILDINGS

Their buildings are principally the morais, or places of worship, which have been described by Captain Cook. Some of them are amazingly large piles of stone that must remain as monuments of their ingenuity for ages. They are regularly and exactly built without tools or cement and can receive no damage but from time. Of these, every family of note has one of size proportional to the wealth of the owner, and in them, as said before, they perform their religious rites with becoming decency and awful reverence.

Their houses are neat thatches made of the palm leaves and supported on posts and are of different sizes according to the owner's abilities. The dwelling houses are mostly railed round with wattles, and in bad weather, they screen them in with coconut leaves woven into a kind of matting, which they remove in fine weather. They are exactly calculated for the climate and want no other fence but to keep the hogs out. The common size is from thirty to forty feet long, eighteen or twenty high and about the same broad.

Of these each family has two, one for the males and the other for the females, and some have their hog sties in the middle. They are generally of an oval form, and the eaves come within nine feet of the ground, which is always raised somewhat from the level to keep the floor dry. The floor is always laid with grass or hay to a good thickness, on which some of the family sleep on mats. Others who take the trouble have bedsteads raised with little stools, neatly carved out of the solid for pillows, and sleep on cloth and mats.

Their furniture consists of a large chest or two to hold their property in. On one of these the master of the house and his wife sleep on cloth and mats. Those who have not stools for pillows use the seats of the canoes; one or two large stools for the accommodation of their guests; stools for beating pudding on, with a stone or two neatly cut for a pestle; platters and trays of different sizes; baskets of several sorts; and a post or two to hang their provisions on.

The unmarried women generally sleep near the parents, and the unmarried men and servants generally sleep in the women's eating-house. In fine weather they prefer the open air, as the grass with which the floors are covered, if not frequently removed, produces an abundance of fleas. For this reason they sleep out of doors to avoid these disagreeable companions.

They always divest themselves of their wearing apparel when they sleep, but most of the young men and servants make their wearing apparel serve for bedding also, as they seldom take the pains of keeping too many clothes at one time—except an extra suit for dress, which they do not wear in common. This way of proceeding has its convenience as they always have their bedding with them and have nothing to take care of. They also have small houses for kitchens, as they never dress provisions in the house they eat in, the smoke being not only disagreeable to them, but spoils their clothes.

The houses of the chiefs are not remarkable for being better furnished than those of the common people, thought they are somewhat larger. Like the houses for the reception of travelers, they are generally open on all sides, having a low fence of plank forming a square about them. The part within the fence is either spread with small pebbles or laid with grass. If they intend to reside long in one house or place, they have a neat, small house railed in for their use. They frequently sleep in poor, mean huts and eat in the open air, hanging their provisions on a tree.

Their canoes may be also comprehended in the article of building, and those for war are certainly curious machines when we consider the tools with which they are constructed. Before they had iron introduced among them (and of which they have now but small quantities), their tools consisted of no other than stone adzes of different sizes; leg or arm bones of men for augur, chisel, and gouge; coral and sand to smooth with; and skins of fish to polish. Where fire could be of any use in burning off the rough, it was also used. Now they have axes for the rough work and small hatchets, which they convert into adzes by lashing them to handles, making for quicker work. They also have a number of saws, but can make no use of them. Nails of different sorts make gimbals, chisels, etc.; they are even converted into small adzes for carving with, the adze being their principal tool at all kinds of work.

Some stone tools are nearly of the same construction as in use among the natives of New Holland. It is not improbable that these were the original and only tools in use among other nations before the use of iron was known.

The length and size of the war canoes having been before described, I shall proceed to describe their construction and equipment:

Each canoe (of which there are always two lashed together) is at her greatest breadth about four feet wide and six feet deep, and the whole length from sixty to ninety feet. The bottom is sharp and projects in a straight line to the wale, where the extreme breadth is. There, the round suddenly turns into the side, which rises about fourteen or sixteen inches of one plank in an upright manner, making the midship frame form the figure of a spade—the mark on cards known by that name.

They are built of several streaks securely lashed together with plaited coconut fibers. The keel pieces form the two lower streaks, on which another is raised and on it another that is mostly the wale—which falling as sudden as the quarter of a circle, the side is raised on its inner edge. Each streak consists of several pieces of three- or four-inch plank well lashed together, and the keel is generally composed of two or three lengths. Inside they have three or four timbers of the natural growth to answer for floors and timbers, or rather knees that are firmly lashed to each side as high as the wale.

The proa, or bow, projects with a great rake forward, having no stem, and is closed in with round pieces on the top. The topside is closed in with a square piece answering to the side, like the end of a chest, and in the same manner abaft, where the stern rises suddenly from a full buttock. Being closed in on the upper part, it forms a spire or cone regularly tapered to a point and becoming nearly round as it rises. On the bow and top of the stern are rude figures of men for ornament. The height of the bow is somewhat more than the level of the top of the gunwale, which is without sheer. The height of the stern is nearly twenty-four feet, the image being eighteen inches or two feet higher.

When the canoes are ready for putting together (for they cannot be used singly by reason of the narrowness of their construction), they are placed alongside at a regular distance fore and aft, which is commonly about six feet asunder. They are secured by eight- or ten-square beams of five or six inches square that are fixed on the upper part of the wale of each, at equal distance, and firmly lashed. They are partly let in to the wale and part into the topside, the whole being made secure by lashings.

The frame of the stage is laid with other strong beams on the top of the gunnel, projecting without the wales on either side, being about twenty feet wide and secured firmly to the lower beams by lashings. The stage is then laid with plank, like a deck, with scuttles, or openings, on each side, and in the middle for the paddlers, who are often one hundred and upward.

On the forepart of the stage, a breastwork of plank about four feet high is raised, over which the warriors fight. When they are equipped for war, the decks are filled with heaps and baskets of stones, and every paddler has a sling. They are often managed by sails, the masts being placed on steps on the top of the stage and supported by the rigging.

When under sail, it takes four men with long paddles to steer them and sail at a good rate in smooth water, but in rough weather, they make less way and more water, the motion making them soon leaky. When at sea they often keep six hands bailing with scoops, having no other method to free them of the water with which they are often filled by the surge rolling up between them. Nevertheless, they are in no danger of sinking but drive till they are freed. In port they are always forced to haul them up to prevent their sinking. When they sail in fleets, the chief's canoe has always an altar on board.

In these vessels they frequently go from island to island in large parties, sometimes ten or twelve sail. By means of them the ironwork left at Tahiti is distributed among all the islands they are acquainted with. In return they get pearls, pearl shells, etc. Some of the islands they sail to are at the distance of more than one hundred leagues.

The chief of Tyarrabboo keeps one of these vessels constantly plying between Tahiti and Myetoo, or Myetea, called by us Osnaburgh Island, twenty-seven leagues SE of Tahiti, which is subject to him. In her he sends ironwork and what European commodities he can raise as presents to the chiefs, who in return send back pearls; pearl shells; stools for seats; pillows and pudding stools made of tummannoo, with dishes and trays of the same wood; matting; and cloth, oil, hogs, etc. She seldom returns without a cargo.

By means of this island they have communication with several others to the NE of Tahiti. Taking the advantage of the northerly wind, they reach Myetoo, where they watch wind shifting to stretch to the northward to a group of small islands, the capital of which is called Tapoohoe. By their account, it appears to be the same Tapoohoe where the African *Galley*, one of Commodore Roggewein's squadron, was lost. (He was fitted out by the Dutch West India Company and passed these seas early in this century. His ships were afterwards seized by the governor of Batavia.) [Roggewein called the island on which his ship was wrecked (in 1722) Schaadelyk (Pernicious Island), in what was afterward known as the Palliser Group, the northwest islands of the Tuamotus, in about 16S, 146½W. This seems to be the group to which Morrison refers, while Myetoo is apparently Maitea (also known as Osnaburgh), which is approximately in the position given in the text.]

From this island the first iron was imported to Tahiti, and a beam of oak that we saw at Tetooroa (a number of small islands eight leagues north of Tahiti) is, I have no doubt, a part of that ship—which may account for their knowledge of the use of iron when that island was discovered. From the account of the natives—some of whom are now living who remember the loss of the ship, though they could form no idea of her but from the description of the natives of Tapoohoe—they saw the beam come on shore, which they supposed to be part of the ridge of a house.

It may seem strange to European navigators how these people find their way to such a distance without the help or knowledge of letters, figures, or instruments of any kind, other than their judgment and knowledge of the motion of the heavenly bodies. They are more expert and can give a better account of the stars that rise and set in their horizon than a European astronomer would be willing to believe. This is nevertheless a fact, and they can with amazing sagacity foretell by the appearance of the heavens, with great precision, when a change of the weather will take place and prepare for it accordingly. When they go to sea, they steer by the sun, moon, and stars, and shape their course with some degree of exactness.

At the distance of eight leagues N or N1/2W from Point Venus lie the islands of Tetooroa, in number ten, encompassed by a reef about ten or twelve leagues in circumference. They are all low and for the most part covered with coconut trees, which is all they produce. They are the property of Otoo's family, who keep the inhabitants in subjection by keeping them from planting the breadfruit or other trees. He suffers nothing to grow there except a few taro for his own use, under the charge of one of his favourites.

As these islands cannot be approached by large canoes, he makes them his warehouse for all his riches. A number of canoes are kept there for fishery, and nearly forty small sailing canoes that they haul over the reef are kept constantly plying between them and Tahiti. They bring fish for the king's household and return loaded with provisions.

Besides these, the dolphin canoes trade there when the dolphin fishery is over, carrying provisions and returning with oil, which they make in large quantities; a variety of fine fish; and a sauce made of ripe coconuts called tyeyro. The nuts are gathered before they are too old and grated in the same manner as for oil, which, being mixed with shrimps and left a day or two to ripen, becomes like curds and is excellent sauce for fish, pork, or fowl. This is also made at Tahiti, and a basket of it always accompanies a fish or hog when dressed for a feast; the nuts must not be too old or it will become oily and rank.

Their travelling canoes are different from those of the war build, having low sides, broad sterns, and a flat plank projecting over the stem, which is upright. They are about three feet deep, eighteen inches wide, and fifty or sixty feet long. The bottoms are flat and rounding, the sides flat and rather falling in, and the stern rising with a regular rake for ten or twelve feet—on the top of which are placed pieces of rude carved work of a cylindrical form, two or three feet high. They are hollow, and the open work represents rude figures of men supporting each other on their hands, forming several tiers and with some resemblance of an old round tower. The size of these denote the quality of the owners.

These canoes are also double, being secured by two or three strong bars lashed to the gunnels of each. On the broad planks of the bow, they fix a movable house or awning for the owner and his family to sit in out of the weather. Canoes of this size are paddled by twenty or thirty hands and answer the same purpose as a gentleman's coach in England; in them the people of note travel from place to place. They have these kind of different sizes. The small ones, some of which carry only one or two men, may be used double or single occasionally, with or without masts.

The single canoes have a float supported by two outriggers, one forward and one aft, the float being nearly the length of the canoe. These are chiefly used for fishing and other uses.

The canoes of this build used for sailing are nearly thirty feet long and are either double or single as the owner fancies. They are raised with washboards, and the masts stepped on crosspieces above all. The double ones have two masts, placed one in each canoe at equal distance, one from the stem and the other from the stern, and a like distance from each other, being nearly a third of the canoe's length. The masts are supported by the shrouds and stays, of which they have always one to shift to windward. On the masthead they have a kind of funnel basket fixed by way of ornament.

The sails are made of matting and are long and narrow, being mostly as long as the canoe and the mast one third shorter, the breadth not exceeding five or six feet. The foot of the sail is spread by a short, crooked boom having an elbow or knee on the after part, to which a spreet is securely lashed and to which the sail is laced all up the after leech. Being secured at the masthead by a rope to keep it from splitting the sail, it forms a sweep in which form the sail is cut. The end of the spreet comes directly over the masthead, where it is confined in the form of a fiddle bow by the rope that supports the weather leech of the sail. The sail, being extended on a frame, is quite flat, having no belly but what the wind gives it. At the spreet end hangs a long pendant of feathers, woven on three lines that reach the heel of the mast.

The sheet is generally made fast to the splice or joint of the boom and spreet and is at the command of the man who steers if it is a single canoe. In a double canoe, they must have others to attend them. The sails of the war canoes are made in the same manner, but they, being larger, have a frame ladder to go to the masthead. The others have only a few short sticks seized across the mast to get up to fasten the sail and the line that keeps the spreet in its place.

The single canoes rigged for sailing have only one mast and are rigged with a large float parallel to their keel or middle line. Two-thirds of her length from the side is supported by an outrigger, a little before the midships, consisting of several strong pieces or spars of a proper size, steadied by a single one from the stern to keep it fore and aft.

On the top of the fore-outrigger the mast stands, and two soars are fixed one-third of the canoe's length, supporting a stage of two planks on the opposite side to the outrigger. These also serve to support the mast by making the shrouds fast to them. On this stage they sit when fishing for dolphin or keep their dry clothes on when sailing.

These canoes have washboards of twelve or fourteen inches as well as the double ones, and are preferred to them for fishing. None of them will sail at a great rate, seldom going more than five or six knots per hour. If the floats are not straight or well adjusted, which is sometimes the case, they will not sail so well as that.

They have no method of reducing their sails but by casting off the lower part and rolling it up; should that not answer, as it frequently will not, they must take their chance. As they cannot reduce the sail at head but by casting it off entirely, for which purpose a man must go to the masthead, it would be next to impossible to get them up again from the quick motion of the canoe. For this reason, they let them stand at all events and had rather overset or lose the mast than strike the sail. In squally weather, both these accidents often happen. They are so accustomed to them that they think nothing of either, though by being dismasted they are frequently blown off and heard of no more.

When they are taken in a squall, they luff head to it and shake it out, but should the squall continue too long and the vessel is like to fall off, all hands jump overboard and hang her head to windward till the squall is over, when they get in and steer their course. Should they not be able to hold her on and she gets overset, their first care is to secure everything and make their fish, cloth, paddles, etc., fast.

When the squall is past, they tow the canoe round with the masthead to windward, and making a line fast to the upper part of the spreet, all hands get on the outrigger. Hauling the head of the spreet out of the water, the wind getting under the sail lifts it, when they all swing off with their whole weight together and right her. Some hands then keep her head to windward till the others free her of the water, and then get in and proceed on their voyage.

This frequently happens on their return from fishing, when they endeavour to outcarry each other till they are overpowered by the wind and get overset. Of this they think the danger so little that they never require any assistance except to take in their cloth or such things as may receive damage by being long wet. They frequently lose so much ground as to be forced to run for Morea and sometimes for Hooaheine and Ryeatea, and we have known some of them, who being dismasted, have been nine, twelve, and fifteen days at sea with scarce a mouthful of provisions and no water. They seldom carry more than a few coconuts and a breadfruit or two, sufficient to serve as long as they intend to stay out, and trust to Providence for fish.

Those who sail in the large canoes are better provided and are in no danger of such distress as they can never overset. Should they carry away their masts, they are better able to get them put to rights again, having plenty of cordage and mats to repair the damages.

In building their canoes, they hollow out the bottom or keel pieces, and having fitted them, they smear each part of the butt with pitch made from the gum of the breadfruit tree. This is wrapped round a number of candlenuts reeved on sticks for the purpose, and being lighted and held over a tray of water, the pitch drops in. It is then taken out of the water and made up in balls fit for use.

With this, as said before, they smear the edges and butts of the plank, and having a quantity of coconut fibers beaten up like oakum, they lay it between the pieces. Bringing them together with sets and wedges, they lash the parts firmly together with plait made of the same. After they have passed as many turns as the holes will admit, they caulk them with more of the beaten fibers. Over the seams in the wake of the lashing, they spread more pitch and oakum and lay a piece of bamboo split and soaked for the purpose.

Having formed the bottom they proceed to bring on the next piece, or streak, pitching the seams and securing it as before. They never pay the bottom or sides, though it would be of much service to them, but they cannot bear to touch the pitch. This would be often the case, as they haul all their canoes up as soon as they land.

They have no rule for building but the eye, and have no idea of working by a line. Nevertheless, some of them are built with as much exactness as if they had been planned by able builders. According to the opinion of some good workmen, they are well finished.

The war canoes are built by levying contributions, as are those made as presents to the Deity that are occasionally used for that purpose. These are, in fact, built only by the contrivance of the priests who are in the interest of the king. He tells the other chiefs that the Deity wants such a number of canoes of such a size, and they set about building them immediately.

Each chief who has one to build calls the towhas and ratirras together to a feast, informs them of the request of the Deity, and asks them to collect hogs, cloth, oil, etc., to pay the carpenters, to which they readily agree. The carpenters who are employed go into the mountains and mark their trees. The ratirra on whose land the trees happen to be sends hands to assist in cutting them down, hewing out the pieces in the rough according to the carpenters' directions that it may be the easier brought down. They form each part out of a solid tree and often at some miles distance in the hills.

When they have enough collected to make a beginning, they fix a day to fetch them down, and a house is erected to build the canoe in. When the timber is brought down, a feast is made and an offering of a hog to the Deity to prosper the work. A feast is also made for the workmen. At every piece they make fast, and when the bottom is completed, a grand feast and offering is made. This is repeated at the finishing of every streak till the whole is complete, when a greater feast is made.

The canoes being dressed with cloth, breastplates, red and black feathers, fine matting, etc., they are brought to the grand morai. A man is killed and put on board and offered as a sacrifice. The canoes are hauled up near the morai, where she is covered with thatch till wanted. The priests secure the feathers for the Deity and the other decorations for the king, to whom they are presented in form, as said before. The eye of each sacrifice is presented before him and the body interred in the morai. The war canoes are offered in like manner, but hogs serve instead of men.

When sacrifices are wanted for such occasions, the chief assembles the ratirras at the morai and a feast is made, at which none must be present but those who are by birth entitled to give their opinion. He then informs them of the business, which they however know beforehand. They then agree among themselves about the fittest man. If any have been guilty of blasphemy or has been a most notorious thief and has escaped punishment, they fix on him.

One of themselves undertakes to kill him and watches his opportunity, the business being mostly kept a secret till he is killed, which is generally in the night. The man appointed to kill him, finding where he sleeps, knocks him in the head with a stone and gets his servants to make a large basket of coconut leaves, into which they put the body and convey it to the canoe to be offered into which they put it. They are careful not to disfigure the face, as that would make it unfit for an offering, and another must be got instead. For this reason they mostly strike them on the back of the head or neck.

If they can find none whose crimes deserve death, they tell the chief and a hog must be killed instead. They will not kill a man to gratify a private pique of any man, even if the chief insists upon it. If he persists in having one, he must kill him himself, and should he be killed in the attempt, the man killing him comes to no harm.

If such a thing is insisted on, they never fail to give notice that such as think themselves in danger may keep out of the way. Should any man be killed without sufficient cause (though they never admit them to be present at their trial), his friends instantly make war on the offenders. But if he is known to be guilty of the crimes laid to his charge, no notice is taken of it, as every one deems it right. The man who kills him is justified as having been the executor of justice.

If a man of property is found guilty of a crime that deserves death, he is punished as well as the poorest in the island. We saw an instance of this at the time the Young King was invested with the royal marro. One of the first men in Morea was sacrificed for attempting to stop the flag from passing through his land on that island.

During the celebration of that ceremony, numbers of human sacrifices were made. Many who knew themselves guilty took sanctuary about our houses, where they knew themselves perfectly safe, as they knew our aversion to such horrid practices. But we could not protect all, though we often tried in vain to dissuade the chiefs to drop their barbarous customs, who always gave for answer, "If we do there will be no chiefs." However, we protected all who took sanctuary with us, and though surrounded by the most notorious thieves on the island, our property was always safe.

But this was only a temporary respite, as they seldom fail at one time or other to be found, and should they fly from one district to another, their character always follows them. Should a sacrifice be wanting, the chief of the district in which they have taken shelter always points them out before one of his own people, by which means he secures the love of his own and is dreaded by others.

If a man under such circumstances submits himself to be bit by a woman so as to draw blood, he is thereby rendered unfit for a sacrifice and saves his life—but can never be admitted to partake of any religious ceremony, being ever after deemed on an equality with women's food, and must be a woman's servant ever after. They never sacrifice a woman, nor is she or any of her servants, as before said, permitted to be present at or partake of a feast made on the morai; nor must she eat of any food that has been touched by a sacred person, though it were her own husband.

In their common way of life, their food is the animals and vegetables before described, but is chiefly vegetables and fish, of which they have an abundance. Their cookery is simply baking and broiling, having no vessel that will stand fire; nor do they understand the method of converting clay to that use. However, they lose little or none of the substance of their food by baking, and fish dressed in that manner are preferable to boiled.

The men and women eat separately, and for this reason each family has two houses, except when a man chooses to reside in his wife's house, and then each takes one end.

The children eat with the mother till their restrictions are taken off, though she cannot eat of the food that is the child's or that it has touched. The child's provisions must not enter the house by the same entrance at which the mother's come in. When traveling they must have separate canoes for the men's and women's food, of which the children may partake.

The women have their own particular trees for bread and can eat no other, and must have particular people to catch fish for them. Should a shark, turtle, porpoise, albacore, dolphin, or cavally, which are sacred fish, be caught by their fishermen, they cannot eat of them but may dispose of them to whom they please.

It has been supposed by most former voyagers that they were also forbidden to eat pork, but in this they were most certainly mistaken. If any woman has an inclination to keep her hogs penned up and prevent them from feeding on any other ground than their own, they may eat pork. As this is troublesome (and should the hogs get loose and run on the land of their male relations, they become unfit for them to eat, or should any of their male relations or the chiefs touch the hogs, it is the same) and attended with difficulty, they seldom attempt it.

They have the greatest variety and abundance of fine fish. Nevertheless, they often kill and eat pork under that denomination, taking care to keep such men as are not of their retinue out of the secret. Their servants, always agreeing on this score, are sure not to want for part of what the mistress possesses.

The men may partake of any of the women's food but must not touch any but what is given them. Though they enter the eating house of their wives, they must not touch any of her culinary utensils. Otherwise, she must not use them again, but he may apply them to his own use. Then she must provide herself with a new set or as many as he has touched.

No woman can eat in a house where a chief has been unless she is of the same rank and authority with him; then she may eat in his presence. If any woman of inferior rank should trespass in eating in any house, canoe, or ship where a chief has been, they would not only be severely striped but lose their possessions. For this reason they are careful how they infringe on these laws, as they know that few are given to keep a secret—for which reason they always refuse to eat when invited before men, but would take the food offered them and give it to their relations. This may also account for a number of the chief women who refused to dine at table, yet ate hearty with the servants.

They eat fish of all kinds that the sea or rivers produce, as they hold that nothing unclean can be the produce of water. From our being so fond of flesh they at first conceived that we were cannibals, as they have an account of the inhabitants of an island to the east of them who eat each other. It was with some difficulty that we were able to persuade them to the contrary, as they were in some measure confirmed in their opinion by Brown (the man left by Captain Cox), who threatened to put a child into the oven. The mother of it could never be persuaded to believe that he was not in earnest and would never suffer the child near him afterwards. They were also further confirmed, as some of our people had said foolishly that they had eaten part of a man.

They make three regular meals in a day when at home and eat hearty, and nothing can give them more satisfaction than to see a stranger do the like when they invite them to eat. This they are ever ready to do, always parting with what they have cheerfully, be it little or much.

When they are from home and numbers are met in one district, provisions grow scarce from the rahooe before described, and they are sometimes whole days without any. When they get any, they eat so large a quantity as would readily give a stranger an idea that they were mere gluttons. It would certainly appear more so to those who were perhaps sated with the abundance of good provisions around them, which these people had most likely stinted themselves to supply them with. They always endeavour to surpass each other in their presents and giving away what they stand in immediate need of themselves.

In general, they cannot be called (except at such times) immoderate eaters, though their method of stuffing their mouths as full as they can hold has the appearance of it.

They sit cross-legged, and having a place spread with leaves for a tablecloth (often under the shade of a tree in fine weather), they sit at a distance to prevent offending each other by flapping the flies away, which are often troublesome. They are always swarming where any provisions are, especially fish, which draws whole swarms about them.

Having some clean leaves laid for platter and dishes, the provisions are set before them. They cut their meat or fish with a piece of bamboo or knife and put it into a coconut shell with salt water and the sauce before described. Having washed their hands in another shell, they proceed, sucking the flesh or fish and repeatedly dipping it in the sauce, eating large quantities of breadfruit or taro, and drinking clean water or coconut milk.

After their pork or fish is done, they have a sort of pudding made of breadfruit called popoe, of which each has a shell. They then wash their hands and mouths, using a piece of the husk of the young coconut to clean their teeth, of which they are particularly careful.

When they drink yava, they are forced to eat as fast as possible after it, or they would not be able to eat at all, as it takes such immediate effect. It is no disgrace for either men or women to be intoxicated with this root, but the women seldom take the pains to cultivate it, and the chief women who use it can procure it without that trouble.

They have several sorts of puddings besides the popoe, the method of making which is this: The popoe is made of baked breadfruit and mahee (breadfruit of the last season made into sour paste) beaten together on a stool with a stone, both kept for the purpose. It is mixed with water, and when done is not unlike what we call flummery, and is eaten with water or coconut milk. It is made of either separately, but the mixture is preferred by most, and it is excellent food that may be made either hot or cold.

Another sort is made with the mountain plantains mixed with mahee, which when made ready is equal to, if not superior to, gooseberry fool and may be made of any consistency, either for knife or spoon. This is called popoe payee.

Paypay is another sort made of the breadfruit that gets too ripe or falls from the tree, which, being beaten up with coconut milk and baked, is delicious food.

Poe atdutarre is another sort made of the breadfruit before it gets too ripe— which, being baked and the core and rind taken away (as for any other use it is), is mixed with juice squeezed from hard coconuts, which is white and thick as cream. Wrapped in plantain leaves, it is put into the oven and baked again.

Poe parro is made by grating the taro down on a rough stone and mixing it with some of its own young leaves and sweet herbs, along with the juice of the ripe coconut.

Poe peea is made in the same manner by mixing the juice of the coconut as before, the nut being grated as for oil, and the juice wrung out with the mo'oo, which serves as a strainer on all occasions. This is mixed in a tray, and they throw in some hot stones, which harden it in the same manner as batter is hardened in a frying pan. If this is eaten in large quantities, it causes giddiness in the head for some time after, though it has no bad effect attending it.

Another method of dressing the peea, which takes off the cause of the giddiness, is by mixing the peea and the grated nut together with water and baking them in the oven. When done this way, its taste and appearance is not unlike a yeast dumpling, but somewhat sweeter.

Tooparroo, or teaparroo, is an excellent pudding made of taro (or breadfruit), ripe plantains, and coconuts grated and squeezed and wrung out as before. The whole is strained through the mo'oo (or fibers of the stem of the cyprus grass) to take out the strings of the plantains, and being baked in leaves is as good as a custard. The juice of the coconut being mixed with some of the milk answers the purpose of milk and butter; the milk, being tart, takes off the luscious sweetness of the plantains and gives the whole a pleasant taste.

As they make this in large quantities, they make the leaves of the plantain tough to contain it by searing them over the fire. Tying up five or six quarts in a bundle, it is put it in the oven, where it remains all night. When taken out, it is put by for use and will keep for several weeks.

As they seldom have plantains sufficiently ripe for this purpose, they gather them a few days beforehand and bury them in the earth (with some ripe palm nuts, which gives them a fine flavour), putting grass all round them to keep the dirt from them. In this manner they ripen all their fruit when they have not sufficient for their purpose ripe on the tree.

They have a superstitious notion that should they bathe in the sea while the plantains are in the earth, that they would never ripen properly—this only extends to the person who puts them in the earth—nor could we persuade them out of this foolish notion, though we showed them to the contrary. They always insisted that we had more than common power to prevent the fruit from spoiling. Though we persuaded them to try, they still affirmed that it was on our account and that were they to try it, the fruit would certainly spoil or rot before it was ripe.

They get fire by rubbing two sticks (commonly dry poorow, but breadfruit or any other dry wood will answer the purpose) together thus: They take a long piece sufficiently large that they may hold it fast by sitting with their feet on it. They cut a groove on the upper part five or six inches long, with a shell to receive the point of a smaller piece that they hold between their hands, and begin chanting a prayer (without which they suppose they could not get the fire).

They rub the point of the small piece in the groove of the larger one and, shoving from them, increase their motion from a slow, easy stroke to a quick, smart one. The dust made by the friction takes fire, which they put into a leaf with some dry grass and wave it about till it communicates to the whole, when they have more leaves and wood to make their fire.

When they make an oven, they make a hole in the earth of a proportional size to the provision they have to dress. Making their fire, they build it up with wood that they pile round with stones, throwing the bottom ones up as the top falls in till the wood is all burnt to coals and the stones red hot. They then level the stones, and the coals being free from smoke, they spread the oven over with leaves or the trunk of the plantain.

The provisions, being wrapped in and covered with leaves, are covered with grass, the earth thrown up on the top, and the provisions left to bake a proper time, according to the quantity. Meanwhile, those who were employed at it go to the water and wash themselves all over. When the oven is opened, it is done so carefully that the least particle of earth or sand does not come to the provisions, which are taken out clean and well dressed.

They are very expeditious in preparing their food and will dress a hog whole (which they always do, never cutting them to pieces till they are baked) and let it be sufficiently well done in two hours, though it were three hundred pounds weight. They like their food well dressed, though they frequently eat fish raw. When they dress a large hog for a small company, they never dress it thoroughly, so the visitors may not have it spoiled for a second dressing, as they always take away whatever has been provided for them.

When they kill a hog, they strangle or drown it; the former method is preferred and is done by putting a rope round its neck that they heave up with a stick or lever till the hog is choked. They then stop its nose, fundament, etc., with leaves or grass, and the animal expires after a few struggles. They then wet it all over and lay it on the fire, or make a fire round it, if it be large, with dry leaves and grass, scraping it clean with sticks and coconut shells.

Then they take it to the water and scrub it clean with rough stones, open the belly with a piece of split bamboo or knife, and take out the bowels and blood, which, having burst its vessels, runs out of the flesh and is found in the belly. With the blood they mix the fat of the guts, putting it into coconut shells with hot stones into it and making a kind of black pudding. This serves the cooks with some other fragments for a relish while dinner is dressing.

The hog is washed clean and laid on leaves till the oven is ready. The pluck is either broiled or washed and wrapped in leaves and put in the oven. The guts are also cleaned and baked, and as they have plenty of assistance, the whole is soon ready. The guts, being kept fast to the craw, are ripped from end to end and well washed. They are laid on the hot stones to scald, being shifted alternately from the stones to the water, till they are perfectly sweet and clean. Wrapped in leaves, the whole is put in the oven with split and scraped breadfruit, which is all the preparation it wants; taro; mahee; etc.; and covered up as before.

In this manner they dress all their food. The breadfruit will broil or roast on the fire, which method they use for a small quantity. Fish wrapped in the breadfruit leaves and put on the fire are better than boiled, being dressed by their own moisture, which is prevented from evaporating by the leaves—which have as much substance as those of a cabbage. If they have a pig of ten or twelve pounds to bake, they will dress it sufficiently in half an hour.

In the time of gathering in the harvest of bread for store, they make an oven in which they bake fifteen or twenty hundredweight of bread, which when baked becomes sweet like gingerbread. Of this they make a sweet pudding, and on this the children (male and female of or belonging to the family who make it) feast while it lasts, which is generally six weeks or two months.

During this time they are kept covered from the sun and are restricted within their respective bounds, which are houses fenced round in squares for that purpose. At the end of that time they are liberated, but are so fat that they can scarce breathe, and are some weeks before they can walk any distance. During this time they lose the tanned colour of their skin and assume their own natural one, which is agreeably fair and clear. They are so tender that the sun scalds them as fast as it would the fairest European, and those who expose themselves to the weather soon alter their complexion.

When a chief or ratirra wants one of these ovens of bread made, they inform their tenants, who go in a body and bring wood from the mountains. Meanwhile, others collect the stones, and while the fire is burning, every man brings his load of bread, which is put into the oven whole and without further preparation. It is covered with leaves, thatched over with grass, and the earth thrown up over it. They do not open it for three or four days, when they take it out for use every day as it is wanted, keeping it covered till the whole is expended. They repeat this every harvest. The bread thus dressed is called opeeo, has a very agreeable taste, and the colour is changed to brown throughout.

The poorer people are not excluded from this method of feasting their children, though they have not sufficient bread for the purpose. They have to do nothing more than signify their intention to their neighbours, who bring their proportions of bread and assist them to collect wood and make their oven. Sometimes they join two families, making one oven between them.

At this season they make their mahee, a sour paste made by fermenting the ripe breadfruit, by which means they keep it till next harvest. While the bread (which they have the whole year round, but not in such plenty as to serve) is scarce, it may be eaten by itself or by being beaten up in puddings. When mixed with the new bread, it makes the best popoe.

The process of making it is this: The bread being gathered in, they scrape off the rind with shells ground sharp for the purpose and lay it in heaps to grow mellow, where it lays for three or four days. Pits are then made in or near their houses, and being well lined with grass and leaves, the bread is thrown in, being first split in pieces with a wooden adze made for that use. They include a few of the ripe fruit that have fallen from the tree to hasten the fermentation, and the pits, being filled and heaped up, are covered with leaves and grass and large stones put on the top to press it into the pits. In this manner it ferments, and when it settles, they shift the leaves that are bad. Taking the core or hearts out, they fill one pit out of another and cover it up for use.

Some take out the hearts at first, but though that method renders the mahee whiter than the other, yet the bread will not ferment so soon without the assistance of some old mahee, nor will it keep so well. The men and women, each having their own trees, have also their own mahee, and should a man who is not the servant of a woman touch even the covering of the woman's mahee, it is rendered unfit for her use. This accounts for Sir Joseph Banks's having spoiled a quantity that belonged to a woman by his wanting to see the nature of the process of making it and examining the contents of the pit—which was not only rendered of no use to the woman, but the place in which it was underwent the same fate, and no woman could ever use it afterwards.

If the crop on any individual's land should run short of his expectation and he has not sufficient to make as much mahee as he wants or thinks will serve, he makes a number of garlands of a shrub called pirreepirree and takes one to every house or as many as he thinks proper. He throws them in without saying anything except to tell the day he intends to send for it or have it brought home, everyone knowing what the garland means.

If he has hands sufficient to scrape the whole at once, it is brought home to the house, each man bringing the garland left at his house as full of bread as it can be made fast. Laying it down at the door, he returns without any further ceremony than bidding God bless his work.

If he has not sufficient help to take the whole in hand at once, he makes it known and either goes himself for it when he wants it or has it brought at the time he nominates to those who supply him—who are ever ready to assist every man according to his abilities. If he goes for it himself, he always finds the garlands already filled at the appointed time.

By this method of assisting each other, they never feel the least inconvenience from having a scanty crop. If a chief wants a supply for the purpose of making mahee, he sends a bit of coconut leaf to all, or as many of the inhabitants of his district as he shall think proper. On the appointed day they bring each a load, which is generally accompanied with a hog by some and fish by others, according to their several abilities. But this they have seldom occasion to do as they are always well supplied, and when supplies are raised this way, the people bring it in such a manner as bespeaks at once their regard for their chiefs and fear of displeasing them—always testifying their sorrow that he should be so far neglected as to have the trouble of sending for bread.

They make an offering of their first fruits to the chiefs besides those made to the Deity. This ceremony is called eehee aree and is thus performed: The fruits being ripe, the towha, or lord of the manor, informs the ratirras, or squires, that on such a day the offering is to be made. It is proclaimed throughout the district by a crier to inform their respective tenants, the mattaeyna or mannahownes, who on the day appointed each gather some of every species. Having put them into a basket that is hung round with a piece of cloth, it is tied to a pole, which is balanced on their shoulder by a suckling pig hung by one foot to the other end.

They repair to the house of their respective ratirras, who then head their own people and proceeds to the house of the towha, who with his priest and orator heads the whole. The procession proceeds to the house of the chief, sometimes four or five hundred in a body.

When they arrive, the towha, by means of his priest and orator (who always attend on such occasions), makes a peace offering of a young pig, a plantain tree, and a small tuft of red feathers. These the priest offers, as usual, and the orator makes a long speech on behalf of the towha and ratirras, expressing their loyalty and the love they have for their chief. The ratirras having, by means of their priests (each family having one or more in or depending on it), made their peace offering, the fruits are deposited before the chief and they retire and return home. When this ceremony is performed for the king, the chiefs of the district always head the procession.

This ceremony is then performed by the ratirras for their respective towha and afterwards by the tenants for their ratirras, after which they carry in as much bread as they think will be sufficient. They put it in large baskets made of coconut leaves, which when filled are as much as two men can carry. With each they send a small fish, intimating that they do not offer bread alone, along with a baked hog and several small baskets of bread, taro, coconuts with the husks peeled off, plantains, etc. These are carried to the house of the chief, towha, or ratirra, each in their due proportion.

They are continually making such presents as this to their chiefs, etc., and never send a fish, hog, or fowl without a proper quantity of vegetables with them. When the bread is scarce, they substitute mahee, in lieu, though they always have some. The mahee, being wrought up like dough, is rolled up in leaves to the size of a penny loaf or roll and baked with the other provisions. Payee, or mountain plantains, are also substituted for bread, and when gathered green answer very well, being much superior to the common plantain to eat as bread.

They often go into the mountains, in companies, to cut timber, gather herbs and sandalwood for their oil, cut rafters for their houses, paddles for canoes, etc., and for the purpose of dying cloth, which takes them several days. There, they subsist on birds, fish, etc., using the mountain plantain and wild roots for bread. The land produces plenty of birds and the springs plenty of fish.

They catch the birds by fixing the gum of the breadfruit on long bamboos, and setting them up, take the birds that perch on them as we do with birdlime. Others who are used to this method of living can, with much exactness, knock them down with a stone that they throw by hand. They point at the bird with the forefinger of the left hand, as it were to take aim, while the stone is prepared in the right. If the birds are sitting they seldom fail to bring it down, but cannot bring one off the wing.

When a party goes into the mountains on any of the aforesaid occasions, their first care is to send a party in search of provisions (as they never carry any with them), while others erect huts for their lodgings made of reeds and covered with the leaves of the tee. Others procure fire and fuel. As they seldom take the trouble to make an oven, they roast their roots and plantains and dress their fish or birds in pieces of green bamboos.

The provisions, being put into the bamboo and stopped up with leaves, are laid on the fire and kept turning round like a spit till the contents are sufficiently dressed. The moisture inside keeping the bamboo wet, it keeps its form though burnt nearly to pieces. In this manner they live when on these excursions, and though they have hard labour in hand, they turn the work into pleasure. Taking no thought for tomorrow, they leave off and return when they think proper.

As they are very fond of the tail feathers of the tropic birds, which they esteem for dressing their parais, or mourning dress, they go two together to hunt for them.

As the birds build in the face of the highest cliffs, it takes much trouble to get them. Their method is this: The bird catchers are provided each with ten or twelve fathoms of rope of sufficient strength to bear their own weight, and having fixed their place of abode near the cliff, where provisions are in the greatest plenty, they proceed together to the top of the cliff.

Bending their ropes together, they make fast a stick of eighteen or twenty inches long by the middle and lower it over the face of the cliff, having a stake fixed to make it fast to on the top. If a tree is not convenient, one hand then stays by the rope to haul up or lower down as the other shall order, who goes down. Seating himself on the cross stick, he swings from hole to hole in search of the birds, holding on by the points of the stones that project or the shrubs that grow among the fissures of the cliff.

When he catches a bird, he hauls out the tail feathers, which he secures in a bamboo that he carries for the purpose, and lets the bird fly. Having examined all the holes within his reach, or if he tires in the search, he goes up and either shifts the rope to another part or attends it for his partner, who takes a spell.

Though this may appear dangerous to us, it is no more than amusement to them and seldom attended with any accident—though they hang some hours in this manner, sometimes twenty, thirty, or forty fathoms from the top, and often four times that from the bottom. Sometimes they do not get a single feather in a whole day's search.

The shining black feathers of the man-o'-war birds they also hold in high esteem, for which reason they always watch their coming, as they seldom visit this island except when the westerly winds and thick weather prevail. They afford diversion for numbers as they are only to be caught at the beach, or when it happens to fall calm, when they perch on the coconut trees. Then they are caught by a snare fixed to the end of a long stick, with which a man goes up and puts the noose over the bird's neck while it is asleep.

This happens a few minutes after it lights, and letting the stick go, it brings the bird to the ground. While they keep on the wing, they entice them down by a fish into which they thrust a piece of poorow to float it and throw it into the water. They keep it within reach of their wands, of which each man has one of fourteen or sixteen feet long. As soon as the birds observe the fish, they instantly make towards it, sometimes eight or ten together, and the men stand by and knock them down as they attempt to seize the fish—which they all attempt to do. If they do not receive a blow before they get near enough, these birds always seize their prey in their claws, which are long, sharp, and webbed only to the first joint.

They are inhabitants of the low, uninhabited islands in the neighbourhood of the Society Isles, and never come from home but in thick weather. Their feathers are held in such esteem that the natives will give a hog of one hundred pound weight for one of them, for making their war and heiva dresses, etc. They never eat the bird. During our time we shot several that were deemed grand presents; but we thought the powder of more value, and therefore made but little waste of it for that use, and seldom took that expensive diversion. The cock birds are the most valuable, and the back feathers are those they prize highest for their beautiful shining black.

DRESS, ETC.
The dress of both sexes is nearly the same, except that the women's lower garments are somewhat longer than the men's; being put on in a kind of neat negligence, together with the cleanness of their clothes, sets them off to great advantage. As they wash regularly three times a day, they are free from any disagreeable smell, and a stranger suffers nothing but heat in the midst of a thousand of them.

Their clothing when put on has some resemblance to the dress of the natives of Peru and Chile, from whence it is possible that it might originally have come. The present natives of these islands are known to drive about those seas to the distance of some hundreds of leagues and might in all probability have been at first driven from the continent to these islands—first to these near the continent and afterwards to the more leeward ones.

It consists of square pieces, and the men's dress is first a long, narrow piece called marro, which passes between the thighs and round the waist. One end hangs down near the knees before and the other, being tucked in behind, hangs down in the same manner, serving for breeches. This is made either of cloth or matting for dry and wet weather. The oblong piece is two yards long and one to half a one wide, in the center of which is a slit to let the head pass through; it hangs down before and behind. This is also of cloth or matting and is called teeboota. A square piece is doubled so as to pass once and a half round the middle over the ends of the teeboota, which is tucked in on one hip, and hangs as low as the knees. When worn by women it is to the midleg or ankle; this is called parew. Round the waist they wear a sash or girdle made of braided hair, and wrought into a network called tamow.

All these are common to both sexes except the marro, which the women never wear but when they are fishing or at wrestling—when they are in danger of having their parew hauled off. In lieu of the marro they wear a shorter parew by way of an inside petticoat, and a large piece of cloth by way of a cloak, consisting of several fathoms folded up in a square. Over their eyes they wear a kind of shade like the forepart of a bonnet made of coconut leaves, which they weave in a few minutes and change several times in a day; they never carry one of them over sacred ground. For these shades, which they call tow matta (the same name they give our hats), they prefer the yellow leaves to the green and are proud to get one of that kind. Sometimes they must tear it in pieces in half an hour after they have made it and look for another.

These and garlands of flowers are the only things they ever wear on their heads, except at heivas, and then none can wear anything on their heads but the performers, who wear a kind of turban. Every other person must be uncovered in presence of a chief. In war or mourning the men may wear turbans and other headdresses made of wickerwork, covered and decorated with feathers, and breastplates of the same work. They are ornamented with dog's hair, pearl shells, shark's teeth, red and black feathers, garlands of feathers, etc. The heiva dress shall be described in its place.

They have also garlands for mourning made of the fibers of the coconut, curiously plaited, in which they fix the fingernails of their departed friends, with bits of pearl shells cut into many forms; of these they are particularly careful. The children of both sexes go naked till they are five or six years old, and at about thirteen or fourteen the males cut their foreskin, not from any religious custom but from a notion of cleanliness. It is split only on the upper part with a shark's tooth, and after the blood is stopped by putting ashes on the wound, it is suffered to get well as it may, and nothing more being applied. It is sometimes a month or more before it gets well, though their flesh in general heals quickly.

This, like the tattooing or puncturing their hips, etc., is at their own option; but a person who is deficient of either is reproached and told of it in public, and it is as bad to lack these marks as it would be among us not to be christened or to go naked, though some want both. They have their tattooing begun about the same age, and both these offices are performed by a particular set of men who make it a trade, subsisting partly by it and always getting well paid for their work.

The instruments used for the tattooing are made of hog's tusks fixed to a handle in the form of a hoe, the instruments being of different sizes and having from three to thirty-six teeth about one eighth of an inch long. These they strike in with a little paddle made for the purpose. When they tattoo or puncture the skin, they dip the teeth of the instrument into a mixture of soot (prepared from the candlenut) and water, which being struck into the skin leaves the mark of a black or bluish colour. With this the hips of both sexes are marked with four or five arched lines on each side, the uppermost taking the whole sweep of the hip from the hipbone to the middle of the back. There, the two lines meet on one that is drawn right across from one hipbone to the other, and on this all the other lines begin and end.

Under this centerline are generally four or five more sweeping downwards. Most women have that part blacked all over with the tattooing, but everyone pleases their own fancy in the number of lines or the fashion of them. Some make only one broad one, while others have five or six small ones ornamented with stars and sprigs, etc.

They also mark their feet, legs, thighs, arms, etc., but the women never mark higher than their ankle, and few mark their arms. They have only some fancy spots on their hands, and it is accounted foolishness to have any other marks except those on the posteriors, feet, and hands; but in men it is taken no notice of.

The tools used for the first time on a chief or the heir of a large family must be destroyed as soon as they are done with and deposited in the morai. When all the amoas (except those of marriage or friendship) are performed, they receive a small spot on the inside of each arm, just above the bend of the elbow. This signifies that they are free to eat and drink of their parents' food and that their parents may eat of theirs. This mark they never receive till these rites are performed, nor is it always done at the time of the last being performed.

The tattooing is performed at the pleasure of the parties who have it done and will not suffer the performer to leave off while they can bear a stroke. Sometimes they make such lamentation while they endure the pain that a stranger would suppose it was being done against their will and that they were forced to suffer it contrary to their inclination. The young females are more remarkable for bearing it than the males, though they cannot suffer more than one side to be done at a time. The other side may remain perhaps for twelve months before it is finished, till which time they never conceive themselves company for women—being only counted as children till they have their tattooing done.

While the girls are having it done, they are always attended by some of their female relations, who hold them while they struggle with the pain and keep their clothes from being kicked off. Should they from their tears draw pity on themselves, and the person who holds them should persuade them to leave off, they are often in such a passion as to strike even their mother if she should happen to be performing that office. This she must not return on pain of death. They often suffer so much to be done at once (through their pride, it being a disgrace to give out till one side is finished), as throws them into a fever.

EXERCISES AND DIVERSIONS

They have several exercises of which wrestling and throwing the javelin are the most common. They are very expert wrestlers, both men and women, but never box, though this diversion is common at Ryeatea and the other islands. When they assemble to wrestle, as they do at all public feasts, a ring is made, into which the wrestlers walk round, clapping with the right hand on the bend of the left arm, which is bent so as to bring the hand to the breast, making a loud din. If anyone has a mind to accept the challenge, he returns it with a clap and puts himself in a posture to receive his opponent; they close immediately.

If either finds the other too strong for him, he signifies it, and they part. If not, one must fall, and the women of the victor's party strike up a dance and song, the victor clapping round the ring till another takes him up. The vanquished retires peaceably, thinking nothing of his disgrace. They generally wrestle one district against another, and the women always wrestle first, but are more vicious than the men and cannot bear to be worsted. At this sport Eddea and her sister are always first and often come off with victory. Eddea always directs the ceremony and fixes the number of falls that must be wrestled, and whichever side attains the number first is declared victorious.

The wrestling being finished, dancing takes place among the women, and the men go to throw the javelin.

Their javelins are from eight to sixteen feet long, being made of wands of poorow with the bark stripped off and pointed with the fwharra, or palm tree. With these they heave at a mark at thirty or forty yards distance with great exactness and count their game by the uppermost javelin that has held in the mark, which is mostly part of the plantain stock. Their method of throwing is underhanded, poising the javelin on the forefinger of the left hand while they send it home with the right—or the contrary if left-handed. The women also play at this game but never for any wager. The district in which they play always provides a feast.

Another diversion is with bows made of poorow and arrows of bamboo pointed with toa. With these they shoot for distance or up the side of a hill without any mark. After this game they have also a feast made as before. The women shoot as well as the men but by themselves, and those who follow it must have clothing sacred to the game that must not be worn at any other time. For this reason it is left chiefly for those of rank who can pay the proper attention to it; these bows are for diversion only.

They practice the quarter staff from their youth, are well versed in the use of it, and defend themselves amazingly well—it being no honour to receive a wound in war except from a spear, and even them they hide as much as possible.

They also practice the sling and will throw a stone with some exactness and great force. The sling is made of plaited coconut fibers, having a broad part woven in the center to contain the stone (which is mostly of the size of a hen's egg). There is a loop at one end to put over their wrist to keep it from flying away when they let go the other end. When they throw a stone, they keep the sling across their shoulders and with their thumb keep the stone in its place, when by a quick motion let go the stone. At the same time they jump off their feet and, grasping the right wrist in the left hand, swing the stone three times round their head before they discharge it. It flies with such force as to break the bark of a tree at two hundred yards distance, keeping in a horizontal direction nearly the whole way.

Heiva is the general name of diversion, whether music, dance, song, etc. The dance called heovra is performed by two, four, six or more neatly dressed young women and any convenient number of men, with one who is prompter or director. Drums and flutes play through the whole performance, the women beating regular time with various motions of the hands as well as feet. This dance is generally performed on mats spread for the purpose, and at night it is always under cover of an open house or shed built for the purpose, with torches and other lights.

The dress of the women in these dances is elegant and their figure graceful. It consists of a turban of tamow or plaited hair several hundred fathoms long, decorated with shark's teeth, pearls, and flowers. Their arms and shoulders are bare, and a kind of vest of white or coloured cloth covers their breasts, over each of which a large rose of black feathers is fixed.

On their back are several pieces of cloth in regular folds, painted with a red border, and so fixed as to represent wings on each side, from the hip to the shoulder. From the waist depends a kind of petticoat that reaches the feet; this has also a red border and a stripe of the same colour with another of yellow, each about an inch broad and about ten inches from the bottom. From the waist also depends several tassels of black feathers that reach the knees, and two or three red or black feathers on each forefinger.

When the women retire to take a breath, their place is supplied by the music and singers, which is no way disagreeable when understood, being soft and pleasing. At other times a set of actors supplies their place. The principal part that they perform is satire, which is often directed at their chiefs. They never fail to expose such characters as draw their attention, and though they treat their chiefs with great freedom, they incur no displeasure, so long as they keep to the truth. By this method they rebuke them for their faults in public, having first diverted them to draw their attention.

This is done in a kind of pantomime, at which they are so good that any person who knows the man they mean to represent may easily perceive who they are making the subject of their sport. Nor was it so badly done before we became acquainted with them as to prevent every spectator from observing that one of their plays at which our commander [Bligh] was present was entirely a representation of himself—and of which he was a most distinguished character. This was performed at the request of Matte, or Otoo, and several of the officers and crew of the *Bounty* were present.

The houses where they hold these plays or dances are commonly nothing more than a shed open at the front and both ends, the back part being screened in with coconut leaves, woven into a kind of matting for the purpose. The back part generally forms one part of a square, which is railed in with a low railing. The whole square is laid with grass and the part they perform on laid with mats. Outside the railing, which is not more than a foot high, sits or stands the audience. They sometimes may act at the houses of the chief, when they leave all the dresses as a present. Many of them contain from twenty to thirty fathoms of cloth from one to four wide, with the matting, cloth, and feathers.

The hewra is the dance performed by the relations of warriors slain in battle when they make friends with the man who killed him or them. As these dresses are very expensive to those at whose expense they are found, they seldom have more than four and oftener two than any other number—though they may have twenty if they can afford it.

Another dance is the ponnara, which is performed almost every evening in every district throughout the island. To this dance the women of every age and description resort to dance. Young and old, rich and poor mix promiscuously, but no men join with them. When they attend the ponnara, they are always neat and dressed in their best, their heads decorated with garlands of sweet-scented flowers.

Having fixed on the ground, they divide themselves in two parties and separate thirty or forty yards from each other. Then one of the best players, having been provided a small green breadfruit for a ball, runs out about halfway between the two, kicking the ball with as much force as she is able. She strikes it with the upper part of the foot, near the instep. If she sends the ball through the other party or past it so as none can stop it till it stops itself, then the opposite or her party strikes up a song and dance, beating time to it with hands and feet with much exactness and regularity.

After they have finished their dance, which lasts about five or six minutes, the other party kicks the ball, which, if it passes, they who kick it dance. But if it is stopped by those who danced first, then they dance again. In the meantime the others stand still.

After they have played at this for some hours, they kick the ball to one side, and both parties strike up together, when each—to draw the spectators to their exhibition—produce two or three young wantons, who strip off their lower garments. They cover themselves with a loose piece of cloth, and at particular parts of the song, they throw open their cloth and dance with their forepart naked to the company, making many lewd gestures. However, these are not merely the effects of wantonness but custom, and those who perform thus in public are shy and bashful in private. They seldom suffer any freedom to be taken by the men on that account.

The single young men also have dances wherein they show many indecent gestures that would be reproachable among themselves at any other time but at the dance. It is deemed shameful for either sex to expose themselves naked, even to each other. They are more remarkable for hiding their nakedness in bathing than many Europeans, always supplying the place of clothes with leaves at going in and coming out of the water. The women never uncover their breasts at any other time.

Besides these amusements they have several others and are very fond of cock-fighting, which is mostly their morning diversion. They never trim the cocks or use any spurs but their natural ones. While the cocks are fighting, the owners are praying for the success of their cocks. As soon as they appear fatigued by the heat, they part them till they are recovered and then put them together again.

They never fight for any wager but merely for sport, and sometimes two hundred cocks are brought to the pit, one part of the district fighting their cocks against the other. A feast is provided by the party who sent the challenge, whoever wins or loses.

In the evenings they play the flute and sing till bedtime. Sometimes they accompany their music with drums. Their flutes are made of bamboo, having only three holes; consequently, they have but few notes. However, they vary and tune to each other, and their sound is soft and not inharmonious. They blow the instrument with one nostril, stopping the other with one thumb, and with the second finger of the same hand stop the second hole. The third, being near the lower end, is stopped or opened by the forefinger of the other hand.

Their drums are hollow, cylindrical pieces of wood covered with a shark's skin, on which they beat with their fingers. They are loud and clear, and generally have two, for bass and tenor. One is about four feet high and ten or twelve inches over, and the other of the same diameter but only eighteen or twenty inches high. They have also large bass drums in their morais, which, with conch shells, are used by the priests on solemn religious ceremonies. These drums are constantly beating when anything ails the chief.

When the westerly winds prevail, they have a heavy surf, constantly running to a prodigious height on the shore. This affords excellent diversion, and the part they choose for their sport is where the surf breaks with most violence. When they go to this diversion, they get pieces of board of any length, with which they swim out to the back of the surf, when they watch the rise of a surf sometimes a mile from the shore. Laying their breast on the board, they keep themselves poised on the surf so as to come in on the top of it, with amazing rapidity, watching the time that it breaks. Then they turn with great activity and diving under the surge, swim out again, towing their plank with them. At this diversion both sexes are excellent, and some are so expert as to stand on their board till the surf breaks. The children also take their sport in the smaller surfs. As most learn to swim as soon as walk, few or no accidents happen from drowning.

They resort to this sport in great numbers and keep at it for several hours. As they often encounter each other in their passage out and in, they require the greatest skill in swimming to keep from running foul of each other. Sometimes they cannot avoid it, in which case both are violently dashed on shore, where they are thrown neck and heels and often find very coarse landing. However, they take little notice of this and, recovering themselves, regain their boards and return to their sport.

The chiefs are in general best at this as well as all other diversions, nor are their women behindhand at it. Eddea is one of the best among the Society Isles and able to hold it with the best of the men swimmers.

This diversion took place during the time the *Bounty* lay in Matavai Bay, when the surf from the Dolphin Bank ran so high as to break over her, and we were forced to secure the hatches, expecting the ship to go on shore every minute. After they have been at this sport, they always wash in the fresh water, as they always do when they have been out in their canoes or have been wet with salt water.

They have also a diversion in canoes, which they steer on the top of the surf with great dexterity, and can either turn them out before it breaks or land safe, though it break ever so high.

Their natural aversion to filth, which they detest, and their unparalleled cleanliness of body and clothes not only renders their persons agreeable to strangers and themselves, but keeps them free from many disorders that we have—nor do they give way to sickness till death stops their career. Young and old constantly bathe in running water three times a day, some oftener. When they become too old to walk far, they fix their habitation near a stream to enjoy that convenience.

They always wash their hands and mouth before and after meals, and when they are not at some diversion, either go to sleep in the heat of the day or employ themselves trimming their hair, beards, etc. A black coconut shell serves for a looking glass when filled with water and fish scales for tweezers. They pick their beards into form, and the hairs from the legs, arms, armpits, and other parts of the body that are apt to gather filth from sweat and dust. A shark's tooth answers every purpose of scissors for trimming their hair, which they keep always in neat order.

Both sexes have their ears bored, in which they wear flowers or hang their pearls, on which they set much value; they mostly wear three in a bunch, hung two or three inches from the ear, seldom having both ears decorated in the same manner. Coconut oil is used for pomatum, and their combs are made of bamboo. Their clothes are always neat, and they take a pride in shining at public assemblies.

Their disorders as said before are few, and for any inward complaint they have no remedy unless it is applied by chance, though they always administer some medicine with their prayers. In surgery they are excellent and make surprising cures. We have been eyewitness to some—one of which was from a musket ball that a man received in his breast and passed through the shoulder blade; another with his arm broke by a ball; a third having a ball through his thigh; and a fourth who received one through his thigh while stooping, which passed under his ribs and out by the collarbone.

There were several others wounded with stones, all of which were perfectly cured within two months. Among those wounded with stones was one who had all his upper jaw stove in and six or seven teeth knocked out. Several splinters of the bone were extracted, and the juice of herbs with clean water was the only remedy we ever saw used.

They cannot bear their wounds bound up and are constantly washing them to keep them from smelling. For this reason should they get a leg broke it is certain death; they cannot be kept from the water, though they know the consequence, always flying to the water as soon as the smell becomes disagreeable. They often grate sandalwood on the part to take away the smell. For splints they use bamboo and often repair broken arms, whether gotten by war or accident.

Their chief disorders are madness or insanity, agues, coughs and colds, swelled legs and arms, swellings under their ears like the King's Evil [scrofula], ruptures, and some few others.

The insanity is only temporary and perhaps may proceed from too great a flow of blood and spirits and a want of exercise, as it generally commences when the bread begins to be ripe. At this season others are troubled with boils on their legs and thighs, this being the wet season, and the sun overhead when they are more confined to their houses by the rain. This generally leaves them when the sun returns to the northward, and it is not common for a man or woman to have it return, though during its stay with them they are very mischievous and go quite naked.

With some it stays longer than others, and they have it in different degrees, from a heavy, dull melancholy to raving mad. They never bind them but let them run, and some travel all round the island naked in the time of their madness. None interrupts them unless they do some mischief, as they suppose them possessed with some evil spirit. This is common to women as well as men, who are not restrained but suffered to take their own course till the spirit leaves them—when they return home and wear their clothes as usual.

The ague is a common disorder for which, as well as madness, they have no cure. This carries them off, as does that terrible disease the venereal, for which death is their only remedy. Such was the fate of those who contracted it from the Europeans, for as soon as anyone is known to have it, no person will touch them or theirs, nor will they bathe near them in the river. Their food is also carried to them, they not being suffered to touch any but what is for themselves. Their companions forsake them, and they languish out the remainder of their days in a miserable manner; though they want no food, yet they pine at seeing themselves neglected and soon die.

They know that this disorder was brought by the Europeans but are not certain whether by the Spaniards or French, for which reason they blame both. Nor do we escape blame in all points, for they charge us with several other disorders with which they say they were unacquainted before they knew us, particularly with bringing fleas among them, which they say were brought by the cats. However, it is possible that they may be natives of their own country, as it is clear that most of their disorders are. The ague is from the effects of the sudden heats and colds that they often experience, as they always jump into the river when they sweat to cool themselves, and often sleep in heavy dews.

Their coughs and colds are often gotten in the same manner, and their hot bath, into which women go after childbearing, is sufficient to carry off those of the best constitution. This is made by screening in part of a house or erecting a hut or tent of cloth and mats, into which they bring a quantity of hot stones and spread grass and herbs over them; the person intending to bathe then goes in with a shell of water.

The place is shut close, and the water, being sprinkled on the grass and stones, makes a steam. In this they stay as long as they are able. Then they throw a cloth loosely round them, come out, and run directly to the river, into which they plunge head foremost. This bath is also used by both sexes, merely for the sake of making themselves thoroughly clean when their skin appears too rough or greasy to be cleaned in the river. This we have seen often repeated by both sexes, without any immediate good or bad consequence.

The swelled legs and arms are a disorder perhaps peculiar to themselves. These swellings often break out in small ulcers but never diminish. They seldom affect them above the knee or elbow, being confined to the arm and leg, which swell to a prodigious size. The swellings under the ears are like the King's Evil, making large scars. For these they have no remedy but clean washing, never suffering their head to be bound up, which often occasions large wounds in their necks. Although we often convinced them that binding up their wounds would be the means of a speedy cure, yet as they must either stay at home or remove their bandage every time they pass over sacred ground, they could never be persuaded to do it.

Ruptures are very common, frequently swelling to a prodigious size. These are perhaps occasioned by too great an exertion of strength when wrestling, which we were not able to persuade them to believe. Nor is it possible to persuade them that disorders proceed from such things as sleeping on damp ground or in heavy dews, etc. They believe that all their diseases are immediately sent from the Deity as a punishment for some fault; consequently, it is impossible to prevent or escape it.

They have few cripples, though they have several blind and dumb. Most of the deformities found among them are from accidents. Their limbs in general are straight, and it is very rare to see a bowlegged or knock-kneed person. Their children are free from the rickets, and the mother takes many pains to form the features and keep the limbs in their proper places while they are young. If a child is not very deformed, they will bring it into shape before the bones are set. If the child has any of these faults, the mother is blamed, and any stranger will tell her that she does not understand how to nurse her children.

They also have a kind of leprosy that changes the body to a dead white in some parts, while the natural colour is heightened to black. This change of colour extends to the hair on the head and body, some of which is as white as snow, while the rest is jet black—which gives them a very odd appearance. Some are changed all over, but this does not affect their health or strength.

These are their principal disorders, and it appears to me that they live to a good old age and are vigourous and healthy. Several are now on the island who were alive at the time the African *Galley* was lost (the ship spoken of before) on Tapoohoe, an island to the NE of Tahiti. Many of them mentioned by Captains Wallis and Cook are still hale, hearty men—and many who appear to be near one hundred years old are sturdy men.

The women in this climate, as in other warm ones, are sooner ripe than in the colder northern and southern countries, and generally marry at thirteen or fourteen years. But those of rank often reach sixteen or eighteen years, by which time in this country they are grown women. They also appear to fade sooner. Nevertheless, handsome features may often be traced under grey hairs, and it is something remarkable that many who were once faded revive and hold their beauty with all the sprightliness of youth at fifty. Others who have broken their constitution in their youth by their dissolute manner of living are perfectly withered at thirty.

MOURNING RITES

When any person dies, the relations flock to the house in numbers, making much lamentation. The women cut their heads with shark's teeth, and both sexes cut their hair off different parts of their heads, sometimes cutting all but a lock over one ear, sometimes over both, and the rest close cut or shaven. The women often cut themselves on these occasions till they bring on a fever, and I have known a woman to cut herself for the loss of a child till a delirium was brought on, which ended in the total loss of her reason.

For the loss of a relation, they cut a square place bare on the forepart of their head, which they keep bare for six moons or longer, according to the love they bear the deceased; but for a favourite child, they wear it so for two or three years, and all the hair they cut off is either thrown into the sacred ground or carried to the morai.

If any person dies of a disorder, they are buried in their own ground, and a priest always puts a plantain tree into the grave with them. Some of the relations put them in the grave, praying them to keep their disorder in the grave with them and not afflict any person with it. When their soul is sent on that business, they also bury or burn everything belonging to them or that has been used by them while in their sickness—house and furniture—to prevent the disorder from spreading or communicating to others.

These are the only people that have any funeral prayers. Those who die without disease are either laid on a bier or embalmed. Their method of embalming is by taking the bowels out and stuffing the body with cloth and grated sandalwood, anointing the skin with coconut oil scented with the same wood. The body is laid on a bier in a house by itself and covered with cloth, which the relations present as they come to the place—which they all do if they are in the island.

The body is often dressed in the same manner as it was while alive. The head ornamented with flowers, the house is fenced in and hung round with finely scented cloth. The bier is ornamented with garlands of palm nuts, which, having an agreeable smell, keep off any foul one.

The tears shed on these occasions are saved on pieces of cloth, together with the blood from their heads, and thrown within the rail of the sacred house. They suppose this gives satisfaction to the departed soul, who is hovering about the body while it remains without mouldering. Others are hung up on a bier under a thatched covering, covered and dressed with cloth. They are also ornamented with palm nuts and coconut leaves, plaited in a curious manner and railed in with reeds. The man that is appointed to take care of the body keeps this in repair. He is obliged to have a man to feed him, as he must not touch any sort of food for one month after he has touched a dead body or any of the things which belong to it. They also offer provisions, etc., near the corpse, not for it but for the Deity who presides over it.

The body is called toopapow, the bier fwhatta, and the house wherein it is contained farre toopapow. Those who are embalmed are called toopapow meere. They are kept each on their own land and not carried to the morai, where none are interred but those killed in war, for sacrifice, or the children of chiefs who have been strangled at their birth.

When chiefs or people of rank die, their bodies are embalmed and they are carried round the island to every part where they have any possessions, in each of which the tyehaa, or weeping ceremony, is renewed. After a journey of six or eight months, they return to their own estate, where they are kept till the body decays, when the bones are interred. Some who have a great veneration for the deceased wrap up the skull and hang it up in their house in token of their love, and in this manner the skulls of several are kept.

These bodies, while they are whole, are liable to be taken in war, and the man who takes one of them gets the name and honours as if he had killed a warrior. Should the body of a chief be carried off in this manner before another was named, the district would fall to the conqueror as if he had killed him. For this reason they are always removed, having each a steady man to carry them away into the mountains, if they should be at war. In this manner Captain Cook's picture is also removed lest it should be taken. While the body remains, they keep the bier well supplied with cloth, and new is always substituted in lieu of that which is decayed. The cloth is in general good and neatly painted.

Besides weeping and cutting their heads, they have another mourning ceremony wherein they wear the parais, or mourning dress, described by Captain Cook. This is mostly worn by two or three of the nearest male relations, each of which is armed with a weapon called paaeho, edged with a row of shark's teeth for three feet or four of its length. The upper part forms a blade like that of a gardener's knife. They are attended by forty or fifty young men and women who disguise themselves by blacking their bodies and faces with charcoal, spotting them with pipe clay.

These seldom wear any other clothes but a marro; each is armed with a spear or club and parades about the district like madmen. They will beat, cut, or even kill any person who offers to stand in their way. Therefore, when anyone sees them coming, they fly to the morai, it being the only place where they can be safe or get refuge from the rage of the mourners, who pursue all that they see.

The morai alone they must not enter, and while this ceremony lasts—which is sometimes three weeks or a month—they pay no respect to persons, nor are the chiefs safe from their fury unless they take sanctuary in the morai. The women and children are forced to quit the place, as they cannot take refuge in the morai.

If any person is stubborn or foolish enough to stop one of the mourners, or not get out of their way, and is killed, no law can be obtained nor anyone blamed but himself. The mourners are looked on as lunatics, driven mad through grief for the death of their relations. Therefore, none attempt to obstruct them, but fly at their approach. This ceremony is also called tyehaa, or mourning. The performers are called naynevva; madmen, hewa tyehaa—mourning spirits, ghosts, or spectres.

These are the whole of their mourning rites and are of longer or shorter duration, according to the circumstances of the family who have lost their relation. They are more particularly observed for children than grown persons.

Among their societies (of which they have several) is one in particular distinguished by the name of Areeuoy, a name that signifies a restless or unsettled chief. This society is composed of a set of young men of wild, amorous, and volatile dispositions, who, from their infancy, devote the youthful part of their lives to roving, pleasure, and debauchery. They are continually going from one island to another and from one district to another in companies of four or five hundred together upon parties of pleasure, and as nearly all the chiefs are of this society, they always meet with the best entertainment from them all in their respective districts.

So greatly are they respected throughout all the islands, that if any of the members takes a liking to the clothes that they see any person wearing, they are never refused them or anything else they may choose to demand. They are always sure to carry off the finest women in the country. The old members of this society are distinguished by having a black oval tattooed under their left breast and one on the right side of the back below the shoulder. Their legs and thighs are entirely blacked from the ankle to the short ribs, and their arms from the finger ends to the shoulder. They are always well dressed with the best cloth that can be made, their hair scented and adorned with various kinds of odoriferous flowers.

The younger members, and indeed all in general being fond of variety, seldom remain any length of time with one woman but are constantly changing, and if any of their wives prove pregnant, they go away and leave them immediately on the first discovery. They do not want to be obstructed in their future pursuits and enjoyment of pleasure by the domestic cares of a wife and child.

It is deemed highly reproachful for a child not to know who his father is (which would be almost impossible in that society). When they are pregnant with a child of whom they know not the true father, to prevent its being treated with indignity in its passage through life (and as it could have no inheritance without a father), it is no sooner born than someone strangles the little innocent and buries it. These Areeuoy ladies of pleasure easily agree to this, as they think that nursing children spoils their beauty in the prime of youth and debars them from the happiness of having so many suitors as before.

If an Areeuoy preserves any of his children (which they seldom do till they advance in years and the fire of their youthful passions is a little quenched), they are not treated with so much respect as when bachelors. They are then denominated Areeuoy Fwhanownow, or a childbearing Areeuoy. They are not entertained at the feasts till after the bachelors are served, though they are always looked on as part of the society and treated as such. They are never called upon in war and may pass through the countries at war without molestation and be well received, though part of them belong to the enemy's district.

If any person wishes to have his son or daughter instituted into the society, he procures an Areeuoy to be his son or daughter's friend and adopts him for his son by performing the amoa (before described) towards him and his son or daughter at the morai. The child is acknowledged an Areeuoy immediately after the ceremony is over and may continue to follow their methods while he or she thinks it proper.

There are many people who are not of this society that kill their children for this reason: If a man takes a wife of inferior rank to himself and has a child by her, it is strangled immediately when born to prevent its bringing disgrace on the blood of his family. If he wished to preserve its life himself, his relations would oblige him to kill it or declare himself no longer of their family.

It is the same if the wife be superior in rank to the husband, both of which frequently happens. If the child should chance to cry out in coming into the world, or should the mother chance to see it before it is killed, nature takes place of custom and the child is saved.

Such was the case with the present Tommaree, the only child that Pbooraya saved. Being delivered by herself she saved the child, though she had killed several others, both her and Oammo being of the Areeuoy society. For this reason he left her, but they afterwards became friends and the boy was acknowledged their heir.

Here it may not be improper to remark that the idea formed of this society, and of the inhabitants of this island in general by former voyagers, could not possibly extend much further than their own opinion. None remained a sufficient length of time to know the manner in which they live. As their whole system was overturned by the arrival of a ship, their manners were then as much altered from their common course as those of our own country are at a fair—which might as well be given for a specimen of the method of living in England.

Such was always their situation as soon as a ship arrived, their whole thought being turned towards their visitors and all methods tried to win their friendship. In the meantime they were forced to live in a different way of life, that they might better please their new friends.

Their general notion of delicacy is undoubtedly different from ours, perhaps from their want of refinement, without which many of our own countrymen would be as bad, if not worse, than they—many of whom would not keep within bounds but for fear of the law.

A woman is not ashamed to show her limbs at a dance, or when bathing, if they are perfect. If they are not, she will avoid being seen as much as possible. Though the men and women frequently bathe together, they are more remarkable for their decency than frivolity at such a time.

They have no walls to their houses nor do they require any, notwithstanding which they cannot be charged with holding carnal conversation in public, and like privacy in such cases as much as we do. Nor did I see anything of the kind during our stay in the islands, though they are not remarkable for their virtue. Yet, this is not their general character, and the large families of some show that there are some of that stamp.

Their actions might possibly be for the sake of gain, brought to a style of what we call indecency, but where are the countries that do not produce women of the same description? Iron is to them more valuable than gold to us, for the possession of which some of our own countrywomen would not stick at acts of indecency nor even horrid crimes that these people would tremble to think of. Nay, they challenge us with the very crime and say we are ashamed of nothing, using these things that we knew they were fond of to persuade them to commit such acts as their innocence had taught them to be ashamed of.

If they can purchase iron at the expense of their beauty or are able to get it by theft, they will—neither of which methods I hold to be a crime in them. They know its value and think no price too great for it. Gold is preferred in other countries and some, as fine women as any in Europe, are said to prefer it to virtue; yet we upbraid these untaught and uncontrolled people with such actions as we ourselves help them to commit.

They lay no restraint on their children because they are the head of the family and therefore do as they please. Having no law or custom to prevent them, they have a number of amusements that would not suit the ideas of Europeans. However, they are dropped as they grow up, when they become ashamed of these childish sports—although they are not compelled to unless they think it proper themselves. As there are always enough people in all countries to promote evil practices, they who do not like them can only reform themselves, having no power over others; for which reason they are suffered to proceed in their own way.

Those who make a trade of beauty know how to value it, and when they come on board bring with them their pimps or procurers, under the denomination of relations, to receive and secure the price. These ladies are as well qualified to act their part as any of their profession in other countries and are in no way bashful in making their demands.

When a man makes a friend, that friend can never have connections with any female of the family except his friend's wife—every other one becoming his relatives, which they hold an abomination to have any connection with. Nor can they be persuaded to alter that custom on any consideration, detesting incest as much as we do.

The women of rank are most remarkable for their licentious practices, and many of them have a number of favourites in which they pride themselves. Many of the lower class are what may honestly be called virtuous, never admitting a second to share in their favours.

The famous queen Pbooraya being herself an Areeuoy, it is not to be wondered that every licentious practice was carried on by her followers and attendants, her court being filled with such as preferred the rites of Venus to those of Mars. She saw that they were also more agreeable to her visitors (the general case with sailors after a long voyage). They were, no doubt, practiced and carried to the utmost verge of their latitude, it being in all countries the case that those in power always lead the fashions, let them be good or evil.

However, the ladies who act these parts are not to be taken as a standard for the whole—no more than the nymphs of the Thames or sirens of Spithead are to be taken as samples of our own fair countrywomen.

Their ceremonies have also been misunderstood by former voyagers. The flies being numerous, they are forced to use fly flaps, and when they have none they use branches of the first tree. With these they are ever ready to supply every stranger, especially if any food is at hand. They cannot bear to see a fly touch what they eat and have a number of hands always employed to drive them away with these branches.

The other branches used in ceremonies are the rowavva and are commissions borne by substitutes for chiefs. Every person bearing one of them is treated in the same manner as the chief would be if he were present. These commissions or emblems of truth are never assumed by any unless on such occasions, as they would suffer death for such fraud. The plantain, as before mentioned, is the only emblem of peace. When any person is sent with such a commission, he gives a leaf to each of the party to whom he is sent, on the receipt of which, and being informed who sent him, his word is never doubted.

Besides the different classes and societies already described, they have a set of men called mahoo. These men are in some respects like the eunuchs in India but are not castrated. They never cohabit with women but live as they do. They pick their beards out and dress as women, dance and sing with them, and are as effeminate in their voice. They are generally excellent hands at making and painting cloth, making mats, and every other woman's employment. They are esteemed valuable friends in that way, and it is said, though I never saw an instance of it, that they converse with men as familiar as women do. This, however, I do not aver as a fact, as I never found any who did not detest the thought.

The manners and customs of the other islands are nearly the same as those of different counties in the same kingdom, and their produce nearly the same. The inhabitants of all the Society Isles are one and the same people. Tahiti is by much the largest and most powerful when the strength of the island is united and is, therefore, acknowledged mistress paramount of the whole. They all distinguish their language, customs, etc., by the name of Tahiti as well at home as when they are at Tahiti. There are few men of property who do not visit Tahiti once in their lifetime, and many visit it frequently.

It must be acknowledged that Captain Cook, when he first thought of stocking these islands with cattle, poultry, and the fruits and roots of Europe, intended it for the good of mankind. But these people knew not the value of them, and for want of Europeans to take care of them, they were soon destroyed. The curiosity of the natives to see such strange animals made each wish to have one, by which means they were separated and their increase prevented. The poultry soon became extinct; the sheep, which did not as in other warm climes lose their wool, died for want of shearing; the black cattle alone thrived, though kept mostly separate.

The seeds and plants were destroyed by being removed as soon as they made their appearance. Everyone wishing to possess some part of the curiosities that they esteemed the whole and would part with the best cow for a good axe. They set no value on them for food, though they killed several and ate part of them in the wars. Having no method of taking the hides, they cleaned them as hogs and could not fancy they were good. Therefore, they took no pains to save a breed.

They could not abide the rams and male goats, from their disagreeable smell, and many of the goats were banished to the mountains. Their flesh was not a compensation for the mischief they did to the cloth plantations. Those they keep now are always tied if they are near one of these plantations and, at best, are not esteemed equal to a dog. This method of treating them prevents the island from being overrun with them, which it soon would be if they were suffered to range at large.

Notwithstanding their having lost all these valuable curiosities, they still remember Captain Cook for bringing them and take more care of his picture than all the rest. They made frequent enquiry after him and Sir Joseph Banks, both of whom will never be forgotten at Tahiti. They were exceedingly sorry when they heard of Captain Cook's death and wished that his son might come and take possession of his father's land, he being acknowledged chief of Matavai—and will be as long as his picture lasts.

They were also very inquisitive about all their friends and were happy when we entertained them with an account of their welfare. Their language is soft and melodious, abounding in vowels. They have only seventeen letters, yet they can express anything with ease—though for want of the others that compose our alphabet, they never could pronounce any English word that contains them.

They count their time by years of twelve months, which they have names for, and calculate it by the sun's passing and repassing over their heads. They call the month marrarna, or moon, though they do not always begin or end with the moon. They have names for every day of the moon's age and can tell her age to a certainty at first sight, without the assistance of figures.

As they never keep an account of their time, they can easily reconcile any mistake in their reckoning at the end of the year, when the sun is over their heads. They divide the day and night into twelve equal parts, and can tell their time exactly by the sun in the daytime and the stars at night.

They have also names for every wind and are excellent judges of a change and can tell whether the season will be uncommonly dry or wet before it commences. They have no method of measuring distance but by the length of time it requires to pass it, but can measure any depth of water with exactness by the fathom, yard, or span—all of which they name alike with the addition of longer or shorter.

They are able hands at conversing by signs and perfect masters of the language of the eyes. I have seen a dumb man so well learned that he might be sent to the distance of sixty miles with a message, and return with his answer, as well as if he could hear and speak.

They are forever changing their names from making new friends and many other accidents, and though they do not lose their former ones, it would be difficult for a stranger to know who they were talking of, or what about, or be able to find an old acquaintance by his name. No word must be used that contains any of the syllables of the chief's name while he is alive.

They never compare any kind of food to a man's head, for which reason the heads of animals have a different name—nor can they think of eating anything that has touched a man's head, and nothing can offend them more than laying a hand on their heads. Brown, who was left here by Captain Cox, was thought worse than a cannibal for carrying provisions on his head, of which none ever partook with him. However, they were always ready to excuse him, saying he knew no better, which in fact was nearly the case. But it was his sole study to be contrary to them in everything, and he took more pains that way than in conforming to their ways, which made him disagreeable to them all.

Such is the best account that I have been able to collect of these islands and their inhabitants, who are without doubt the happiest on the face of the globe. I shall now proceed to give such a vocabulary of their language as we were able to obtain during our stay among these islands.

The End

Glossary of Nautical Terms

Aft—At, near, or toward the stern (back) of a ship.

Articles of War—The disciplinary code that specifies naval crimes and punishments.

Backing and filling—Pushing a sail out, letting the wind fill the opposite side. This is performed to slow down a vessel.

Ballast—Weight placed at the bottom of a vessel to provide stability.

Bare poles—This term describes the appearance of the masts when sails have been taken down in heavy weather.

Batten down—Securing the deck hatches before or during severe weather.

Binnacle—The mount and housing for a ship's compass.

Boom—A long pole used to extend the bottom of a particular sail.

Bow—The front (forward) part of a ship.

Bower anchor—The anchor at the bow of a ship.

Bower cable—The cable attached to a bower anchor.

Bread—Ship's biscuit.

Burgoo—The nautical term for gruel or porridge made from oatmeal.

Caboose—A ship's galley or kitchen.

Cable—A strong, thick rope used to hoist and lower the anchor of a ship. The term also is used as a nautical measurement of distance: one cable length equals one-tenth of a nautical mile, one hundred fathoms, or about two hundred yards.

Chock—A wooden block or wedge to keep objects, such as a ship's boat, in position and secure on the deck.

Coaming—A low vertical lip or raised section around the edge of a cockpit, hatch, etc., to prevent water from running below the deck.

Cockpit—Junior officers' quarters in the hold (below lower deck).

Cooper—A craftsperson who makes and repairs barrels.

Crossing the Line—A ceremony performed when a ship's crew or passengers cross the earth's equator for the first time. In the Royal Navy, the ritual frequently included ducking in the water.

Deadlights—Ports in a cabin or deck to admit light that are fixed in place and do not open.

Driver boom—The boom used to extend the bottom of a driver sail.

Fathom—A unit of measurement relating to the depth of water or to a length of cable; one fathom equals six feet.

Flummery—A custard or pudding made from oatmeal or another grain.

Fore—Something positioned at or close to the bow of a ship. Often used as a prefix such as "forescuttle" and "fore-topsail yard."

Forescuttle—A small hatch or round window that may be securely fastened or opened for light and air.

Four-pounder—A ship's cannon capable of discharging a four-pound shot.

Gang cask—A small cask used to bring drinking water on board a ship.

Gangway—A narrow portable platform used as a passage by persons entering or leaving a vessel moored alongside a pier.

Gimbles (Gimbals)—Two concentric brass rings that suspend a ship's compass in its box. They counteract the effect of the ship's motion.

Grapnel—A small anchor frequently used on small boats.

Grog—A mixture of rum and water given to sailors in a daily ration.

Halyard—The line that either hoists or lowers a sail, flag, or spar.

Hatch—An opening in the deck that provides access to the space below, or a deck opening provided with a watertight cover.

Heave to—To stop a ship and hold it in position, particularly in stormy seas.

Jymbals—See "Gimbles."

Kedge—A small auxiliary anchor. Sailors "kedge" a vessel, such as a grounded boat, by throwing a kedge and pulling on its line to move into deeper water.

Keel—The backbone of a vessel, running along the center line on the bottom of the hull.

Kelson—A piece of timber placed in the middle of the ship that binds the floor timbers to the ship's keel.

Lacing—A thin rope used to attach a sail to a spar.

Larboard—An old term for the left side of a ship. The name eventually was changed to "port."

Launch—Long-boat, the largest of a sailing-ship's boats. The *Bounty* also carried a small cutter (jolly boat) and a large cutter.

Leech—A sail's after (trailing) edge.

Leech Line – The line that tightens a sail's leech.

Marlinspike—Pointed tool used for line work, for opening line strands for splicing and especially for prying tight knots apart.

Moor—To attach a vessel to a mooring, dock, post, anchor, etc.

Nun Buoy—A type of navigational buoy, with the shape of a cone.

Pinnace—A small, two-masted sailing vessel that sometimes includes oars.

Portable beef broth (portable soup)—An early dehydrated food that kept well for an extended period of time. It had a jelly-like consistency and was believed to help prevent scurvy.

Puncheon—A large cask for storing liquids. Also, a pointed tool used for piercing.

Qr. (Quarter) gunner—A sailor in charge of four cannon.

Quarters—Living space for the crew.

Reef—To reduce the extent of a sail by taking it in or rolling up a section of it.

Round and grape shot—Different shapes of iron ordnance shot from a ship's cannon.

Scud—To run before a gale with reduced sail or bare poles.

Scupper—An opening in a deck, toe rail, or gunwale to allow water to run off the deck and drain back into the sea.

Ship—To take an object aboard, such as cargo or water.

Sheet—A line that adjusts or controls a sail.

Sinnet (Sennit)—The braided rope used to rig a ship.

Spar—The round, wooden pole that supports a sailing ship's rigging.

Spinnaker—A large, triangular sail.

Sprit—A light spar that crosses diagonally across a four-sided fore-and-aft sail to support the peak.

Stay—A long rope that helps support a ship's mast.

Stem—The front part of a ship.

Stern—The back part of a ship.

Streak (Strake)—A line of planking that runs from the bow of a ship to the stern, alongside the hull.

Swivel—A rotating fitting used to keep a line from tangling.

Sweet wort—An infusion of malt, similar to unfermented beer.

Tack—The lower forward corner of a triangular sail; the direction that a boat is sailing with respect to the wind.

Tacking—Changing a vessel's direction by turning it into the wind.

Thimble—A pear-shaped, grooved metal fitting around which an eye splice is made.

Trades (Trade Winds)—The steady winds that occur in a belt around 30° north and 30° south of the earth's equator.

Unreeve—To run a line completely through and out of a block, fairlead, etc.

Waist—The middle part of a ship between the fore and main masts.

Weather—The direction from which the wind blows, as in "weather side" of a sailing vessel.

Weatherboard—The windward side of a ship.

Yard—A spar from which a square sail is hung.

Yardarm—The section of yard that lies between the lift and the outboard end of the yard.

Yaul (Yawl)—A sailboat equipped with two masts. The shorter mizzenmast is placed aft of the rudderpost.

Bibliography

Anthony, Irvin, ed. *The Saga of the* Bounty: *Its Strange History as Related by the Participants Themselves.* New York: Putnam, 1935.

Barrow, Sir John. *The Eventful History of the Mutiny and Piratical Seizure of H.M.S.* Bounty: *Its Causes and Consequences.* London: John Murray, 1831.

Belcher, Lady [Diana Jolliffe]. *The Mutineers of the* Bounty *and Their Descendants in Pitcairn and Norfolk Islands.* London: John Murray, 1870.

Bligh, William, and Edward Christian. *The* Bounty *Mutiny.* Introduction by R. D. Madison. New York: Penguin Classics, 2001. Reprinted in 2003 with new "*Bounty* Chronicles" cover artwork by John Hagan.

Bligh, William, and others. *A Book of the 'Bounty.'* Edited by George Mackaness. New introduction by Gavin Kennedy. London: J. M. Dent and Sons, 1981.

Campbell, I. C. "James Morrison of Tahiti." In *"Gone Native" in Polynesia: Captivity Narratives and Experiences from the South Pacific.* Westport, CT: Greenwood Press, 1998.

David, Andrew C. F. "Broughton's Schooner and the *Bounty* Mutineers." *Mariner's Mirror* 63, no. 3 (August 1977): 207–13.

De Lacy, Gavin. "Plagiarism on the *Bounty.*" *Mariner's Mirror* 83, no. 1 (February 1997): 671–73.

Dening, Greg. *Mr. Bligh's Bad Language: Passion, Power and Theatre on the* Bounty. Cambridge, UK: Cambridge University Press, 1992.

Du Rietz, Rolf E. "Note sur l'histoire des manuscrits de James Morrison." Introduction to *Journal de James Morrison, Second maître à bord du* Bounty. Paris: Société des Océanistes, 1966.

———. *Peter Heywood's Tahitian Vocabulary and the Narratives by James*

Morrison: Some Notes on Their Origin and History. Uppsala, Sweden: Dahlia Books, 1986. (*Banksia 3.*)

Fletcher, William. "Fletcher Christian and the Mutineers of the '*Bounty.*'" *Transactions of the Cumberland Association for the Advancement of Literature and Science,* part 2 (1876–77): 77–106.

Grant, James Shaw. *Morrison of the* Bounty: *A Scotsman: Famous but Unknown.* Stornoway: Acair, 1997.

Greatheed, Samuel [Nausistratus, pseud.]. "Authentic History of the Mutineers of the *Bounty.*" *Sailor's Magazine and Naval Miscellany* 1, no. 10 (October 1820): 402–6; 1, no. 12 (December 1820): 449–56; and 2, no. 1 (January 1821): 1–8.

Grocott, Terence. *Shipwrecks of the Revolutionary & Napoleonic Eras.* London: Chatham Publishing, 1997.

Hamilton, George. *A Voyage Round the World in His Majesty's Frigate* Pandora, *Performed under the Direction of Captain Edwards in the Years 1790, 1791 and 1792.* Berwick, UK: Printed by and for B. Law and Son, London, 1793.

[Haweis, Thomas, ed.]. *A Missionary Voyage to the Southern Pacific Ocean, Performed in the Years 1796, 1797, 1798, in the Ship* Duff, *Commanded by Captain James Wilson.* London: Gosnell for Chapman, 1799.

Haweis, Thomas. "Curious tradition, among the inhabitants of Otaheite." *Evangelical Magazine* 5 (January 1797): 23–25.

———. "On the Otaheitian sacrifices." *Evangelical Magazine* 6 (March 1798): 110–12.

Henderson, George C. *The Discoverers of the Fiji Islands: Tasman, Cook, Bligh, Wilson, Bellinghausen.* London: John Murray, 1933.

Joppien, Rüdiger, and Bernard Smith. *The Art of Captain Cook's Voyages.* New Haven, CT: Yale University Press, 1985.

Lamb, Jonathan, Vanessa Smith, and Nicholas Thomas, eds. *Exploration and Exchange: A South Seas Anthology, 1680–1990.* Chicago: University of Chicago Press, 2001.

Langdon, Robert. "'Lost' Manuscript May Tell . . . Have These Men a Place in Fiji History?" *Pacific Islands Monthly* 32, no. 1 (August 1961): 29–33.

———. "Lost 'Pandora' Logbook Turns Up in U.K. after 170 Years." *Pacific Islands Monthly* 36 (April 1965): 33–35.

———. "The Lost Tahitian Vocabulary of Peter Heywood." PAMBU, no. 3 (October 1968): 6–10.

Leeson, Ida. "The Morrison Myth." *Mariner's Mirror* 25, no. 4 (October 1939): 433–38.

L'Estrange, Alfred Guy Kingan. *Lady Belcher and Her Friends*. London: Hurst and Blackett, 1891.

Levy, Robert I. "The Community Function of Tahitian Male Transvestitism: A Hypothesis." *Anthropological Quarterly* 44, no. 1 (January 1971): 12–21.

———. *Tahitians: Mind and Experience in the Society Islands*. Chicago: University of Chicago Press, 1973.

Marshall, John. "Peter Heywood, Esq." In *Royal Naval Biography*, 2, pt. 2. London: Hurst, Rees, Orme, Brown, and Green, 1825, 747–97.

Maude, H. E. *Of Islands and Men: Studies in Pacific History*. London: Oxford University Press, 1968.

———."The Voyage of the *Pandora*'s Tender." *Mariner's Mirror* 50, no. 3 (August 1964): 217–35.

Maxton, Donald A. *The Mutiny on H.M.S. Bounty: A Guide to Nonfiction, Fiction, Poetry, Films, Articles, and Music*. Foreword by Sven Wahlroos. Jefferson, NC, and London: McFarland and Co., Inc., 2008.

McDonald, William N., III. "*Bounty* Mutineer: James Morrison of Lewis." *Highlander* 26, no. 1 (January–February 1988): 52–53.

———. "James Morrison of Lewis: Saga of a *Bounty* Mutineer." *Pitcairn Log* 20 (December 1992–February 1993): 6–8.

Montgomerie, H. S. *The Morrison Myth: Pendant to William Bligh of the* Bounty *in Fact and in Fable*. London and Woking, UK: Unwin Brothers Ltd., 1938. Privately printed.

———. "The Morrison Myth." *Mariner's Mirror* 27, no. 1 (January 1941): 69–76.

Morrison, James. *The Journal of James Morrison, Boatswain's Mate of the* Bounty, *Describing the Mutiny and Subsequent Misfortunes of the Mutineers, Together with an Account of the Island of Tahiti*. With an introduction by Owen Rutter and five engravings by Robert Gibbings. London: The Golden Cockerel Press, 1935.

———. *Journal de James Morrison, Second maître à bord du* Bounty. Translated by Bertrand Jaunez. Paris: Société des Océanistes, 1966; Papeete: Société des Etudes Océaniennes, 1966.

———. *Journal de James Morrison, Second maître à bord du* Bounty. Translated by Bertrand Jaunez. Introduction by Eric Vibart. Rennes: Editions Ouest-France, 2002. This edition reprints only the first part of *Journal de James Morrison*.

Neill, Anna. "James Morrison's Tahiti." *The Center and Clark Newsletter On Line* (Spring 2000).

Reid, Alan. "Broughton's Schooner." *Mariner's Mirror* 64, no. 3 (August 1978): 241–44.

Rogers, G. A. "Sojourn of the *Pandora's* Tender at Ono-I-Lau, Fiji." *Mariner's Mirror* 69, no. 4 (November 1983): 452–55.

Rowe, Newton A. *Voyage to the Amorous Islands: The Discovery of Tahiti.* London: Andre Deutsch, 1955.

Rutter, Owen, ed. *The Court-Martial of the "Bounty" Mutineers.* Notable British Trials. Edinburgh and London, UK: William Hodge and Company, 1931. Reprinted in 1989 as part of the Notable Trials Library, with an introduction by Alan M. Dershowitz.

Tagart, Edward. *A Memoir of the Late Captain Peter Heywood, R.N. With Extracts from His Diaries and Correspondence.* London: Effingham Wilson, 1832.

Thomson, Basil, ed. *Voyage of H.M.S. 'Pandora,' Despatched to Arrest the Mutineers of the 'Bounty' in the South Seas, 1790–91.* London: Francis Edwards, 1915.

Index

tuoy, 99, 140
turbans, 208, 211
turtles, 59, 62–63, 108, 130, 145–46, 197
Tyarrabboo, 70, 72–73, 75, 133, 135. *See also* TahitiEete
  and traffic (trade), 190
  violence in, 80–88, 163
  and Young King's investiture, 104, 106–8, 161
tyehaa, 219–20
Tyepo, 88
Tye tabboo, 109–10, 112
tyeyro, 191, 198

Union Jack, 44, 51, 56, 106, 109
urre heiva, 166
urtica argenta, 141, 146, 155

Valentine, James, 20
Vay-heeadooa, 70, 73, 80–84, 86–88, 163
vee, 90, 138–39
venereal diseases, 216
Venooa, 157–58
Venus (dog), 89
Venus (planet), 169
vermin, 61, 115, 162, 187
volcanoes, 31, 35, 136
Voyage Round the World, A (Hamilton), 116
Vreedenbergh, 128–29
Vyeerre, 82, 89, 100, 106, 157
Vyeerre Harbour, 99, 102
Vye Heereea, 154
Vyeooreedee, 81, 154, 157
Vyeooroo, 158
Vyeowtaya, 83, 86, 158

Wahlroos, Sven, 4
Wallis, Captain, 163, 218
war, 159, 161–67, 171, 183
  and adopted friends, 98, 165, 167, 179
  and Areeuoys, 221
  clothing for, 207–8
  council of, 96
  deceased warriors, 57–58, 67, 92, 95, 166–67, 174, 219
  declaration of, 165
  deity presiding over, 167
  marro eatooa, 93
  and mourning rites, 219
  and O'Mai, 104
  and priests, 165, 172

  sea actions, 166
  on Tahiti, 92–103, 106–8
  on Tubuai, 43–45, 49, 56–58, 63–66
  and Young King's investiture, 106–8
war canoes, 93, 96, 104, 140, 162, 166, 188–90, 192, 194–95
war clubs
  on Annamooka, 33–34
  on Tahiti, 139, 166, 220
  on Tubuai, 43, 53, 56–57, 59, 63–64
warriors, 64, 94–96, 162, 165–66, 189, 212, 219
  deceased, 57–58, 67, 92, 95, 166–67, 174, 219
watches, 91–92
water
  on Annamooka, 34
  on *Bounty*, 12, 14–15, 17–20, 26, 28–29, 31–32, 34, 58, 70
  on open-boat voyage, 37–38
  on *Pandora*, 116–17
  on *Pandora*'s open-boat voyage, 121–23
  on *Vreedenbergh*, 128
  on Wreck Island, 120–21
Wa Vaheine, 85
Webber, John, 25
Well's Reef, 117
westerly winds, 134–35, 144, 206, 214
West Indies, 1, 12, 146
whales, 14, 145–46, 151
Whappai. *See* Tew
white salmon, 62–63, 145, 149
wickerwork, 143, 155, 208
widows, 175
Williams, John, 12, 39, 41, 69
wine, 12, 17, 37, 46, 68–69, 73–74, 114, 120
women, Annamookan, 33–34
women, Tahitian. *See also names of women*
  and amoa, 176–79
  barred from the sacred, 62, 105, 146, 160, 169, 177, 196–97
  on *Bounty*, 24–25
  as chiefs, 160–61, 199
  and childbirth, 173, 216–17
  clothing for, 54–55, 207–8, 211–12
  and cookery, 196–99
  cutting head with shark's tooth, 115, 178–80, 183, 218, 220
  estates of, 60, 175–76

About the Editor

Donald A. Maxton is the author of *The Mutiny on H.M.S.* Bounty: *A Guide to Nonfiction, Fiction, Poetry, Films, Articles, and Music* as well as specialist articles on the history of HMS *Bounty* and Pitcairn Island. He has written extensively on the history of his home state, New Jersey, and received a New Jersey State grant to research and write *The Rahway Valley Railroad*, published in 2003. He is the director of public relations for New York City's largest hospital network and resides in Manhattan.